VE MAR 2013

02 NOV 13

A Mad, Crazy River   SA SEP 2016

A Mad, Crazy River

Running the Grand Canyon in 1927

CLYDE L. EDDY

UNIVERSITY OF NEW MEXICO PRESS
AVANYU PUBLISHING
Albuquerque

© 2012 by Avanyu Publishing
All rights reserved. Published 2012
Printed in the United States of America

Originally published in hardcover as
Down the World's Most Dangerous River
by Frederick A. Stokes Company, 1929.

17 16 15 14 13 12   1 2 3 4 5 6

Library of Congress Cataloging-in-Publication Data

Eddy, Clyde, 1889–1954.
A mad, crazy river : running the Grand Canyon in 1927 / Clyde Eddy.
    p. cm.
"Originally published in hardcover as
Down the World's Most Dangerous River
by Frederick A. Stokes Company, 1929."
ISBN 978-0-8263-5155-5 (pbk.: alk. paper)
ISBN 978-0-8263-5156-2 (electronic)
  1. Colorado River (Colo.-Mexico)—Description and travel.
  2. Colorado River (Colo.-Mexico)—Discovery and exploration.
  I. Title.
F788.E25 2012
917.91'304—dc23

2011037549

Contents

Foreword to the Paperback Edition

When Clyde Eddy and his team of novice adventurers shoved off into the current at Green River, Utah, on June 27, 1927, a crowd of townsfolk showed up to wave good-bye. Caught up in the fun, a gang of boys raced along the river, scrambling up over an embankment to get one last look at the strangers as their three boats disappeared around a bend. I'm sure nobody expected to ever see them again. A dozen expeditions into the Grand Canyon had met with disaster during the previous decade and a half, and nearly fifty men had died. There was no reason to think Eddy would do any better. In fact, as he and his crew had sat around a table in a Green River restaurant a few days before, a local teenager had come up behind them, tapped one of them on the shoulder and blurted out, "In two weeks you'll be dead." He was just saying out loud what everybody else was thinking.

What qualifications did Eddy have, after all, to embark on such a risky endeavor? Was he a seasoned boatman who had spent years running lesser rivers before taking on this, what he describes as the "most dangerous river in the world"? Not hardly. Eddy was a middle-aged office worker from New York City who had visited the Grand Canyon once on his honeymoon. The closest he'd gotten to the river was to study the reports of those who had actually gotten wet: John Wesley Powell, who explored the Grand Canyon in 1869; Emery and Ellsworth Kolb, who ran the river in 1911; and Col. Claude H. Birdseye, who led a 1923 expedition down the Colorado for the U.S. Geological Survey.

How did Eddy plan to compensate for his own lack of experience? Did he enlist the most knowledgeable river men he could find to join his expedition? No way. He did exactly the opposite, posting advertisements on the bulletin boards of college fraternity houses to attract young men "fresh from their sheltered homes and schools." His theory, as he states it in the first chapter of this volume, was that a man "need not be tough-whiskered to be brave and that a 'pink wristed' college boy will stand up as well in the face of long continued danger as, for instance, the average 'hard-boiled' army sergeant." He had learned this lesson, he said, as a soldier in France during World War I. (More about that in a minute.)

If Eddy didn't put much stock in training or in experience, however, he was keenly interested in publicity. As David Lavender points out in his book, *River Runners of the Grand Canyon*, Eddy had made a deal with the International Newsreel Company to film his adventure on the Colorado River, possibly as a documentary for Metro-Goldwyn-Mayer. That explains why, before leaving New York, Eddy stopped off to buy a bear cub from the zoo. He thought the animal would make a "picturesque addition" to the party, he said. His interest in movie making may also help explain why he chose to run the river in early spring, at high water, the most dangerous season in the Grand Canyon. It seems he'd learned that another group was planning to make a film on the Colorado that summer and he wanted to beat them to the punch.

To be fair, Eddy was no different in this respect than many early adventurers in the Grand Canyon. John Wesley Powell used his celebrity as "Conqueror of the Colorado" to launch a career in Washington. When he returned to the Canyon in 1871, he took a photographer with him, planning to use pictures to impress lawmakers. Robert Brewster Stanton also took a shooter in 1889. He was hoping to attract investors for a railroad he wanted to build through the canyon. Newspaper publisher Charles Silver Russell included a photographer in his 1907 expedition, a publicity stunt to promote mining in the canyons. Ellsworth and Emory Kolb were photographers before they ran the river in 1911. The documentary they made—the first motion

Clyde Eddy's signature from 1927, Grand Canyon, near Mile 117. (Photo by Robert Southwick.)

picture made in the canyon—was a tourist attraction in their studio on the canyon rim for almost seventy-five years.

Vanity alone didn't drive Clyde Eddy to risk his life on the river, however. As you'll see for yourself in the pages that follow, he was driven by other motives, including a powerful urge to test himself as a leader. For this, I believe, Eddy could thank his wartime experiences a decade before. A number of times in his story he recalls his memories of the war, in particular of the fighting at Verdun, in France, where some 750,000 men were killed or injured on both sides of the trenches. Listening to the ominous roar of the river above one of the last big rapids, he writes, "I felt as I did the last night of the war when I lay in an open field a few miles from Verdun, listening to the explosions of heavy aerial bombs aimed as us in the darkness from enemy planes flying over-head—resentful toward the dangers that threatened to destroy us at the last minutes, within sight of the journey's end."

Something interesting happens to Eddy under the pressure of such stress: he comes to grips for the first time with the deadly seriousness of his great adventure. Standing on the river bank watching one of his boats plunge through a dangerous rapids, he is surprised to find tears in his eyes. "I realize that nothing can be achieved without risk and I know there will always be young men who are eager to gamble

The expedition (including bear cub mascot in the back of the first boat, left) arrives safely at Needles, California, after forty-two days on the Colorado. (8:11 screen shot from DVD movie.)

their lives against the vagaries of air currents, the whims of a river, or the chances of death on mountain heights but that day I came near resolving that when I go adventuring again I shall take with me old men with whiskers down to their waists and if they get killed it will be their own responsibility."

To me, Eddy redeems himself at such moments. He turns off that imaginary movie running in his head and takes responsibility for his living companions. At such times, he seems to understand that the point of his great adventure is not to make a name for himself, or to profit from a documentary film, or even to prove that quiet men of intellect can be as courageous as brawny frontiersmen. The point is the journey itself, the satisfaction of attempting the near impossible, and of surviving to tell the tale.

In the end, as Eddy and his teammates float into Needles, California, forty-two days after shoving off from Green River, there would be no crowd on hand to meet them. No band. No pretty girls. No running children. The only witnesses to their arrival would be two Native Americans sitting on the bank, Eddy writes, and they "showed not the slightest interest in us when we ran our boats ashore."

And that was just fine with Eddy.

Peter Miller
National Geographic Magazine

Introduction

*P*ublic interest in the Colorado River recently has been accelerated by the proposition for the Federal government to build, in Black Canyon, a dam more than 550 feet in height—the highest dam anywhere in the world to-day. The harnessing of this great river will regulate the erratic flow of the turbulent stream, protect the vast investments in the Imperial Valley, supply a prodigious amount of electrical power, and give the population of Southern California a chance to secure additional and abundant water now absolutely necessary to the continued development of that portion of the United States.

Mr. Eddy's book is timely in that it emphasizes again the uncontrolled fury of this extraordinary stream in its headlong descent from the mountains of the north. In 1700 miles the river falls 14,000 feet. It loses 2225 feet of altitude in the 278 miles of Grand Canyon from Lee's Ferry to the Grand Wash. It is plain to any thinking mind that the river must, sooner or later, be brought under control. If it is not, the fertile fields of the Imperial Valley will be irretrievably lost and the Californians there must cease their progress. The power that now yields nothing will continue to run to waste. Salton Sea will be augmented until every vestige of farming will be destroyed for so long a time we may call it forever.

Read Mr. Eddy's chapters on running through the Grand Canyon on high water and the evidence is clear that the waste of water is something gigantic. Fortunately, we are meeting this problem in time.

Each new descent of the Colorado is a freshly adventure—a new exploration. That is to say the problem of navigating the river is always a changing one. The powers of erosion are at work unceasingly. While the results as a rule are not immediately perceptible the denudation proceeds year in and year out through the ages, bringing continual changes of current, of bed, of banks.

The bed of the Colorado has a tremendous declivity and the river, accordingly, is swift. The swifter water runs, the more silt it will transport in suspension, so the swiftness of the Colorado enables it to carry an unbelievable quantity of silt, especially at flood times. Then the surface of the water in the seething, whirling currents appears to be well-nigh solid, not water at all, but merely mud, slick, smooth, oily mud. This indeed it largely is and the gigantic lake resulting from the dam in Black Canyon is expected to receive this mud, drop it to the bottom and deliver to the thirsty lands of Southern California fresh, clear water.

It is this huge amount of mud in suspension which bestows on this stream additional power, for the great weight, combined with terrific speed in rapids, gives the big waves the force of trip hammers. The power of the river can hardly be described. It is fierce, unrelenting, demoniacal. If the navigator for a single moment is caught off guard, his boats may be destroyed and he is lucky if he does not go to the bottom. With this terrific current and the loaded character of the water the very bed of the river is kept in motion. Bowlders weighing tons are shoved, rolled, tumbled along like pebbles, often with a noise like distant thunder.

Stones of the hardest kind are dovetailed into each other so intimately by the unremitting oscillation, if they happen to be in a measure protected from rolling, that the zigzag line of joining can be detected only by close examination. The two big stones have become one. Other blocks half as big as a house perhaps, and standing part way out of the water, are rocked gently, as if by a submerged engine, back and forth endlessly, till all beneath is crushed, crumbled, pulverized to gravel, sand, silt. Finally, the big rock itself settles down and succumbs in its turn to the mighty power of the Colorado.

The silt thus formed is augmented by that from the surrounding region brought down by torrential rains—the wreckage from the cliffs and mountains which are gradually being carried away by this destroying river aided by wind, frost and rain. This is the irresistible work of erosion operating through millions of years, pouring thousands of tons of the land into the sea, every day, month, year. The task will not be completed until the great Colorado Plateau is worn down to plains and prairies some millions of years hence.

The results of this tremendous and endless activity of the waters of the Colorado are continual alterations in the character of the river bed and therefore in the river itself and of course in the rapids. No two years, almost one might say, no two days, are exactly alike. Every rise and fall of the water also creates new situations in the rapids and in the numerous whirlpools and suction holes. On one stage of water, no whirlpools—on another many whirlpools turning boats around and around before permitting them to go on their way.

Generally speaking, the highest water is the most dangerous, the lowest the safest for, on high water, boat control is more difficult than on low. Mr. Eddy chose as his first venture the high stage imposing thereby on himself a most dangerous task. The second Powell expedition experienced phenomenally high water, rising further one day at the rate of four feet an hour, from the Little Colorado to the Kanab Canyon, and they found that while some stretches were turned to enormous billows others were so furious in the plunges against the cliffs that only the exercise of patience and hard work carried the party through. Mr. Eddy found the same thing, and then not satisfied with running on high water, he tried it again on low as far as Bright Angel Creek.

There are several statements going the rounds as to how Bright Angel came to be named. Permit me to insert here the true story which I had, in 1872, at Bright Angel from the one who named it— Major Powell. The men emerging from Cataract Canyon, 360 miles up stream, were on the watch for a clear stream wherein to slake their thirst. Jack Sumner was the first boat to run into the mouth of a new tributary. "How is she, Jack?" called one from the rear. "Oh, she's a dirty devil," replied Jack, and the name Dirty Devil was ever the name of that river. Arriving at the mouth of a beautiful clear stream in the Grand Canyon, the Major said some atonement should be made for applying the name of Dirty Devil, so he called this clear water, Bright Angel. As he looked at it on the occasion of telling me this, he observed that it was muddy, also, from the torrential rains, and he exclaimed with a quizzical expression, "But it appears to be a soiled angel now!"

Jack Sumner was chief boatman on the 1869 expedition, a man of iron nerve, but he conceded that the Colorado is a serious opponent. After days of bad rapids, the party at length with their water-logged boats, reached a place where they encountered, says Sumner, "a stretch of water that made my hair curl."

This was the now famous Sockdolager Rapids which is ferocious in appearance from above but is not so difficult to navigate as some of the other drops. Mr. Eddy and his collegiate band ran it without any trouble and so too have others like the Kolb brothers, those specialists in running rapids.

Mr. Eddy deserves the highest credit for putting through his expedition with such complete success. The loss of one boat was a drawback but it did not prevent the carrying out of his full plans. Journalist, explorer, lecturer, and active member of the Explorers Club, with the enthusiasm of youth, with abundant physical strength, and a clear head, Mr. Eddy will proceed now to conquer other rivers. Nowhere will he find one more hazardous than the one he describes in this admirable volume.

Frederick S. Dellenbaugh
New York,
January 26th, 1929.

Foreword

*T*he following pages are with only slight elaboration the field notes of the leader of the only expedition that ever has successfully navigated the troubled waters of the Colorado River during the annual period of high water. They are set down here in the same tone as they were written, under the stress of the supernormal conditions that evoked them, because their value seems to the writer to lie in their truth to the actuality of that stress and its effect upon a comparatively prepared mind.

The magnifications they contain and the obliviousness they disclose to every consideration beyond the safety and success of the trip belong to them. Thus when Holt's individualism led him off on a solitary exploit that endangered the success of the venture as a whole; when Bradley refused to look upon the danger as a sporting proposition instead of an irrational straining of the routine of his job; when Jaeger, who fortuitously joined us as a sportsman and an amateur, did not prove to have the foresight and the experience of a seasoned professional; it appears that I felt aggrieved. Sustained and necessary concentration can breed this intolerance. I can see in half a glance that it bred it in me. I hope and believe I kept the manifestation of it to myself and my journal.

The leader of an exploring expedition during the time he is putting his obsession into execution is a curious natural phenomenon. I think I may call him natural. I am sure he is a phenomenon. He wants to do something that will constantly risk his life, that sometimes has an all but imperceptible pragmatic value, that in most cases will bring him a mere modicum of notice, not fame, and will cost him more than he can possibly yield. But that it shall be done seems to him a compelling thing, worth the danger to life and limb, the thirst, the weary round of monotonous food, the risk of starvation, the grinding drive of sleeplessness and the ache of back-breaking toil. He cannot tolerate the realization that it is less compelling to those who associate themselves with him.

The youth of the personnel of this expedition, and their insouciant approach to the dangers involved, increased the stress, for though they proved themselves men in stature and capacity, this was the proving ground. Too young at the time of the War to have a part in its carnage, fresh from their sheltered homes and schools, they never before had led dangerous lives and, until the Colorado taught them, had only a romantic conception of what dangers meant. That the Colorado had a chance to teach them was my doing and many times during the six weeks chronicled here I felt the effect of the added weight of that responsibility. When I wondered at times if they could push the undertaking through to a successful conclusion it was not because I doubted their individual courage but only that I did not know whether any man could so long withstand the ceaseless buffeting of the swollen stream.

A voyage down a river beset with rapids differs from almost every other exploring expedition in that the effort demanded is sharper and more insistent. Danger crowds upon danger, each one is in plain view and is apprehended by the consciousness. Every move is a menace, nearly every breath a strain—and not to move means disaster. The necessity for speed gives the human beings concerned no recuperative periods, no chance to rebound. Then, too, the Colorado trip is unique because during the entire period both ear and eye are assailed with a violence which only the word insanity can describe. The almost subterranean effect created by the overhanging walls, especially when those walls are of granite, somber and dispiriting, adds to the nervous strain while the incredible, incessant, deafening roar of the river that pounds, pounds, pounds day and night in a welter of monstrous sound magnified and reverberated by the cliffs that are the scars of its fury's creation, eats into any mechanism made of flesh and blood.

Even a minor exploring expedition takes an enormous amount of preliminary thought and labor in its organization. Each and every danger, each and every ounce of endurance, each and every element of strength, time, food, accident and division of responsibility and labor must be calculated and provided for. The men doing this calculation are thus mentally prepared in some measure for the exigencies of the trip. In this case I was the only person concerned with this work and thus the only one except Galloway who had any conception of what lay before us.

It is true that I told each man who volunteered as much as I could of the nature of the river and the conditions that would confront him. I described the fate that had befallen previous expeditions and furnished the men with published data concerning the dangers of the river trip. I tried to impress it upon them that the exploit was no gay adventure to be undertaken lightly, but an affair of life and death instead. Even so, no one of them had wrestled with the possibilities as I had wrestled with them trying to assemble the proper paraphernalia to withstand the attack of the river. It is true that I had never navigated such a stream, and that reality transcended my keenest imaginative anticipation, but I had visualized in some measure the hazards of the adventure and I am convinced that they had not. I salute them, therefore, for the gallantry with which through peril, privation and pressure they carried the venture through.

It is most keenly and terribly true that, provide all the physical equipment he may, display the most penetrating foresight, the most admirable ingenuity, the leader and the expedition must succeed or fail according to the strength of the spirit of the men. So it is with profound gratitude and affection that I acknowledge my debt to that superb river man and genial companion, Parley Galloway, to W. Gordon Adger, and to each of the others who did his share and endured to the finish. Even that old devil Colorado was not too much for them.

Clyde L. Eddy

CHAPTER I

A Mad, Crazy River—
Boyhood Dreams—
Plans and Preparations—
The Start from Greenriver.

*A*way at last! With the aid of the long stern sweep I pushed the boat out into the stream. Then, the current caught us and we were swept quickly under the two bridges, around a bend in the river and out of sight of the people on the shore. The other boats followed close behind and we were started on our journey. Compelled to pay quick attention to our oars to save the boats from being carried against the midstream bridge supports, there was no time even to wave our hands in farewell to the people who had come down to see us off. We had a hurried glimpse of the men, women and children standing at the water's edge—the younger boys breaking away from the crowd in a fruitless effort to scramble up the railroad embankment in time to see us again before the river swept us out of sight—and then there was nothing along the shore but willows seeming to pass in swift procession up stream and, in the distance, the sagebrush-covered mesas, shimmering in the desert sun.

Three boats, thirteen men, an Airedale dog and a cub bear were floating down the world's most dangerous river. Eight hundred miles of perilous going lay ahead. Three hundred bad rapids barred the way. Steep canyon walls more than a mile high presently would hem us in. The swift current was sweeping us down into the deep and narrow gorges, from which escape would be impossible if we should lose our precious boats.

The Colorado River is a mad, crazy stream. Even in times of normal flow its rushing water carries six-tenths per cent of sand and silt and is so turbid that the eye cannot penetrate an inch beneath its swirling surface. At flood tide the stream carries an incredible volume of sand and gravel and moves great bowlders and rock masses down stream over its smoothly polished bed. Its water is so heavy with suspended sand that it rolls along like a river of quicksilver, sweeping everything irresistibly before it. When men are thrown into the stream their clothing fills with sand and the very weight of it drags them down to death. Then the cruel and cunning river hides their bodies in backwaters in its lonely canyons and covers them with sand, burying them there forever.

The Colorado is one of the great rivers of the earth and the suddenness with which it drops 14,000 feet from its source in the mountains of Wyoming and Colorado to its mouth in the torrid Gulf of California gives it tremendous power. Great bowlders sometimes fall into the stream from overhanging cliffs, or are wrenched loose from its banks in seasons of high water, and then the current picks them up and rolls them along the river's bed with roars that echo and reëcho through the mile deep canyons it has dug. The river represents 5,700,000 continuous horsepower, the ceaseless power and energy of that many million untamed horses, and yet, because of its inaccessibility, the stream, until it emerges from its canyons, is practically useless, either for power or irrigation.

The amount of water in the river varies greatly from one season to another, the stream being thirty to fifty times larger when spring floods are crashing through its narrow canyons than it is at low water during the winter months. The river, in the Grand Canyon, averages about 300 feet in width, is thirty feet deep and, with a velocity ranging from eight to thirty miles per hour, has an average volume of 20,000 cubic feet of water per second. The stream is subject to sudden floods and its volume may multiply many times in a single night, raising the level of water sixty feet in half a dozen hours, sweeping away the boats of luckless voyagers, leaving them to die of hunger in the canyons whose cliffs they cannot climb. In the Upper Granite Gorge I found water-piled driftwood a hundred feet above the normal level of the river!

The Grand Canyon of the Colorado was discovered in 1540 by Coronado on his historic northward march from Old Mexico through our great Southwest, and the region is so remote and inaccessible that three hundred years elapsed, while the western tide of civilization flowed around it toward the gold fields of California, before the canyon was first explored, in 1869, by John Wesley Powell.

Few expeditions on the Colorado have escaped disaster. Powell and his men, exhausted by twelve weeks of battling with the river, reached a rapids at last which three of his men refused to run. They were unwilling to go ahead. The meager supply of food was divided and the three men set out to find a way up the steep canyon walls while Powell and the others turned their attention again to the river. Four days later Powell splashed through the last bad rapids and arrived safely at the end of his journey. The three who left him at the tumbling stretch of river now known as Separation Rapids finally found a way out of the canyon, and were killed on the rim by Indians.

Frank M. Brown fought a gallant but hopeless battle with the river in 1889 and his ill-fated expedition was abandoned only after Brown and two others of his party were drowned in the whirlpools of Marble Gorge. John Vartan was wrecked in Cataract Canyon but managed to find his way to the rim, and was insane with fear and suffering when a searching party found him weeks later wandering about in the arid Land of Standing Rocks. Charles Smith ventured alone into Cataract Canyon and was never seen again, the only clew to his fate being parts of his boat which were washed ashore later at Lee's Ferry, 186 miles down stream. I have actual records of twenty-nine fatalities in Cataract Canyon since Brown's successful passage in 1889—and Cataract, forty miles in length, is one of the lesser canyons of the Colorado.

Nine expeditions were destroyed during the twenty years between 1889 and 1909 while attempting to pass through Cataract Canyon, 120 miles below Greenriver, Utah. On two occasions sole survivors of shipwrecked parties escaped the river and found their way to the Hite ranch at the foot of Cataract, arriving there half dead from hunger. Small wonder that the people of Greenriver speak of Cataract Canyon as the "graveyard" and regard as next to impossible the navigation of the cliff-bound stream.

If Cataract Canyon, with fifty-four bad rapids, can so consistently destroy the men who launch their boats upon its perilous water-way, what of the Grand Canyon itself, with 245 bad rapids lying in wait to smash the boats of explorers voyaging between its granite walls? The answer to that question is found in the pitiful record of twelve major expeditions that met with defeat or disaster during the sixteen years that preceded my adventure on the river—a record, surely, that justifies me in calling the Colorado the most dangerous river in the world. Easy of access where it is crossed by the railroad in eastern Utah, and not quite impossible to navigate, it invites exploration—and has destroyed more men than have succeeded in their efforts to navigate its troubled course. At the time of my voyage on the river fewer than twenty men then living had seen the Grand Canyon throughout its length in the only way that it can be seen, from boats. Fewer than fifty men in the history of the world ever had made the voyage through from Greenriver, Utah, to Needles, California. At least that many had died in vain attempts.

And there I was, on the morning of June twenty-seventh, 1927, afloat on the muddy river, being carried along on a ten-mile current between the narrowing walls of Labyrinth and Stillwater canyons toward Cataract. One of my childhood dreams was being realized and twelve other men were sharing its thrills, its hazards, with me. As the current swept us along and the muddy water splashed against the sides of my boat, a line that I had read somewhere years before came back to me, "Be careful what you set your heart upon, for some day it will be yours." Into what dangers was my childhood's dream, my heart's desire, now leading me?

~~~~~~~~~~~~~~

It had been a dream of mine for years to go by boat down some turbulent river. As a boy in Utah and Colorado I watched the mountain torrents plunging over their rocky beds and picked out precarious channels through which a boat might find its dangerous way. Swift streams fascinated me and "white water" rivers swept gloriously through my childhood dreams. Then, years after in the spring of 1919, I visited the Grand Canyon and saw the Colorado River at the foot of

Hermit Trail. There was the river of my dreams, excepting only that the water was filled with sand and silt instead of being crystal clear. My wife was with me and as we gazed at the turbid stream I said to her, "There is my river." But it was not actually in my mind at that time to attempt a journey through the canyons. The Colorado was a new discovery to me and there was much that stood in the way of making it "my river." It was months before I realized that dreams were giving way to plans and that my heart was set on making the river trip.

Eight years passed while I dreamed my dreams and made my plans. I read the published reports of Powell's explorations and the successful journey made by Emery and Ellsworth Kolb in 1911, and by the United States Geological Survey expedition, under the leadership of Col. C. H. Birdseye, in the winter of 1923. I profited from the experiences of the few successful navigators of the river and learned what I could from the failure of the others. Knowing the importance of careful planning I gave much thought to stores and equipment and believed that at last, without ever having been on the river in a boat, I had a list which included everything needed to make a successful voyage through the canyons. With everything else in readiness, I began assembling my crew.

I have a theory concerning men. It is my belief that a man need not be tough-whiskered to be brave and that a "pink wristed" college boy will stand up as well in the face of long continued danger as, for instance, the average "hard-boiled" army sergeant. I saw my theory proved in France during the war, when men of great apparent physical strength exhibited less endurance than softer looking men whose minds were trained and tough if their bodies were not. Social experience tends to toughen minds and knowing that the river trip finally would become a test of sheer endurance, where courage would count for more than brawn, I determined, if possible, to enlist a crew of young men who were still attending, or recently had been graduated from college. I felt reasonably certain that if I could secure such a crew and get them started on the river my chances for success would be reasonably good. But I knew, too, that such men would be intelligent enough to withdraw if, before the start, they decided that the hazards were too great. For that reason I had advertisements inserted in outdoor magazines as well as in several western newspapers and enlisted an entire second crew, upon which to my great satisfaction I did not have to draw.

I began advertising for college men early in the spring, using the columns of school and fraternity papers and having notices posted on bulletin boards in the fraternity houses. I learned that a motion picture company was planning to launch an expedition on the river sometime during the summer and in order to keep my plans secret I did not announce where I was going but purposely made it appear that I was going some place else instead. Here is the call for volunteers, to which more than a hundred college men responded, eager to go even though they were to be required to pay their own rail fares and do their share of the "chores."

EXPLORERS WANTED

Volunteers are wanted for an important geological-geographical expedition scheduled to leave New York City about June 10, to be gone six or eight weeks. Preference will be given to men who have had outdoor experience and no one will be accepted who cannot swim, handle a boat, do his share of camp "chores" and handle himself in the woods. No one should apply who is afraid of cold, or of high altitudes. A fine opportunity for geology students, or younger members of teaching faculties, to do field work in virgin territory.

No salaries will be paid but rations, transportation and camp equipment will be supplied. Each member of the expedition will have to furnish his personal equipment, and will have to pay his own fare to the point where the expedition leaves the railroad. In applying to join the party, state whether or not you are an American citizen.

Send photograph and complete biographical information in your first letter.

Eager requests to be included in my party came to me from college men all over the United States and, after carefully studying their qualifications, I sent letters to forty of the applicants which I told them where I proposed to go, and described to them as well as I could the dangers of a journey through the Grand Canyon and the other wild and desolate gorges of the Colorado River. Many of the volunteers then withdrew and, from the remaining applicants, I selected to accompany me on the journey: Robert H. Weatherhead, John H. Marshall and Frederick L. Felton, of Harvard; Edward L. Holt and Vincent F. Callaway, of Coe College; Robert F. Bartl and Vincent F. Carey, of Notre Dame; and O. A. Seager, of Northwestern University.

Meantime, working on my second crew, I was given the name of W. Gordon Adger, of Shreveport, La., who had made application through the American Museum of Natural History to join one of the Roy Chapman Andrews expeditions to Mongolia. Adger did not qualify as a college student but he was young, cultured, handsome, and eager to go. He accepted my invitation and became an invaluable member of my party.

Those nine young men were the "pink wristed" members of my expedition, but wrists can tan and toughen in the hot Arizona sunshine as events were soon to show.

I had three special boats constructed, two of them twenty-two feet long, and the other one sixteen feet in length. The large boats, similar to those used by Powell in 1869, were built of half-inch Mexican mahogany. They were five feet wide in the beam, pointed at one end and were intended to draw about eighteen inches of water when loaded with twelve to eighteen hundred pounds of men, food and equipment. The keels and ribs were of well seasoned oak and the ribs were placed very close to each other to give added strength, being only three inches apart, center to center, near the bow and stern and five inches apart amidships. Each of these boats had three waterproof cabins, four feet long, and two open cockpits. They were intended to be unsinkable and were built to withstand severe pounding on the rocks. The boats were named the *Coronado*, the *Powell* and the *Dellenbaugh*, in honor of the discoverer, the first explorer, and the principal historian of the river. I have been asked many times why I did not use canoes. It is my opinion that canoes would be battered to pieces very quickly in the rock-strewn rapids of the Colorado.

The sixteen foot boat also was five feet in the beam and was built of cedar planking five-eighths of an inch thick, securely fastened to heavy oak ribs and keel. This boat had no closed compartments but was decked over for four feet both forward and aft and was equipped with high splash boards to keep out the waves. Life lines were attached to all the boats and they were equipped with cork ring buoys and extra oars. A life preserver was furnished for each man, with a half a dozen extra ones packed away in the boats.

I provided, in duplicate, saws, hammers, copper sheeting, marine glue, paint, canvas—everything needed for repairing the boats. Two complete medicine kits were supplied, and carefully stowed away in different boats so that we still would have everything needed if one of the boats was lost. There are many rattlesnakes in the canyons and the adjacent desert country and our first aid equipment included two packages of especially prepared snake serum.

There are only a few places in the 800 miles of wilderness through which the river flows between Greenriver, Utah, and Needles, California, where it is possible to obtain provisions and only three places in the entire distance where wagons or automobiles can be brought down to the river's edge. It was necessary for me, therefore, to determine in advance about how long it would take me to travel from one point to another, and to provide sufficient provisions to carry us through. There are only two places on the Colorado below Greenriver where provisions conveniently can be brought in; at Lee's Ferry, 332 miles below Greenriver, and at the head of Bright Angel Trail, eighty-nine miles farther down stream. I decided to start with a supply of food stowed away in the watertight compartments sufficient to last us three weeks. I believed I could cover the next lap of the journey, the eighty-nine miles between Lee's Ferry and Bright Angel Trail, in ten days and arranged to have provisions for that length of time trucked in to Lee's Ferry, ninety-five miles over the desert from Kanab. I believed that I could make the final lap of 367 miles in three weeks and arranged to have food for that part of the trip delivered to me at the head of Bright Angel Trail. How nearly we could keep to schedule, and how adequate our supply of food would prove to be, I realized depended largely on the whims of the river.

Then, I shipped the boats, notified the men to meet me at Greenriver and left New York City on Saturday, June 18. That was a year of great floods in the Mississippi Valley and, at Omaha, Nebraska, I saw buildings that had been demolished a few weeks before at the peak of the flood on the Missouri River. When my train reached Canon City, Colorado, I looked at the noisy, muddy water of the Arkansas and noted with misgiving how furiously it swept over the rocks in the Royal Gorge. Eagle River, on the rocky banks of which I had dreamed of boats when I was a boy, was higher than I had ever seen it and when, at dawn the next morning, I cross the Green River itself, a mile east of the town, I saw that it, too, was high with late spring floods.

I reached Greenriver several days later than I had planned and all of the men were there ahead of me. Felton and Marshall had been there for a week and in that time the river's volume had increased from 15,600 to 30,700 cubic feet of water per second. The river, already high, had doubled in size in seven days and was still rising when I arrived. I hastened to tell the men that I did not intend to leave until the flood had subsided and they felt reassured when I finished showing them how well equipped we were for almost any emergency that might arise.

The people of Greenriver had seen many expeditions start upon the journey through the canyons and, knowing as they did the evil character of the stream, exerted their best efforts to dissuade us from going. The younger men of my party stayed together much of the time and the very fact that there were so many of them gave them added courage. But Bradley, the camera man who was being sent with us to make motion pictures for one of the weekly newsreels, clearly was little inclined to venture on the river. From the first, he was not one of us but kept to himself a great deal or visited with the townspeople, and listened to the gloomy tales they had to tell. After his first day in Greenriver I made it a point to be with him as much as possible and, day by day as the level of the water dropped at the rail-road bridge, I felt his spirits rise. I took him with me when I talked to L. M. Chaffin, who actually had been through Cataract Canyon at low water one winter on a trapping trip, and he heard Chaffin tell me that we probably would be successful in our venture, the first encouraging words that we had heard. Chaffin also told us that his sons herded cattle along the rim of Cataract and that, while there were only two places in forty miles where it would be possible for us to climb out in case of shipwreck, he would have his boys watch for us as we voyaged through.

I talked with Harry Howland, government water gauger, and after assuring myself that he thought we might get through if we waited for the flood to pass, I had him talk to Bradley. I concluded finally that I had the camera man in a cheerful mood and then, one day when we were having lunch together in the only restaurant in town, all the courage that had been built up in him was destroyed in a moment. We were seated at a table and Bradley had his back to the door. A boy about sixteen came in and walking up behind my companion tapped him on the shoulder. Bradley looked up and the boy, pointing his finger at the camera man, said slowly, "In two weeks you'll be dead." Bradley's face paled and he smiled a wry smile. I knew instantly that he would not start with us down the river if he could find a way to avoid going, and I was right. He hurried off to the railroad station after lunch and wired to New York for permission to leave the expedition, while I went down to the river to see if we could get away before he got an answer to his telegram. We did get away, but his answer followed us, where no other telegram ever has been, before or since.

We were at Greenriver five days and during that time the level of water at the railroad bridge dropped steadily. It fell a foot between Wednesday and Sunday and I decided to start as early as possible on Monday morning.

In the meantime there had been several additions to the crew. I already have mentioned Bradley. Parley Galloway was engaged as guide. Galloway had not been through the canyons below Greenriver but had hunted and trapped in the up stream canyons and was familiar with boats and rapids. On our last day in Greenriver a hobo asked me for a job. I explained to him that what I had in prospect was not a job at all as that word usually is understood but an expedition instead and when I told him we were about to start on a voyage down the river, 800 miles to Needles, he asked to be included in the party. He told me his name was McGregory and that he had been a sailor. He professed to know all about boats and said that during the war, as a member of the British Army, he had accompanied an expedition through the upper canyons of the Euphrates River and, therefore, knew all about rapids. I did not believe much that he told me but decided he might prove a valuable addition to the party. I bought him a pair of shoes, a shirt, a blanket and some overalls, and he joined us. Knowing that a cub bear would be a picturesque addition to the party I had brought one with me from New York. Later we named him "Cataract," because he was so rough. To serve as mascot I had a dog which had been sent to me from the dog pound in Salt Lake City. The party was then complete, thirteen men, three boats, a dog and a bear.

The citizens of Greenriver turned out, to the last man, woman and child, to see us off. The younger men in my party already were heroes to the girls and young women of the little town and I suspect that tears were mixed with smiles when farewells were said and we launched our boats on the treacherous river. Three girls, Margaret McClurg, Caroline Beebe and Marjorie Bennett, had been selected to christen the boats. At one-thirty, on the afternoon of Monday, June twenty-seventh, with the water down to 10.1 feet at the railroad bridge—the lowest it had been in ten days—the *Coronado*, the *Powell*, and the *Dellenbaugh* were shoved out into swift current. We had been in Greenriver only a short time but the members of my party had made many friends and I knew that day, as I caught a last hurried glimpse of the people lined up along the shore, that all of them were concerned for our safety and that, as they saw our boats whisked away from them and swept down toward the first of the canyons, they sent after us their heartfelt wishes for a successful voyage on the river.

A clear, hot afternoon, reeking with desert sunshine, thirteen men, a cub bear and a dog afloat in three boats on the world's most dangerous river; a dream come true; my long-planned expedition was under way at last.

CHAPTER II

The River Shows Its Teeth—
Man Overboard—Wind and Rain—
Organizing the Expedition.

From the moment our boats were launched on the river it was necessary for us to pay close attention to navigation. Just below the railroad bridge the current was split in two by a wide, flat sand bar and we had to pull hard on the oars to keep our boats from piling up against its willow-bordered shores. Then, clear of it, we were swept swiftly by, barely missing the willows, swaying crazily on the swollen stream. The noise and excitement of Greenriver were left behind; we were alone on the river; alone in a wilderness of scattered buttes and mesas. There was no sound except the rustling of the water in midstream and occasional noisy splashes where it poured over infrequent rocky ledges jutting out from either shore. The current was flowing from six to eight miles per hour and we had to be constantly on the alert but the going was relatively easy, even for my untrained crews.

We had been under way less than an hour when, for a few exciting minutes, the river showed its teeth. Where the railroad crosses at Greenriver the stream flows through a broad, level valley and the low banks of the river are lined with trees. A mile below the bridge, high gravel banks and low cliffs began to hem the river in. The stream narrowed, friendly willows and cottonwoods along the shore gave way to walls of rock and gravel. There was a sharp bend in the channel and the muddy, hurrying water, piling up against a rocky wall on the right, was turned abruptly toward a crumbling gravel bank on the other side of the river. The main body of water rushed diagonally across, sweeping furiously against the opposite shore. Where the apex of the current swept across the stream there was a moving ridge of water three feet or more in height and it was only by turning the bows of our boats against this cross current and pulling stoutly on our oars that we avoided having our boats upset in midstream, or carried against the gravel bank on the left. However, that skirmish stands out only because it was our first brush with the river. There were to be many such encounters, some of which were not to terminate so happily.

I had placed the *Dellenbaugh* in Galloway's charge and with him in the boat were Seager, Holt and Callaway. Adger was in charge of the *Powell*; the other members of the crew being Bartl, Felton and them as passengers. Carey, Weatherhead, McGregory and the bear were with me in the *Coronado* and, as it was not necessary for us to row, we turned our boats about and floated stern first down stream. In that position we could see where we were going and could use our oars to maintain our positions in the river. There had been little time in Greenriver for me to get acquainted with the men and, as the current carried us rapidly along between walls growing gradually higher, I had my first long talk with Weatherhead, who pulled oar with me in the stern of the *Coronado*.

Weatherhead, from the beginning, was a man apart. Most of the others had come in pairs, or had quickly allied themselves with one or another of the groups into which the men had naturally drifted. But Weatherhead apparently was self-sufficient. He was friendly with everybody and intimate with no one. He spoke with a marked Boston accent and was accused by Felton and Marshall, fellow students at Harvard, of "high hatting" even them. I watched him ride off alone on horseback one evening at Greenriver and later he described to me the magnificent sunset that he had watched from the summit of a mesa south of town. Another time he went with two or three of the other men to a sociable in the Mormon meeting house and, confining his repertory strictly to classical music, played the piano magnificently to a surprised and delighted audience. He affected certain mannerisms not calculated to make him popular with his companions and endured, without seeming to notice it, a little gentle chaffing from the other members of the party.

It was partly for that reason that I had him with me on the *Coronado*. One has only to be different to lay oneself open to ridicule and Weatherhead clearly was unlike the others. It was my intention simply to shield him as well as I could from further raillery until our struggle with the river had given him time and opportunity to prove that he possessed qualities which would place him in a class with the best of his fellow voyagers.

He was far from being a second Kit Carson but I had not selected Weatherhead at random and when I saw him at Greenriver, apart from the others, keenly interested in exploring the country, scornful of the calamitous prophesies of the townspeople, I was more certain than ever that I had not been mistaken in my choice. Weatherhead was the youngest of several brothers and sisters and, like every son so situated in his family, grew up with the feeling that much was expected from him, so much perhaps that he could not hope ever to measure up to the others, who were and always had been older and wiser than he.

Give any healthy boy a handicap, whether it be in stature, a difficulty in his speech, his physical appearance, or even his position in the family and then provide the right ideals and inspiration and, in overcoming his disadvantage, he is likely to go ahead and conquer his whole world. The pages of history are crowded with the achievements of men who never knew when they had compensated enough for some real or imaginary inferiority. I felt from the start that, whatever may have been his handicap, Weatherhead possessed ideals and I believed that, ably or otherwise, he would do his share of the work and endure the buffetings of the river as long as any of us.

We talked about the country through which the stream was hurrying us and it was clear that he had read much about the river since I had told him where we were going. He commented upon the stark, rugged beauty of the buttes and mesas and seemed little concerned over the hazards of the river trip. He spoke with a cultured accent and a purity of English which later brought down upon his unheeding shoulders the ridicule of certain other members of the party. Later, 500 miles down stream when Weatherhead said to me, "It is hotter than hell," I made a note of it in my dairy. His habitual conversation contained no such expressions of opinion concerning anything. He told me he was majoring in English and spoke glowingly of Edward Arlington Robinson's *Tristram*, a copy of which he had with him in the boat.

We passed Dellenbaugh Butte at four-thirty and, a mile below, ran ashore to make some photographs. The bow of the boat was headed in and when we were thirty or forty feet from the bank McGregory stood on the deck of the forward cabin with the line in his hand ready to jump ashore as soon as we should draw near enough. The murky, quicksilver-like water hides everything that lies beneath its surface and when the boat still was thirty feet from shore it struck a submerged rock and tipped enough to throw McGregory into the river. He dropped the line and struck out for shore. The current carried him rapidly down stream and I called to him to come to the boat instead. I tossed him the end of the stern line and he clambered into the boat. The river had tried on us another of its many tricks.

We got away again in a few minutes and I began to watch for a place to spend the night. The river had narrowed still more and the current carried us along at increased speed. There were low bushes along the bank and I noted with concern that their lower branches were submerged in the muddy water. Buttes and mesas crowded close to the river's edge and in many places walls of rock rose sharply a hundred feet or more above us. So far as we could see in all directions there was a vast wilderness of barren rock—flat-topped mesas whose banded walls rose high above their talus slopes; distant buttes, thrown into clear relief again the sky; rocks in a thousand forms, devoid of trees, offering insecure foothold even for sagebrush, sparsely scattered on the gentler slopes. The river trench narrowed as we approached the first of the canyons.

We ran the boats ashore at five-thirty and made camp on the left bank at a wide bend in the river, opposite a high cliff of smooth, orange-colored sandstone a mile or two above the mouth of the San Rafael River. The Colorado was about 350 feet wide and the rock wall on the opposite shore, rising four or five hundred feet sheer from the water's edge, threw back to us some marvelous echoes.

"Here, Rags," one of the boys called out, and the dog looked expectantly across the river when the echo, clear and distinct, came back to us.

"Hey, Ruth," became another favorite call; Ruth being one of the young ladies of Greenriver who, apparently, had made a favorable impression upon some of the men. "Hey, Ruth," came finally to be the official echo-tester of the expedition. I do not even know who Ruth was, but certainly the canyons of the Colorado are familiar with her name.

We came early to distinguish two separate and distinct kinds of echoes: the one that comes back alone, after a long pause; and another that brings back with it other echoes of its own making. At Camp No. 1, for instance, there was a single cliff against which the sound of our voices rebounded and "Here, Rags" was returned to us as "Here, Rags" and nothing more. The distance across the river was considerable, however, and we found that we could say whole sentences and have them tossed back to us. We could count to ten, stop, and then the cliff would repeat the count to us. In other places in the canyons there would be a very labyrinth of cliffs and when we called "Here, Rags" the cliffs would toss the call back and forth to each other and we could hear the words repeated distinctly as many as seven times, with Rags looking eagerly in all the directions from which the call had come. Then he would bark furiously as if he knew he had been hoaxed.

Galloway, squatting on his heels, assisted in cooking the evening meal and I appointed Bartl and Carey kitchen police, with the other members of the crew to take their turns on succeeding days. There was some confusion attendant upon the establishment of our first camp and it was dark before I had an opportunity to give any thought to where I should sleep. We had unloaded the boats for more systematic re-packing on the morrow and our tents were stretched over our equipment, and as many of the boys as could crowd in with it. Felton and Marshall produced a pup tent from the voluminous duffel and spread their blankets on the ground beneath it. I slept out, covered with my blanket and a waterproof poncho.

I lay on the sand near the river and listened for a long time to the rustle of the water as it swept by our camp. I never have quite explained the sound the water makes as it hurries along through the upper canyons but more than anything else it sounds as if the grains of sand carried in suspension are being audibly ground together by the water, or perhaps it is caused by the suspended sand being ground again the rocky bed of the river. But I fell asleep presently, only to be awakened in the night by rain beating in my face. A fierce gust of wind blew part one of the tents away and sent me hurrying to keep our provisions covered. Adger and McGregory got up and we soon had everything secure. We even found cramped quarters in one of the tents where all three of us could sleep partly under shelter, leaving only the bear and the dog exposed to the rain, which continued to fall the rest of the night.

"To bed again," I set down in my diary. "Rain dripping on my poncho and in my face. Ground wet but poncho keeps me dry. The rain is a little discouraging on account of what it may do to the river, but not very. Wet camp, bear and dog out in it."

It is significant that Adger was up looking after things with me that first night on the river. He was twenty-three when he joined the expedition at Greenriver, weighed 156 pounds and was five feet, eleven inches tall. He was lean and graceful and his finely molded muscles were as modest and unassuming as the man himself. He was as handsome a man as I have ever seen and there are several young women in the Greenriver who, I venture, remember to this day the gentleness, the modesty and the rare good looks of the unattainable young man in my party who spoke with the faint suggestion of a Southern drawl. I had known from our first day together that he was one of the men around whom I would build the success or failure of my expedition and had given him responsibilities while we were in Greenriver that quickly brought out his qualities in leadership. Then, I had appointed him captain of the *Powell*. Adger was destined to play an important role in our six weeks' battle with the river and the fine qualities he showed before we started were made apparent a hundred times on the long journey to Needles.

We were up at five-thirty on the morning of the twenty-eighth and although the camp was a wet one everybody seemed cheerful. The water in the fiver was excessively muddy. "Unfit to drink," I wrote in my diary, "but we drink it." Logs, twenty to thirty feet long and two to three feet in diameter, floated by, indicating unusually high water in the upper canyons. We finished with breakfast; stowed away the provisions and equipment; tightened down the hatches and, at eighty-thirty, resumed our journey down the river. Later, I set upon five o'clock as the hour for reveille and we learned to break camp and start away by seven, but that was lower down the river when there was less duffel to stow and we had acquired more experience in stowing it.

I rearranged the crew of my boat, the Coronado, and had McGregory in the stern, pulling oar with me. He was a more skillful oarsman that Weatherhead and I concluded that it would be better for him to serve as stroke oar for his side of the boat—and he thoroughly enjoyed the advantage his position gave him over the man from Harvard. It was only by close coöperation that we could hope to work effectively against the swift current in the river and the cruise though Labyrinth and Stillwater canyons was to be practice for the harder going in Cataract. Accordingly, we drilled. We were floating, stern first, with the current and Carey, sitting back of me in the bow of the boat soon learned to do with his oar precisely what I did with mine. McGregory was quick to execute the orders that I have him. With Carey and me backing water on the starboard oars and McGregory and Weatherhead pulling on theirs, the heavy boat would turn around and around in the swift current. We learned gradually to handle the boat rather skillfully and, so far as possible, without spoken orders because I knew that later on, when running rapids, it should be impossible for me to make my voice heard about the roar of the river. As the day passed McGregory assumed full responsibility for his side of the boat. "Pull Weather'ead," he would roar, and "Weather'ead" would pull, or "Back water, Weather'ead," he would command and "Weather'ead" to the best of his ability, would obey.

We had been under way only a few minutes when we reached the mouth of the San Rafael River. The walls were much broken down and there were cottonwood trees along the shore on the right. Nearby on the left were buttes of many colored rock, ranging from gray to red, purple and brown. Far off to the east of us was a clump of mountains which I knew were the Sierra La Sal, fifty miles away.

A short distance below the San Rafael we entered Labyrinth Canyon, where cliffs of dark red sandstone rose hundreds of feet above us on both sides of the river. At ten o'clock I recognized Trin Alcove on the right and gave the signal to run ashore but the current was so swift it swept us by and we landed half a mile below. It was possible in a few places to climb up to the rim of the cliffs and from there we looked out across an arid waste of solid rock. The surface of the plateau is covered with the same red sandstone that forms the cliffs and as far as we could see there was nothing but naked red rock—red rock carved into gullies, ravines and canyons; naked red rock everywhere. The sandstone surface of the plateau crumbled under our feet and crunched like snow when we walked on it.

Rain began to fall late in the morning and magnificent cascades plunged over the canyon walls, falling 500 to 800 feet into the river. How this can happen is explained by the fact that the river has cut its canyon though a great plateau. The country on top is practically level, except that it is sprinkled about with buttes and mesas and is honeycombed with thousands of deep and narrow side canyons though which smaller streams find their way to the river—and the greatest and deepest canyon of them all. There is no vegetation to hold the rain that falls and after every storm each drop of water grasps a grain of sand and rushes away to join its fellows. Presently a stream is formed, which roars furiously though some ravine and leaps at least into the canyon of the Colorado. That is why, after every rainfall of any consequence anywhere in the 1700 miles of upper and lower canyons, there may be sudden floods on the river. There may be a violent rainstorm or a sudden melting of the mountain snows 200 miles up stream, which starts a torrent or turbid water hurtling through the narrow canyons, causing the water to rise ten or twenty or forty feet in a few hours' time. When that happens woe betide the canyon voyager who has made his camp at the foot of a sheer cliff up which he finds it impossible to drag his boats when the wall of water sweeps suddenly down upon him.

Dellenbaugh describes cascades that plunged over the walls of Labyrinth Canyon when he went though with Powell in 1871 and as we drifted along that morning in the rain, I thought of John Wesley Powell, first navigator of the Colorado, and of Dellenbaugh. Theirs was a valiant band. I had the assurance at least that boats had navigated the river. Powell knew only what he had learned on a visit to a few points along the rim of the canyon. Against that he had to weigh the stories of the Indians who assured him that there were great falls between perpendicular walls and that, in places, the river ran entirely underground.

Just before noon we ran ashore at what we thought was Bow Knot Bend, where in a few more thousands of centuries the river may finish cutting its way through 800 feet of rock, 500 feet in height, and so save itself a seven mile journey around the rim of the still uncompleted loop. Or perhaps it is better to describe Bow Knot Bend as an inverted "U" with the free ends of the letter gradually drawing nearer to each other. We ran ashore in the rain and climbed a 500 foot cliff to see if the river was on the other side, and it was not. From the top there was nothing to be seen but a bare, glistening waste of red rock, with pools of clear rain water, which we drank to repay us for the climb to the rim.

We ate a cold lunch, huddled under an overhanging ledge of rock, and after resting for an hour, moved on. I shall say something more about this meal and perhaps should mention here that we had bread, peanut butter, canned beans, jam, and hot coffee with sugar and evaporated milk. Just a lunch to be sure, but I have been on long journeys in midwinter when the noonday meal consisted of cold biscuits with butter, jam, raisins, a bit of chocolate, and hot coffee to wash it down—with no serious results to men or morale.

At four-thirty we reached another place where a marked lowering in the height of the cliff on the right made it seem likely that we had come to Bow Knot Bend and the boats were run ashore. Galloway, Seager, Bradley and two or three of the other men climbed up and reported that we were actually at the Bend, then we dropped half a mile down the river and made camp for the night. Galloway was bareheaded when he returned from the rim and reported that his hat had blown away. Fortunately, he was able to borrow one from Bartl.

An hour or two of daylight remained and even in the midst of getting everything snug for the night, there was time occasionally to stop long enough to drink in the beauty of the scene, to listen to the marvelously clear and beautiful bird calls, and to admire the busy canyon wrens that made them. Their loud ringing whistles, uttered in a steadily descending scale, filled the narrow canyons with clear, cheerful notes. It was as if the birds were saying in surprise, "Well, well, well, well." There was a fringe of willows along the shore and our camp was made on a wide rocky bar. The boats were pulled high up among the willows with their bows resting on solid ground, and the bow lines were carried far back and secured to heavy stones.

That night Felton, as spokesman, complained to me about the quantity and temperature of lunch that we had eaten at noon and I welcomed the opportunity to complete the organization of the expedition by making arrangements to have permanent cooks. Where no one in a party has been employed to do the cooking the only equable arrangement is to have all the men take turns until the "born" cooks come to the surface, and express a willingness to do the work. I had intentionally refrained from employing a cook because I felt certain that the men would survive their own amateur culinary efforts and because I wanted to limit the personnel of the party to men who were qualified for other reasons than that they were good at cooking out-of-doors. Accordingly, I called a conference—primarily to learn how general the complaint was concerning cold lunches and found that only one member of the party "felt weak" after his lunchtime snack of bread, peanut butter, beans, jam and coffee with sugar and evaporated milk. During the next two days I made cooking and dish washing arrangements that endured as long as we were on the river.

Adger and Seager agreed to do all the cooking and the other members of the party were appointed, in teams, to assist as kitchen police. I did not attempt, summarily, to make permanent cooks of Adger and Seager but in our first two days on the river they, with Galloway, practically took the cooking in hand and, when I discussed it with them, they expressed entire willingness to act as cooks for the expedition. These two men were up every morning at four-thirty for six bitter weeks and, by the time the rest of us had our blankets rolled up and camp equipment stored away in the boats, were ready with the welcome call to "Come and get it." Seager was as quick tempered as Adger was calm and tranquil but they worked together perfectly. Adger wrote me later concerning Seager, "One of the men I became very fond of was Seager, who was with me more than any other while in camp. We were the best of friends because we worked together not only on the river but early and late in camp and he never had a cross word to say to me. We never had any arguments about the many things that one can find to argue over while living together as we were."

I have a letter from Seager, also, in which he speaks warmly of Adger. "Among the members of the party smiling Bill Adger deserved a good part of the credit. While in the canyons he never said a harsh word; was continually working for complete unison; and from his very first experience in Rapids No. 5 of Cataract Canyon showed that he was alert to the dangers and could successfully cope with them. In camp he was the first man up and the last man to bed. Morning after morning I watched him get up while the rest of the camp slept on and go forging for wood in order that the fragrance of coffee and frying pancakes should act as an alarm for the less ambitious."

The other men were appointed in groups of two to do kitchen police. Bartl and Carey, from Notre Dame, worked together. Holt and Callaway, from Coe College, were a pair. Felton and Marshall, pals at Harvard, pooled their dishwashing efforts. Weatherhead and McGregory, poet and hobo, were the final two, with McGregory doing his best with stories of impossible adventures to over-awe his sophisticated companion. I paired all but Weatherhead and McGregory as I did because they already had grouped themselves that way and figured that if any man was unfaithful to his job he would accomplish nothing more than disloyalty to his friend. I found later, however, that both would sometimes shirk the dish washing and vigilance was needed to see that the work was not left for the cooks to do. Galloway, as navigating officer, was relived of all work not directly concerned with the boats but frequently helped with the cooking. He was especially good at making flapjacks and it was a treat to watch him, sitting on his heels by the camp fire, smoking a hand-rolled cigarette, calmly tossing into the air—and catching them, cooked-side up, flat in the pan—delicious looking flapjacks an inch and a half thick and a good twelve inches in diameter.

Omitting quantities, here is our ration list for the river trip, replenished at Lee's Ferry and, again, at the foot of Hermit Trail:

Meats, etc.
> Bacon
> Ham
> Dried beef
> Eggs, for two or three days
> Crisco
> Lard
> Evaporated milk

Bread, etc.
> Fresh bread, for two or three days
> White flour
> Corn meal
> Rice

Cream of wheat
Hominy grits
Macaroni
Baking powder

Vegetables
Potatoes
Onions
Carrots
Navy beans
Canned baked beans

Beverages
Coffee, in hermetically sealed tins
Tea
Cocoa

Sweets
Sugar
Jam and marmalade

Acids
Vinegar
Pickles

Fruit, etc.
Dried apples
Dried apricots
Raisins
Peanut butter

Condiments
Salt
Pepper
Mustard
Catsup

The food was carefully divided into two lots and stowed away in the boats so if one of them was lost we would still have at least half of our original supply of everything on the list.

There was no rain during the night we camped at Bow Knot Bend but the ground was wet and the air was cold. Just before dawn I was awakened by the sound of clattering tin and got up hurriedly to drive the dog away from the cold embers of the fire, and a pot of beans intended for our lunch enroute down the river.

CHAPTER III

Morning Finds the River Rising—
Hard Work in Labyrinth Canyon—
Cliff Dwellings—
How the Men Measured Up.

*W*e had hauled the boats half out of the river the previous night with their bows resting on the sloping bank among the willows. When I looked at them in the morning they were floating clear and the willows themselves were all but submerged in the turbid flood. The water had risen several feet and a stake that I had driven in the bank to serve as a marker had disappeared entirely. The river was choked with logs and driftwood and it was apparent that a flood of unusual violence was sweeping through the canyons.

The amount of water in the Colorado varies in average years from 2500 second feet (cubic feet of water flowing by a given point per second) to as much as 95,000 second feet, the low water period being in December and January. The most dangerous floods on the river occur during May, June and July and are caused by melting snow in the upper parts of the river basin in Utah, Wyoming and Colorado. The average discharge for the year is about 20,000 cubic feet per second. When we left Greenriver on June twenty-seventh, the Green was carrying 21,000 second feet and word from Cisco, on the upper Colorado, had been to the effect that even more water than that, 27,000 second feet, was surging through the canyons of the Colorado.

I knew, therefore, that I might expect about 48,000 second feet of water in the river below the junction of the two streams at the head of Cataract Canyon, and hoped sincerely that the level of water would have fallen materially by the time we reached that point. Instead of that, the water rose to 30,500 second feet at Greenriver, on June twenty-ninth, and to 42,800 second feet at Cisco, on the thirtieth. Harry Howland, the government water gauger at Greenriver, became nervous about us and word reached the newspapers that the expedition had been destroyed.

There have been almost unbelievable periods of high water on the Colorado, floods that have caused the river to rise a hundred feet above low water mark. Records extending back for thirty years indicate that the maximum flood in Cataract Canyon has been about 150,000 second feet and, at Lee's Ferry, about 200,000 second feet. Gauge readings and traditional evidence, however, show that a flood of still greater magnitude occurred in 1884. On July fourth of that year a gauge reading of 18.5 feet was recorded by the United States Weather Bureau at Fruita, Colorado. By extending the rating curve for the gauging system at Fruita it has been estimated that the flow of the Colorado at Fruita July fourth, 1884, was about 125,000 second feet. It is reasonable to assume that the Green River was discharging 100,000 second feet at the same time. This would indicate that the flood of 1884 reached a stage of 225,000 second feet in Cataract Canyon!

Jerry Johnson, who was living at Lee's Ferry in 1884, tells how he rescued his cat, which was marooned by this flood and was resting uncomfortably in the forks of an apple tree. As he waded out to get the cat, the height of the water on the trunk of the tree was indelibly impressed upon his mind. It has since been determined by running a line of levels from the apple tree to the present gauging station that the flood of 1884 may have reached a stage of 250,000 second feet at Lee's Ferry. On my journey through the Upper Granite Gorge I found water-piled driftwood lodged among rocks a hundred feet above the prevailing level of the water, left there no doubt by the flood of 1884.

I was thoroughly aware of the danger of sudden floods on the Colorado and viewed with misgiving the sullen, muddy current as it swept through the narrow, high-walled canyons and decided that, in the circumstances, I could do nothing better for the morale of the expedition than to shave.

One learns, finally, to shave under any and all conditions. I remember the difficulties that we encountered when we were on our way to France during the war. There was a scarcity of water and the men were instructed to use none of it except for drinking purposes. Sentries were stationed at the water butts to turn away men who might attempt to fill their mess cups. The guards, however, were left without instructions concerning what should be done when men were seen leaving the water butts with their cheeks puffed out, and hundreds of freshly shaved faces proved alike the ineffectiveness of prohibition, and that wonders can be accomplished even with a mouthful of water. I used cold coffee once or twice but do not recommend it, the army variety at least is likely to leave a stain.

There was a similar scarcity of shaving water on the Colorado. We had filled our large buckets with river water the night before, however, and half a pint of that sufficed. I learned finally to make a cup of water do for brushing my teeth, shaving and washing my face, with enough left over to wet my hair. After that first day in Labyrinth Canyon I rarely missed shaving while the younger members of the party allowed their whiskers to grow "to see how they would look at Needles."

I have said that the water in the river carries six-tenths per cent of sand and silt but that does not begin to tell how much sediment it carries along in suspension. Farther down stream the water is red at times but here it was almost brown, about the color of strong coffee to which a very little cream has been added. The sand that it carried was so heavy that in backwaters where the current was not swift, the debris settled out and re-mixing in the main current was necessary to restore the homogeneous mixture of water and sand.

Galloway showed us how to settle the muddy water by adding to a bucketful of it a few drops of evaporated milk, and stirring it vigorously. Also, he showed us how the same result could be achieved by stringing a few broad, flat cactus leaves on a stick, cutting them open so that the juice would exude and whirling them around in the water. We also allowed water to settle overnight in buckets and, when we started off in the morning, usually had our canteens filled with reasonably clear fluid. But the days were hot and as a rule our quart canteens were empty by mid-morning. We would then scoop our bailing cans full of water and permit it to settle for a few minutes as well as it could in the moving boats before drinking it. There were many days when there was no time for the water to settle and then we simply scooped it up, closed our eyes, drank it down—and then carefully kept our teeth from grinding together until the sand had been washed a little out of our mouths. But our stomachs suffered for that. The Colorado is one river upon which a traveler can almost perish from thirst.

It was five o'clock when I sounded reveille at Bow Knot Bend on the morning of June twenty-ninth, and we were under way at seven. There was some difficulty loading up on account of high water and the impossibility of pulling the boats through the willows up to the new shore line, but even that did not delay us beyond the hour that I had set for our departure. Seager and Bradley did not go with us in the boats but climbed up the narrow part of the bend instead, to make photographs of the country and of us as we drifted down the river.

There are no rapids in Labyrinth Canyon but the current was so swift that we were in constant danger of being swept against sheer walls at every bend in the river. Galloway, Holt and Callaway went first in the *Dellenbaugh* and I, following with McGregory, Weatherhead and Carey in the *Coronado*, watched carefully where Galloway ran his boat, and how he avoided crashes at the river bends. At his suggestion we had long since abandoned the sweeps and used our oars only to hold our position in the channel, the swollen current carrying us down fast enough for our purpose. At one place we saw ourselves drifting down upon a snag of driftwood piled high against a rock in the middle of the river. We started to pull away from it. A long log swung into position parallel to the boat just far enough away to keep McGregory and Weatherhead from dipping their oars into the water and, before we were clear of that obstruction, we had crashed headlong into the pile of drift. Fortunately, the boat swung clear without upsetting.

Bradley made pictures of us when we came into sight around a bend in the river and we ran ashore to pick him up. Seager resumed his place in the *Dellenbaugh*.

There was little opportunity to admire the gorgeous orange and red walls of Labyrinth while we were passing through the canyon and yet the day is crowded with memories of magnificent cliffs rising 500 to 1000 feet above the water's edge—buff, orange and red sandstone

walls with narrow talus slopes on the outer curves of the river's tortuous course, where the current was strong enough to sweep its channel
clear, and wear away the rocky wall besides. In places the walls actually
overhung the river and were not more than 600 feet apart on top.

I remember the shrill whistles of birds, sounds that were beautiful in themselves, and were doubled or trebled in their beauty by
remarkable echoes. The only sounds we heard were the bird calls;
the noisy splashing of water where it swept against a pile of driftwood
held against a rock in mid-channel or against the rocks along the
shore at bends in the river; the sound of oars in their row-locks; and
occasionally the call, "Hey, Ruth," or the startling roar of a pistol
shot as a member of one of the crews tested out a likely looking place
for an echo. But, mostly, there was silence—a vast brooding silence
which seemed to be part of the river and the canyons, a silence
which it seemed a little impertinent for us to break. Here in these
upper canyons is some of the most magnificent scenery in the world,
almost unvisited by man, practically unknown.

Where Green River joins the Colorado.

Before noon the walls began to break away, the river widened and it was no longer necessary to give such close attention to our oars. I carried on a desultory conversation with McGregory who told me that he was thirty-two years old, a native of Scotland and a miner by trade. He said he had been a sailor and had visited many strange corners of the earth. I mentioned the names of several bad rivers and

The nine men who completed the journey. Front, left to right, Weatherhead, Galloway, Clyde Eddy, Callaway, with "Rags," the mascot, and Holt. Back row, Seager, Carey, Adger and Bartl.

Labyrinth Canyon, with the high walls closing in.

when he told me in turn that he had navigated all or most of them, I suspected him of stretching the truth a little to gain his point. He pulled a good oar and when, toward noon, we ran into a strong wind blowing up stream and had to swing the boats around, bow first, and row down stream against it, I asked him to ease up a little. I could not pull against him. Where the river widened the wind blew up some white caps and added to the difficulty, if not the danger, of navigation. The stream was full of erratic cross currents and we settled down to a monotonous grind at the oars.

At one-thirty, in the relatively open country between Labyrinth and Stillwater canyons, we sighted a small, flat-roofed house perched on a hill. We had been told by the people in Greenriver to watch for an ancient Indian fort below Labyrinth and we ran ashore, making our noonday camp under a cottonwood tree on the left bank of the river. We had been under way two days, had come seventy-three miles and were safely through one of the lesser canyons of the Colorado.

After lunch two or three of the men climbed up to the house on the hilltop and found that it actually was an ancient block-house or lookout, built of heavy, flat stones and commanding an excellent view of the surrounding country. In bygone centuries a race of Indians inhabited the more accessible upper canyons of the Colorado and doubtless this old house had been used by a dwindling tribe which cultivated the broken land between Labyrinth and Stillwater canyons. Farther up stream, a few miles below Greenriver, I had found and photographed some interesting, well drawn hieroglyphics. Save for the ruins of their homes in the cliffs, an occasional bit of their sign writing and, less frequently, a block-house such as we found at Indian Fort, no trace remains of the race of people who inhabited these valleys thousands of years before Kit Carson and Jim Bridger, first of the white men, penetrated the region in the years between 1824 and 1840. They were gone and forgotten centuries before William Wolfskill, in 1830, laid out the Old Spanish Trail that crossed Green River where Greenriver City stands to-day—ages before Captain Gunnison, in 1853, first established the latitude and longitude of the crossing, and so gave it his name. Through many miles of canyons there remain to-day, unvisited and unexplored, hundreds of cliff dwellings that offer a rich field of exploration for the archeologist interested in piecing together the history of that vanished race.

For a mile or two below Indian Fort the walls were low, and wide expanses of flat country bordered the river on either side. The Butte of the Cross loomed in the distance. Then the walls rose higher, the river narrowed and, at three o'clock, we entered Stillwater Canyon. We had gone but a short distance between the narrowing walls when we saw a cliff dwelling that looked possible for us to reach and ran ashore. In making the landing, Felton, misjudging the velocity of the current and the weight of the boat, used his oar as a boat hook, and broke it squarely in two an inch or two above the blade. This necessitated unlimbering one of the extra oars, while we still were fifty miles above the first bad rapids in Cataract Canyon. By placing a tall sapling against the cliff to aid us in climbing, we were able to reach the cave but others had been there before us and we found nothing but some blackened corn cobs and a few pieces of broken pottery. The dwelling, like many others that we found in the lower canyons, was simply a shallow cave with a neat wall of flat rocks built across the front of it, leaving an entrance wide enough for us to crawl through. We found corn cobs in practically all the houses we visited, making it seem probable that corn was the principal crop cultivated by the ancient Indian tribes.

The red sandstone walls of Stillwater Canyon rose, in many places almost sheer for a thousand feet, abruptly from the river's edge. The tawny flood of hurrying water filled the channel to the base of the cliffs on either side and, for long distances, there was no place to land. As in Labyrinth, the walls were not more than 600 feet apart on top and the river swept majestically between its palisades. There were few places that offered sufficient room for us to camp in safety and we floated along until nearly six o'clock before we found a likely looking spot. I had to keep in mind the possibility of a further rise in the river and select a camp site where it would be possible for us to climb the cliff, and drag the boats after us, in case of such a flood as swept through the canyons in 1884. Then, as if to compensate for lack of hospitality, and to make amends for giving me some anxious moments when I wondered if we would find a place before darkness came, the canyon opened out at a bend in the river and presented us a wide, willow fringed sand bar, which promised us security for the night. Again, we hauled the boats up among the willows and even found a tree around which we tied the lines. I spread my blankets out in a spot high and dry fifty feet from the river and that night enjoyed a long unbroken sleep, the last I was to have for many weeks.

There was time after supper to set down my impressions of the day, and to observe the men in their various occupations. Galloway, wearing a borrowed hat whose collegiate style clashed oddly with his genial, weather-beaten face, squatted on his heels before the fire and whittled idly with a pocket knife. He knew as well as I the tremendous responsibility he had assumed in agreeing to teach my untrained crews the dangerous art of running rapids, but if he doubted his ability to impart the necessary instructions in time to save the men from being drowned in the treacherous river, no sign of that doubt was apparent in his actions. Puffing occasionally at a hand-rolled cigarette and, with the glow of the fire lighting up his face, he blended perfectly into the rugged picture of swirling river and towering cliffs, a generous and human part of the cold, inhospitable wilderness that brooded everywhere about us.

Bradley, after carefully polishing his camera and stowing his equipment away for the night, joined Galloway before the fire, because it was cool after several days of clouds and rain. He, too, smoked a cigarette but the tranquility that characterized Galloway was totally lacking in the camera man. He was cheerful enough and seemed eager to do the work he had to do but his actions made it clear that the job was one he did not relish doing. McGregory, affecting a superior attitude which he had difficulty in maintaining, sought to align himself with Galloway and to share with him the task of training the young college men in the ways of wilderness going. He struggled to establish himself in a position which already had been freely given him as a member of the expedition and tried to compensate with words for what he sensed he lacked in culture. Weatherhead left us soon after supper and I found his camp a little later comfortably sheltered under a ledge of rock a hundred yards from the rest of us. By his own camp fire, in his own diary, he was setting down his impressions of the day. I talked with him for a few minutes and found him full of the wonders of the canyon and the river, the clouds and the sky.

Adger and Seager, after hurriedly spreading out their blankets for the night, prepared supper, which consisted of fried eggs, carrots, bread, apricot cobbler, pickles and cocoa. Stopping occasionally to chat with the others grouped around the fire, they busied themselves further with preparations for breakfast and for lunch the next day. A great pot of beans simmered on the coals and we knew what tomorrow's lunch would be. From the beginning, they made it a practice to cook the beans overnight and stow them away under the deck of the *Dellenbaugh* when we started off in the morning. With most of us keenly interested in food there were times later on as we came to the rapids, when all eyes would be turned to the *Dellenbaugh*, every one knowing that if she tipped too much or shipped too much water there would be no beans for lunch. Seager worked with the efficiency born of experience gained on many expeditions as a student-geologist. Later, he withdrew from the others and worked up his geology notes for the day. Adger, meantime, joined the group around the fire, lighted his pipe, and lapsed into silence. He and Galloway, unlike in many ways, had many traits in common.

Holt and Callaway withdrew early to one of the tents where the former read and the latter indulged himself in one of a cherished box of cigars. Bartl, Carey, Felton and Marshall argued the relative merits of various forms of college athletics and compared the standing of the eastern and western schools.

As I watched them I realized that I had perhaps as diversified a group of men as ever had been brought together in an expedition. How these men would function as a unit events were soon to show. I sensed tensions that I knew would exist until each member of the party had adjusted himself to each of the others, and to the group as a whole. Very little of what was going on beneath the smooth exterior of our relationships with each other broke the surface but in every contact the men sized each other up. They still were feeling their way about to see what advantage could be gained in one place and what conces-sion was necessary to be made in another to establish themselves as members of the party. The human machine which had thrown down the gage of battle to the river still was no machine at all but a loose aggregation of units adjusting themselves to each other, preparatory to their joint attack upon the river. I endeavored to establish con-tact with all the men, to anticipate their responses, to determine in advance how they would react upon one another. I found ways to ease strains, to encourage better understanding between men who were not so far apart as they thought they were. After leaving Greenriver, until we reached Lee's Ferry, 332 miles below, where four men left the expedition, it was not necessary for me to alter the position of the men in the boats. Differences, in one way or another, were adjusted; they learned to work together and to live together on the river and in camp along the shore. They learned to make necessary allowances for each other's weaknesses and eccentricities, and became a unit in their handling of the physical equipment with which they made their fight. There were weak parts in their machinery but the machine as a whole worked smoothly and was strong and efficient. Once the preliminary adjustments were made, the group held together and worked with little friction during the long, hard weeks that we spent on the river.

CHAPTER IV

Stillwater Canyon—
In Camp Below the Junction—
We Examine Rapids No. 1—
A Mysterious Message.

J was awake at four on the morning of June thirtieth. Adger and Seager began stirring around at four-thirty, and, at five, the shrill sound of my whistle announced to the others that day had come. I did not like to use a whistle for that purpose and tried usually to make reveille sound friendlier and less impersonal by adding, "Let's go," or "Up all hammocks," but doubt if that helped very much, especially on cold, wet mornings when overhanging clouds added to the gloom of the narrow canyons. I soon discovered that Bartl and Carey sometimes required a separate, more insistent reveille and repeated calls of "Yeh, Bartl," and "Yeh, Carey," were needed to arouse them. Weatherhead sometimes was so far away that he did not hear reveille at all and a special expedition was needed to find him, and get him started for the day. However, he usually heard the whistle and when I called out his name, his answer would come back to me from somewhere among the rocks and presently he would join us, smiling and cheerful, with his duffel ready to pack away.

A glance at the boats showed them high and dry among the willows, the water having dropped a foot or more during the night. Logs were floating by, however, and I knew that the river still was unusually

high. We finished breakfast, loaded the boats and were under way a
few minutes before seven. Brilliant sunlight flooded the canyon. We
floated along so quietly that we surprised a small herd of deer and Holt
banged away at them with an ineffective looking pocket revolver.
Later he tested his marksmanship by shooting repeatedly at a young
duck. There are few birds and animals in the canyons and, in the lower
gorges, there are miles where not so much as a blade of grass can gain
foothold along the rocky shore. In Labyrinth, Stillwater and Glen canyons, however, we did see many birds, a few deer and, in one place,
an otter. Galloway was on alert for "beaver sign" and told me that he
planned, some day, to re-visit the canyons on a trapping trip.

At eleven-thirty we reached the junction of the Green and Colorado, completing the journey of 116 miles from Greenriver in almost
exactly three days. In my carefully planned itinerary I had allowed
myself four days for this part of the journey and was, therefore, ahead
of schedule. Our loss in altitude for the distance amounted to 215 feet.
A fall of less than two feet per mile had made fast going through
Labyrinth and Stillwater and I looked forward with some concern
to the next forty miles where, in Cataract Canyon, the fall per mile
amounts in places to nearly thirty feet. Our journey to the junction
had been on the Green, from that point on our voyage would be on
the tawny bosom of the Colorado.

The Colorado River, little known because of its inaccessibility, is
the ninth largest river on the Northern American continent, and the
fifth in the United States. Its basin covers 244,000 square miles, situated in seven states, and the stream, cliff-bound nine-tenths of the
way, is 1700 miles long from its source to its mouth. Its basin is divided
into three parts which are topographically separate and distinct. The
southwestern part, a narrow coastal plain between Grand Wash Cliffs
and the Gulf of California, is in general but little above the level of the
sea, though isolated mountains here and there rise to an elevation of
several thousand feet. The central part, through which the stream has
cut its canyons, is a great plateau region which has a general elevation
of 5000 to 8000 feet. This part is bounded on the east and west by the
Rocky Mountains, which rise to elevations of more than 14,000 feet;
on the north by the Wind River Mountains, in Wyoming, which reach
13,700 feet or more; and on the west by the Wasatch Mountains, in
Utah, which reach altitudes exceeding 13,000 feet.

The differences in the topographic features of the basin account for the great differences in climate in the three provinces. In the desert region adjacent to the Gulf of California the average annual rainfall ranges from an inch and a half to eight inches and the temperature from about thirty-two degrees in winter to 120 degrees in the summer. In the plateau providence, through which our journey took us, the average annual rainfall is about ten inches, with average temperatures ranging from 100 degrees in the summer to zero or below in the winter months. The northern part of the basin, which includes the principal areas of high mountains, has a mild summer climate but very severe winters. Temperatures of thirty degrees below zero are not uncommon, and the annual rainfall ranges from ten inches along Green River to as much as sixty inches along the Continental Divide. Because of the relatively large amount of rainfall in the upper mountainous section of the basin, and the aridity of the plateau and plains regions, seventy-six per cent of the water in the Colorado River originates in the part of the basin which lies above the mouth of the Green at the head of Cataract Canyon.

The actual source of the Colorado is a group of alpine lakes near Long's Peak in Colorado. Joined by the Green, in eastern Utah, the stream plunges through Cataract, Glen and Grand canyons southward into Arizona, then west almost to the Nevada line and, finally, south again, where it forms the boundary between California and Arizona, into Old Mexico, emptying at last in the torrid Gulf of California. In 1700 miles the river falls 14,000 feet and, in its mad rush to the sea, has carved for itself a system of deep canyons more than a thousand miles long with walls so precipitous that access to them is impossible except in half a dozen places where narrow trails cling precariously to the rocky walls.

The amount of work done by the river in cutting its way to the ocean is beyond comprehension. For untold centuries the swift current, armed with sand, has been grinding at the rocks. The canyons gradually were widened and deepened. Stratum after stratum of the softer sedimentary rocks gave way before the attack of the river until at last it reached, and deeply penetrated, the underlying granite, the very bedrock of the world. This work of erosion still is going on and every year the river carries out to sea 170,000,000 cubic yards of silt, enough eroded material to cover 105,000 acres of land to an even depth of one foot.

At one time the Gulf of California extended 150 miles farther inland than it does to-day. The river, then as now, brought down enormous quantities of silt. Year after year it extended its delta across the gulf until, at last, it had built a dam from shore to shore. Then it turned south and found a new channel to the sea. The water left in the area north of the dam evaporated gradually and what once had been the ocean bed became an arid valley, its central portion 280 feet below sea level. This region, formerly called the Colorado Desert, now is known as Salton Basin and its heart is California's rich Imperial Valley.

We reached the junction of the Green and the Colorado at eleven-twenty, and had lunch in a small grove of cottonwood trees. All of us then climbed part way up the talus slope at the foot of the cliff, towering 1300 feet above the river. A tremendous volume of turbid, swirling water was flowing down the Colorado and a great mass of logs and driftwood apparently held back by the larger volume of that stream, partly blocked the mouth of the Green. The river below the junction was 500 feet wide, and according to records that I had, was twenty-five or thirty feet deep.

I had carried my camera up the slope and while I was making pictures a great bowlder slipped its insecure perch on the cliffs above and came hurtling down, narrowly missing us where we stood in a startled group. A few minutes later, before we returned to the boats, I heard the sharp, reverberating crash of another similar plunge and, before we left the vicinity of the junction two days later, heard many of them. Kolb tells how "Jimmie," a member of his expedition, while passing through the canyons above Greenriver, finally lost his nerve when day after day the party had narrow escapes from falling bowlders and, at the first place where it was possible to get out, fled from the river in a panic. This, however, was the only place in 800 miles where falling rocks were a serious menace and I believe that recent heavy rains, loosening the bowlders, were largely responsible for the unpleasant bombardment at the entrance to Cataract Canyon. I never was quite happy, however, when heavy rains compelled me to seek shelter at night under overhanging ledges of rock. There was no way to tell when one of them might slip and crush me under its tremendous weight.

The junction of these two rivers is one of the most remote and inaccessible spots anywhere on the North American continent. Prior to the Civil War the United States Government tried in vain for several years to get an expedition through the arid Land of Standing Rocks to the point where the two rivers join. The country on top is made impassable by a labyrinth of deep and narrow side canyons and Powell, voyaging down the river in 1869, was the first white man to reach the junction. It is possible now to get there either from Moab, on the Colorado, or from Greenriver, on the Green, but the difficulties of navigation are so great that it is doubtful if, even to-day, sixty years after its discovery, more than a hundred persons ever have visited the lonely spot. The river at the junction is 3875 feet above sea level and the broken, jagged walls rise steeply another 1300 feet. A narrow fringe of hackberry and cottonwood trees find scant foothold on the shore at the base of the cliffs.

The augmented river, a tawny, relentless, swirling flood, filled the gorge from wall to wall and the high sandstone cliffs stood as mute reminders of the fate that awaited us if our boats were wrecked in Cataract Canyon toward which the stream was hurrying. L. M. Chaffin had told me before we left Greenriver that we would find a satisfactory camp site in a draw on the right bank three miles below the junction and, after lunch, we set out to find the place. We pulled our boats out around the logs and driftwood and then, hugging the shore, dropped down the river. The cliffs receded on the right and presently we came upon a valley on that side, with willows along the shore and a grove of cottonwoods extending a quarter of a mile back to the foot of the cliffs. We ran ashore and picked out a place to camp. On the way back to the boats we stopped a minute by a bowlder to admire a gorgeous colored lizard. Rags joined us out of curiosity and reached a paw out gingerly to see what the strange creature was. The lizard, startled, gave a wild leap and landed on Galloway, whose turn it was then to be startled. He frantically brushed the reptile off his shoulder and it darted away, with Rags in hot pursuit. The dog learned finally to creep up on the lizards and caught many of them. Because he was not quite an Airedale the men saw nothing wrong in calling him a "lizard hound."

It was then about three o'clock in the afternoon and, leaving the others to unload the boats and make camp for the night, Galloway and I went down along the shore to examine Rapids No. 1 of Cataract Canyon. This is where Brown lost a raft to which he had unwisely entrusted most of his provisions, with the result that his men went through the canyon on starvation rations. The river was high but the rapids did not look impossible to run. I asked Galloway to point out to me in turn each of the danger spots and listened closely while he told me what the perils were that lurked in each of the many dangerous places. We returned to camp and, with the roar of the rapids still pounding in my ears, I remembered that I had not found time at Greenriver to test upon myself the buoyant qualities of my life preserver. All the life preservers had been examined, and even tested by the men, but I still did not know how much swimming I should have to do, and how much I could depend upon my life preserver if I were thrown into the river. Accordingly, I put it on and, before an appreciative audience stepped off, fully clothed, into the river—and was gratified to find that I rose promptly to the surface and floated, shoes, shirt, hat, trousers and all.

Galloway had expressed a desire to stop long enough for him to effect an alteration in the *Dellenbaugh*. I was glad to wait as long as possible for the high water to subside and decided to spend a full day at this comfortable camp. That would give us a day to make motion pictures, rest a little, and further adjust ourselves to one another before entering the forty wild miles of Cataract Canyon.

That was a red letter day on the journey down the river. During the afternoon Bartl played harmonica as accompaniment to Carey's songs. Holt and Seager busied themselves with geology notes. Marshall laid out his blankets and slept for several hours. Felton wrote letters. Weatherhead established his camp somewhat removed from us and wrote voluminously in his diary. Callaway fished but had no luck. Adger, with his shirt off, wander around smoking a pipe. Bradley oiled and polished his camera and Galloway worked on the boat. McGregory talked to any one who would listen. No rain threatened and the only tent that has been put up was intended to protect the rations. We had come that far without mishap. The men—selected at long range upon the basis only of information contained in their letters, most of them strangers to each other ten days before—were demonstrating in greater or lesser degrees the qualities that I had reason to believe they possessed, and were learning rapidly to pull in unison, both in the boats and out of them. We lacked experience but the margin of safety that I had allowed, in extra men and more than enough equipment, I felt would see us through.

In the evening Marshall, Felton, Callaway, Bartl and Carey climbed into one of the boats, thirty feet or more from where the rest of us sat around a pleasant camp fire, and regaled us with songs. John Brown's baby had a cold upon his chest, which required a deal of hilarious dosing with camphorated oil. There were parodies addressed to each of us at the camp fire, college songs, and at least one delightful and clever verse dedicated to the river. Unfortunately, that ribald verse cannot be repeated here. The concert continued until nine o'clock and a few minutes later all of us were asleep.

The next day was devoted to various chores. Motion pictures were made of all the men, singly or in pairs, and in the afternoon Bradley, Carey, Weatherhead and Felton went with me down along the shore to photograph the rapids. I was pleased to see that the river had dropped and that the rapids looked less formidable than on the previous afternoon. On the way back to camp the whirr of a rattlesnake directed our attention to still another danger of the river trip and Carey began searching eagerly for it, poking around under the rocks with a small stick and leaving the vicinity reluctantly when it finally became apparent that the snake had eluded him.

Galloway, McGregory, Holt and Callaway worked most of the day on the *Dellenbaugh*, laboriously sawing off a strip of the boat's two-by-four oak keel. It was Galloway's suggestion and in that, as in everything pertaining to navigation, I welcomed his advice and counsel.

Parley Galloway was forty when he joined my expedition at Greenriver and most of his life had been spent trapping and hunting in and around the upper canyons of the Colorado River. His father, Nathan Galloway, guided Julius Stone's expedition through the Grand Canyon in the winter of 1909, and although Parley's trapping expeditions on the river never had led him below the junction of the Green and the Colorado, he was familiar with the stream, and with the rapids in the canyons above Greenriver. His experience with the river began at the age of fifteen, when he accompanied his father on a winter trapping trip through Lodore and Desolation canyons in northeastern Utah. From that time on, for many years, he and his father built boats in the upper river and spent the winter seasons in the lonely canyons, trapping, hunting and, of necessity, running their boats through the rapids. He was a thoroughly competent river man, quiet, fearless and unassuming. When I made him chief of navigation, I appointed him instructor, as well, of my band of strong, intelligent and eager—but totally inexperienced—band of river explorers. I believe that we could have gone the last 400 miles of the journey without Galloway's help but I am equally certain that we would not have survived the first 400 miles without him. Successful rapids running calls for intimate knowledge of the river, cool judgment, courage, willingness to take appalling but unavoidable chances, and fine skill in handling boats. There are few men in the world who are qualified to act as chief boatmen with expeditions on such rivers as the Colorado and I cannot sufficiently emphasize the importance of placing such a man in charge of navigation. Most of the tragedies that are reported from year to year on the river would not occur if sufficient heed were given to Powell's admonition concerning the unrelenting fury of the river and the ever present dangers of the river trip. The Colorado has amply demonstrated its ability to destroy badly equipped expeditions. Even with Galloway's knowledge, strength and courage to help us, and with equipment that proved its fitness a thousand times, pure luck had much to do with our getting through at last with two of the three boats and nine of the thirteen men who started.

We had supper early and, afterward as they were doing kitchen police together—scrubbing out the pots and pans with soap, sand and muddy water—I overheard McGregory telling Weatherhead about something that happened once on shore leave in Colombo and I judged by Weatherhead's non-committal grunts that he did not believe all he was being told. But it pleased McGregory to attempt in that way to bridge the gap between himself and the young man from Harvard and doubtless supplied the latter some interesting material for his diary.

There was singing again that night but it lacked vigor and did not continue long. The quintette of the previous evening had been reduced to four through the loss of Marshall, who had gone to bed ill, but I suspected that his absence did not account entirely for their failure to sing with the zest of the previous night. During the day all of the men had gone down to examine the rapids and I concluded that an intelligent realization of the dangers confronting them was largely responsible for a noticeable absence of careless abandon in their songs. Finally, the effort ceased. They sang no more that night, and they never sang again during the six weeks we spent on the river until we were safe below the last bad rapids in Lower Granite Gorge.

We went to bed early and as the flames of our camp fire gave way to dying embers the vast, black silence of the wilderness settled over us. Stars sparkled in the bowl of sky that rested on the encircling canyon walls and as lesser sounds died away there came to us faintly the threat and thunder of the distant rapids. I was reminded of a night ten years before when I lay with a group of men in a stable in France listening to the roar of guns along the front and wondered again, as I had wondered then, what would happen the next day to my outfit in its first contact with the enemy. Thirteen men lay courting sleep, each with his own thoughts. We were far away from the busy hum of our accustomed lives, remote, solitary, hemmed in by cliffs, hidden away in the depths of Cataract Canyon. Then, suddenly and unmistakably from the top of the cliffs came the sound of a human voice.

I sat up, wide awake instantly, and listened for the sound to be repeated. Again, came the faint call and putting on my shoes, I hastened out into a clearing and gave an answering shout. Adger joined me and we stood, partly dressed, listening intently and then the words came faintly to us,

"I have a message for you, will be down in the morning."

"Who for?" I called back and the only answer was four pistol shots and though I called repeatedly, no further answer came from the top of the cliff.

There were a few minutes of excited discussion in camp and Galloway expressed his opinion that the four shots were intended to represent the letters of my name, and that the message was for me. I remembered a telegram Bradley had sent to New York, however, and what Chaffin had told me about his sons herding cattle somewhere along the rim of Cataract and determined to station the camera man below the rapids next morning and, if possible, to delay the delivery of the message until we had filmed the running of at least one rapids.

My expedition still was not safely started on its journey, my dream even yet might not come true. I spent another restless night such as I had spent in New York when, at the last minute, certain of my plans seemed destined to fail; such as I had spent at Greenriver when I could not feel assured that all the men would start; and such as I was to spend later at Lee's Ferry and Bright Angel, when there would be the pos-sibility that too many men, or important "key" men, would desert the expedition. So much depends on so little, and there is no sure way to prophesy human behavior. I spent the night with sometimes almost unbearable thoughts and was glad, when at last there was a glow of light in the eastern sky.

CHAPTER V

Through the First Bad Rapids—
The *Powell* Swept Through No. 5—
Wreck of the *Dellenbaugh*—
Adger Kills a Rattlesnake.

*R*eveille was sounded at five o'clock Saturday morning, July second, and immediately after breakfast several of us helped Bradley carry his motion picture equipment down to the foot of the second bad rapids where he made his set-up to photograph us running through. Then, leaving him there to wait, the rest of us returned to camp. On the way back I again examined the river and was pleased to see that, with a steadily diminished flow of water, the rapids looked less dangerous than it had the afternoon before.

When we reached camp I found my worst fears realized, one of Chaffin's sons was there with a telegram from New York ordering Bradley off the river.

The distance from Greenriver to the junction, by water, is 116 miles. In a direct line it is about sixty. How far it is by trail I do not know, but young Chaffin told me that the telegram had been received within an hour of the time we left Greenriver with instructions to deliver it at once at any cost, and that four days of hard riding on horseback had been required to overtake us at the head of Cataract Canyon. I believed I saw a ray of hope in that and asked him how much difficulty there would be getting Bradley and his equipment out. He told me he would have to go on to his ranch for additional horses and for ropes to haul the equipment up the cliffs and expressed the opinion that Bradley could not get back to Greenriver in less than ten days. I then asked him to delay the delivery of the telegram until we had run the first two rapids.

Marshall was not feeling well and Chaffin volunteered to take his place in the boat. Bradley's telegram was turned over to Marshall, the rest of us adjusted our life preservers and shoved the boats away from shore. Galloway went first with Holt, Callaway and Seager in the *Dellenbaugh*. I followed with McGregory, Carey and Weatherhead in the *Coronado*, and Adger brought up the rear with Bartl, Felton and Chaffin in the *Powell*. I watched Galloway, and knew that Adger was watching me. It was our first lesson in rapids running, in a hard school where failure to learn promptly, failure to follow instantly the example of our instructor, might result in disaster.

We swept down into the rapids and found that they were "easy" ones. The boats rolled and tossed. Waves splashed over the decks and water poured over the sides into the cockpits but there were few rocks for us to dodge; the boats were seaworthy and we plunged safely through.

There was bright sunshine in the canyons, we were there in force of numbers and, before we came to the end of the rapids, the men were shouting wildly with the thrill of the adventure. Chaffin seemed especially pleased and his shrill cowboy yells could be heard distinctly above the roar of the cataract. We ran ashore without difficulty and while the men bailed the boats they told each other excitedly about the waves that splashed water in their faces and rolled over the decks of the boats, half filling the open cockpits with muddy water. It was as if they had just enjoyed a ride on a roller-coaster at an amusement park rather than through a dangerous rapids whose rocks and whirl-pools were very real, and very ready to snatch away their lives.

While the boat-loads of gay, excited men still were "in the picture," with their happy shouts still ringing in his ears, Bradley received his telegram. He read the message which released him from the assignment and then we discussed with Chaffin the difficulty of getting out. Chaffin assured him that it would take at least ten days to reach Greenriver and I told him that we should be at Lee's Ferry in less time than that. I did not deliberately exaggerate the difficulties of the return trip overland to Greenriver, nor did I intentionally deceive him concerning the dangers of the river journey. I believe that it was his own zeal for pictures that caused him finally to decide to stay with us. He had made a hundred feet or more of fine, exciting film and saw the possibility of making more. He had watched the boats plunge through the rapids and the danger did not seem as great as he had been led by the people in Greenriver to believe it was. He wanted to stay and, giving as his reason the difficulty of getting his equipment out, wrote a message to his chief saying that he would continue with us as far as Lee's Ferry. I prepared a telegram asking the newsreel organization to have a message for me at the Ferry, and another camera man ready to join the expedition when we reached the foot of Bright Angel Trail. Then, with the telegrams, Chaffin started alone on his long journey back to Greenriver. I breathed freely again and, asking Galloway and Adger to accompany me, went to look at Rapids No. 3. Two bad rapids run, only 298 to do!

Rapids No. 3 did not look particularly dangerous and, with Bradley riding in the *Powell* with Adger, all the boats were run safely through. Where now were the dangers described by the people in Greenriver? The men behaved as if they were at a picnic; my "party" was a huge success.

Then we came to No. 4.

There were approximately 300 bad rapids in the 788 miles between Greenriver and Needles, most of them occurring where great piles of rocks and bowlders have been carried into the river's bed by smaller streams entering through intersecting side canyons. Such a rapids is illustrated in Fig. 1. The débris brought down by the tributary stream forms an obstruction extending out from the mouth of the ravine, part way across the river. The descending water, as illustrated in the diagram, is forced against the river bank opposite the projecting fan-shaped pile of rocks—sometimes with such force that it gradually cuts the cliff away and forms a bend in the channel. As indicated in the drawing, a large eddy or backwater will be formed on the down stream side of the obstruction. The figure does not show rocks in the middle of the river, actually its channel through the rapids frequently is dotted with them. The head of a rapids is the banked-up expanse of eager, restless water which occupies the whole breadth of the channel immediately above the point where the torrent plunges

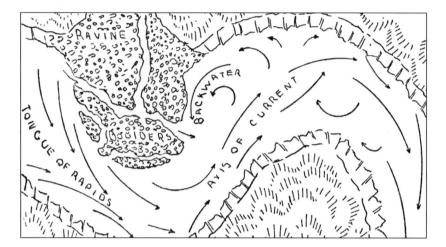

Figure 1. Most of the rapids on the Colorado River are formed by fan-shaped piles of rocks
and bowlders which have been carried into the river's bed by smaller streams
entering through intersecting side canyons. The descending water is forced over
to the river bank opposite the projecting point and a large backwater is formed
on its down stream side. This drawing serves also to illustrate the formation of
the river bed, and the course of the current at Dark Canyon Rapids.

over the obstruction. Its tongue is the "V" shaped, rushing slope of
water whose tip points to the approach, where the axis of the current
continues, a moving ridge of water rushing headlong through the
whirlpools, backwaters and eddies that lurk behind the obstruction
and along the shore.

In entering the rapids illustrated in Fig. 1 the boat, floating stern
first down the stream, would be run fairly close to the pile of bowlders on the left bank and permitted to drop down into the tongue
of the rapids a little to the left of the point of the "V." Then an
effort would be made to keep the boat, still pointing stern first down
stream, just clear of the ridge of waves in the axis of the current, far
enough from shore to avoid being caught in the backwater below the
obstruction. When safely through the rapids the boat would be run
ashore to the left.

Another frequently encountered type of rapids is illustrated in
Fig. 2. This rapids is produced by a sudden narrowing of the walls
that hem the river in. In rapids of this kind there are strong backwaters and whirlpools on both sides of the channel below the projecting ledges and the axis of the current is directly in the center of the

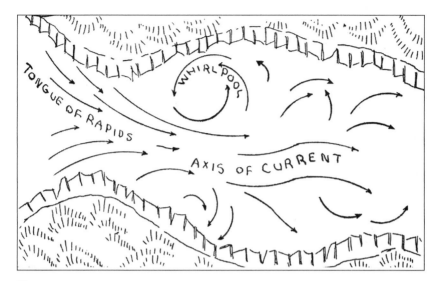

Figure 2. Many rapids are produced by ledges extending from each bank, thus narrowing the channel through which the water has to pass. Whirlpools are produced below the projecting points. The channel in rapids of this type usually is clear of rocks and the apex of the current is near the center of the river.

river. The channel in such a rapids is likely to be swept clear of rocks and the rapids presents few difficulties except at periods of high water when the swollen current backs up before the contracted portion of its gorge and rushes through the narrow place at tremendous speed, producing dangerous whirlpools, both traveling and stationary. Other kinds of rapids are produced by sudden shallowing of the river due to ridges in its bed; to enormous bowlders; or to rocky islands in the river; or to any combination of the causes I have described.

Whirlpools are a serious menace to navigation, especially at high water, and are likely to occur almost anywhere in the narrow canyons. Most of them are caused by rocky ledges jutting out from the banks of the river, deflecting the part of the current nearest shore, causing great variation in its velocity, forcing the main body of water to take a more or less curved or zigzag course through the gorges. Whirlpools occur most frequently along the edges and at the lower ends of rapids but at high water are likely to be encountered in any section of the river where the channel is narrow and tortuous and the declivity is steep enough to impart great velocity to the current. Hundreds of times our boats—the large ones twenty-two feet long and five feet in the beam—were caught in whirlpools and turned around and around in them, with the strength of four men pulling at the oars needed finally to haul them clear. I have seen the bow of one of the large boats sucked down level with the gunwale in a whirlpool, and was grateful that the boat was big and seaworthy. When such a whirlpool draws a man within its fatal coils it sucks him down, smothers him and crushes his body against the rocks that form the river's bed. At high water there are strange and terrible traveling whirlpools which may traverse the whole breadth of the river in their gyrations, and threaten with destruction boats and men alike. Whirlpools are a constant menace. It was largely out of respect to them that we wore life preservers almost constantly and it was whirlpools that I had in mind when I instructed the men to cling to the boats in case of an upset in the river.

I discussed for a long time with Galloway the advisability of attempting to run the boats through No. 4. Considered by itself this rapids was not a bad one but the water was so high that the ridge of waves which formed the apex of No. 4 extended down stream almost to the head of No. 5, whose violent fall made it one of the worst rapids in Cataract Canyon. Would we be able to pull ashore below one rapids in time to prevent our being carried over the other, or would the swift current sweep us to destruction in No. 5? I remembered that the river had outpulled us even in Labyrinth Canyon where there were no rapids. If we did not ship too much water in No. 4 we probably could get the boats ashore but if too many waves broke over us, flooding our open compartments with hundreds of pounds of muddy water, we inevitably would be swept into the fury of the lower cataract—in boats already waterlogged and unmanageable.

All of the men walked down with me and looked at No. 5, and every one of them appreciated its dangers. Few rocks were showing on account of the height of the water but there were many giant waves, such as I had never seen before except in the gorge below Niagara. The waves which form the apex of a rapids are little like the waves of the sea. Waves in the ocean merely rise and fall and floating objects rise and fall with them. The water remains stationary as the form of the wave moves forward before the wind. A boat, unless it is moving in one direction or the other, rises and falls with the rise and fall of the waves. In a rapids the form of the wave remains stationary and the water rushes furiously through it. In the tongue of a rapids the water may plunge down ten or twenty feet, and bring up suddenly in the trough of a wave twenty feet or more in height. This first great wave at the head of the rapids usually is the largest one of all and half a hundred lesser ones may wait below, a series of billows through which the water rushes at a speed of twenty-five to thirty miles per hour. Nor are these waves smooth mounds of hurrying water up and down which a boat may ride with ease or safety. On the contrary the tremendous power and speed of the current seems to heap the water up in the waves, raising it higher and higher until of its own weight it topples over—backward. A boat, swept into such a wave will strike it near its base. The force of the current thrusts it into the wall of water and the toppling crest falls over backward into the helpless craft. If by any chance a boat is turned about in the current so that it is running broadside when it strikes the wave, it is speedily capsized. We spoke of them as "reverse" waves and encountered them in every rapids.

The great wave at the head of No. 5 fascinated me. The river seemed to pause at the head of the rapids, collect its fearful energies and then plunge furiously toward the base of the great wave at the point of the "V" which formed the tongue of the rapids. The wave, a dozen feet high from trough to crest, remained stationary in the river, with its muddy crest rolling over backward up stream. I felt certain that our boats, thrust into that wave would instantly be swamped and their crews thrown into the river. What would happen to them then I feared, as I looked down stream at the series of billows that marked the apex of the rapids, would mark a dismal end to our gay adventure. Galloway expressed his belief that we could pull ashore between the rapids and I gave the order to run through No. 4.

Each man carefully adjusted his life preserver and removed his shoes. Some of the men already had begun to abandon their clothing and doubtless we were a strange looking group of men when we took our places in the boats. Adger and Bartl had abandoned their shirts. Holt wore a close fitting bathing suit. Weatherhead had a "ten-gallon," wide brimmed Stetson hat. No two men were dressed alike, except for our life preservers. Endeavoring not to be too serious about it, I warned the men again to cling to their boats if they were upset and then, with Galloway in the lead, we shoved off into the current.

Turning the bows of our boats toward the opposite shore and pointing them slightly up stream we pulled toward the middle of the river. Then, when we were out far enough to avoid striking the rocks near shore the bows were pointed directly up stream and we floated, stern first, with the current. Again I watched Galloway, who led the way and, again, I knew that Adger was watching me. In that position, stern first floating with the current, we were carried into No. 4. The boats plunged crazily, water poured in over the sides. The stern of my boat was thrust repeatedly into great muddy waves whose turbid water swept over us, wetting, half blinding us. Our oars were all but useless in the smother of foam. Galloway turned the bow of his boat toward shore and I did the same with the *Coronado*. The boat was partly filled with water and we made slow progress against the current. The crew of the *Dellenbaugh* ran their boat near enough shore for one of the men to make a landing. Presently Carey was able to leap ashore with a line from the *Coronado*. We were safe, but the *Powell* was not behind us.

I looked up and was dismayed to see the third boat still in mid-stream, her crew pulling vainly against the swift current. I could hear Adger's voice urging the men to "Stroke, Stroke, Stroke!" Then they realized they could not get ashore.

Adger stood up, waved his hand to us and looked intently down the river. In a second he was down again and in compliance with his orders the men turned the bow of the boat toward the opposite shore and pulled again for the middle of the river. Menacing rocks lay close to shore and I knew that he hoped by this maneuver to guide his boat out around them, preferring to risk the hazards of the long line of reverse waves that formed the apex of the current where it rushed pell-mell through the rapids.

Stern first, with their oars poised to take advantage of any opportunity to get ashore, the men were swept down into the tongue of the rapids. Bradley was riding, an unwilling passenger, in the boat and as it was swept at thirty miles an hour down into the rocks, waves and whirlpools of No. 5, Bradley's professional training, his loyalty and courage, caused him to throw caution to the winds. Partly kneeling on the deck of the 'midships cabin, Bradley pointed his hand camera down stream, released the button and with his eye glued to the finder made motion pictures of the welter of foaming water into which the boat was being swept.

I stood helpless on the shore and saw the great wave at the head of the rapids strike the stern of the boat, roll over the deck and sides, and sweep Bradley back into the open cockpit, carrying his camera overboard. A second later the boat and its precious cargo of human lives had dropped out of sight over the fall into the tumbling waves.

How sick I was of my venture in those first terrible minutes no one will ever know. Four younger men, and Bradley, had been swept into one of the worst rapids on the river. There was no one below to help them out. Whirlpools were waiting to smother them. Great rocks were there to smash their boat. Adger, Bartl, Felton, Marshall and Bradley were at the mercy of the treacherous river.

It would have been suicide to run another boat through. Seizing a cork ring buoy and shouting for the others to follow, I ran down along the shore. Rocks impeded me. I felt that I should never get there and visualized the men struggling in the turbid water, being carried to death in other rapids below.

A thousand yards down stream I rounded a mass of bowlders where they had been piled high by a creek entering from a side canyon on the right—and there was Adger, hurrying back to tell me they had made it safely. There was a great hole in the half-inch mahogany planking of the boat, which had been nearly swamped by the waves but they had made it, and had got ashore below. We made light of the incident but we knew that the men in the *Powell* had escaped death by a narrow margin, and that they owed their lives to Adger's quick decision and to the fact that the boat was built of heavy oak and mahogany, that she was wide in the beam and thoroughly seaworthy.

There was nothing to do but line the other boats around the rapids. Accordingly, the *Coronado* was hauled up on the rocks where the stream could not pound her to pieces, and we were ready for our first let-down. But the cooks had been busy in the meantime and we responded gratefully to Seager's call to "come and get it."

After lunch we had our second lesson of the day in Colorado River navigation. Stout half-inch lines had been securely fastened to the bows and sterns of all the boats and the men were about equally divided between the bow and stern lines when, under Galloway's supervision, we started to edge the *Dellenbaugh* down around the rocks that lined the shore. It sounds fairly simple when I say that the process

"Holes" in the river won the wholesome respect of the members of the expedition. The water, pouring over the great bowlders in the river's bed, forms "holes" to trap unwary navigators.

of lining a boat consists in holding to the lines and permitting the current to carry the boat down along the shore, but actually it is a difficult and dangerous operation. The current is swift and the water, loaded with sand and silt, has tremendous power. Except where rocks actually extend above the surface of the muddy water, it is impossible to know precisely where they are and falls cannot be avoided when the men wade out into the stream to work the boats along. If the boats are kept too near shore they must be lifted over the rocks and if they are run too far out there is constant danger of their being capsized in the river, or jammed against rocks and held there by the force of the current. Always there is the possibility that a man, slipping off the polished surface of a rock, will be caught by the current and swept out into the rapids, or crushed against one of the thousand bowlders along the shore. A broken arm or leg may mean catastrophe.

We started with the *Dellenbaugh*, lifting, tugging and hauling the heavy boat over and around the rocks along the shore, until we came at last to a great bowlder which compelled us, for a moment, to push the boat out into the edge of the main stream, depending upon our skill and the strength of the ropes to snub the craft at exactly the right second and regain control of her after her passage out around

The swift current conspired with jagged rocks to smash the Dellenbaugh.

the rock. Galloway was everywhere and I am not certain that he actually would not have done better if he had been quite alone. We were willing but the work was new to us and when some one, over-zealous and unable to hear Galloway's shout above the roar of the rapids, snubbed the rope at the wrong time, the *Dellenbaugh* swung around in the current, crashed against a rock, turned broadside in the stream, tipped, filled with water and all but disappeared beneath the muddy waves.

Fortunately, there were enough of us to drag her out but the grim determination with which the swift flowing, sand-laden water held the boat pinned against the rock was appalling. The strength of every man was needed on the rope to drag her up on the shore. We found then that a great hole had been smashed in her side and I knew that we could travel no farther that day. The *Dellenbaugh* was planked with five-eighth inch cedar, copper fastened, on one and a half inch by three-quarter inch oak ribs spaced three inches apart, center to center near the bow where the injury occurred. The hole in the boat was as big as a dinner plate, two of the oak ribs had been broken and two others were bent. All this had happened in a relatively quiet stretch while lining the boat along the shore. What chance would we have, boats or men, if we should strike a rock in midstream? We had come equipped with boards, copper sheeting, canvas and paint and by late afternoon the boat, though scarred from its first encounter with the river, was practically as good as new. Later, when our supply of copper was exhausted, we learned to patch the boats with coffee tins.

By the time we had finished patching the *Dellenbaugh* it was too late to complete the let-down and we made camp for the night—or perhaps it would be better to say we made several camps for the night. We always very carefully divided our food between the two larger boats and it was necessary partly to unload the *Coronado* to get out food enough for supper and several trips to the head of the rapids were needed to assemble the necessary variety. The kitchen was down below where the *Powell* had been drawn up on the beach and most of the men were camped down there. Weatherhead, who was ill, went off up a ravine by himself to sleep and I made my camp near the *Dellenbaugh*, drawn up on the rocks midway between the *Powell*, at the foot, and the *Coronado*, at the head of the rapids. Our camp, therefore, was spread out for a thousand yards along the river which was so wide at this point that I felt there was no particular danger of a flood in the night and laid my blankets out among the rocks twenty or thirty feet above the river level. When I went down to the main camp for supper just before dark, Adger showed me a rattlesnake he had killed a few minutes before within twenty feet of the camp fire.

After supper I chatted for a few minutes with the men, then found Weatherhead in his solitary camp, induced him to take some medicine, and returned to the *Dellenbaugh*. By the light of the camp fire I wrote briefly in my diary.

"To-night the *Powell* is down below No. 5; the *Dellenbaugh* is high and dry among the rocks half way down along the shore and the *Coronado* is above, waiting to be lined down. Weatherhead is ill. Total distance for the day not more than 3 ½ miles. Slow going and we must push on in the morning. If we have many such days our rations will not hold out. The waves in the upper part of No. 5, now opposite my camp, are as large as those in the gorge below Niagara, and their threat to-night is roaring in my ears. But for luck there would have been tragedy at No. 5 to-day. The river is still falling and I hope for lower water the rest of the way through. The older men,

Galloway, McGregory, Bradley, are the best workers, the younger men want to ride, and this voyage will not be entirely that. When we hit the big waves the water sweeps over my head and hat, and sometimes almost strangles me. In landing and lining, we are wet to the waist many times."

That night I slept fitfully and made two journeys with my flash-light up stream to see how the *Coronado* was faring, and down to see that the *Powell* was safe. In spite of all that had happened during the day I felt that our first skirmish with the river dragon had disclosed no irremediable deficiencies in the personnel of the expedition and no serious defects in the equipment. I realized, however, that in spite of the possibility of having finally to go on short rations, we might have to go slowly until receding waters robbed the river of some of its tremendous power and we had time in which to become better acquainted with the stream and its dangerous ways.

CHAPTER VI

The Worst Four Miles in Cataract— We Celebrate the Fourth of July— The *Powell* Capsizes.

*M*y call to "rise and shine" aroused the camp at five o'clock on Sunday, July third, and I was relieved to learn that Weatherhead was feeling better. After breakfast all of us went to the head of the rapids, unloaded the *Coronado* and portaged the duffel down to the main camp. Then the boat was lined down part way and both it and the *Dellenbaugh* were run safely through the lower end of No. 5.

Portaging the duffel over the bowlders and driftwood along the shore was a heart-breaking task and even there, at our first long portage, the fat duffel bags with which most of the men had left Greenriver began to lose their rotund shapes. When a man has to make trip after trip, stumbling over bowlders with sacks of flour, potatoes, boxes and bags of canned evaporated milk and other commissary necessities, and then a final one with his duffel bag, he probably will remember items of personal equipment that he does not greatly need. Felton and Marshall sacrificed two expensive but quite useless rubber suits at No. 5. Later other equipment was to go—items that even a seasoned voyager might, in the beginning, regard as absolutely necessary.

The duffel was carefully stowed away in the boats and we were under way again by nine o'clock. Three times in the next four miles we ran ashore above bad rapids, examined them, and ran safely through. At one place Galloway and I, working our way back along the rocky shore toward the boats, discovered the gruesome record of an otherwise unrecorded disaster that occurred on the river three decades before. Scratched on the surface of a flat rock overlooking the river were the words, "Colorado-Pacific Survey Expedition Wrecked Here July 19, 1897." Below the words were crude drawings of three boats, two of them shown broken in half, pinned against rocks in the river. We commented briefly on the pathetic, thirty-year-old monument to the hopes, and perhaps the lives, of an earlier party of canyon voyagers and decided to say nothing about it to the other members of our party. We ran the rapids without mishap and I wondered what cruel combination of rocks and waves had conspired to wreck the boats of our predecessors.

The canyon walls increased steadily in height as we proceeded down the river and brilliantly colored cliffs, composed of alternating layers of limestone and sandstone, towered 2000 to 2700 feet above us. The talus slopes that formed the rocky banks of the river grew steeper and narrower, or disappeared entirely where the walls rose sheer from the water's edge. The stream narrowed to 150 feet and flowed with steadily increasing velocity as it swept relentlessly down into the steep central section of Cataract Canyon. We drifted along for three-quarters of a mile, ran safely through an easy rapids and, at ten-thirty, landed on the right at the head of a cataract whose muddy, tumbling, roaring waves filled the narrow gorge from shore to shore as far as we could see.

The river here drops 115 feet in less than four miles and before us, between narrow, towering walls, was a rapids more than a mile long! A veritable cataract, six thousand feet in length. Restless waves tossed muddy spray, driftwood and great logs alike high into the air, threatening destruction to any one or anything they might seize upon. Steep walls barred our way on the right but a talus slope promised us precarious footing along the other shore, if we could get our boats across the swollen stream above the rapids.

Galloway and I returned to the boats and announced our intention to attempt a landing on the other side of the river. We had run our boats down so near the head of the rapids that it was necessary for us to drag them back up stream to the foot of the fall we had just run through before attempting the quick, hard pull for the other shore. Leaving one man in each boat to fend away from rocks, the rest of us towed the boats up stream to the foot of the rapids we had just negotiated. Then, with Galloway leading in the *Dellenbaugh*, we pointed the bows of our boats diagonally up stream and pulled hard for the opposite shore.

Below us roared the rock-strewn sweep of the most dangerous mile of Cataract Canyon. To point the bow directly up stream would result in the boat being held in mid-channel while the current swept it down into the rapids. To pull too quickly for the other shore would be to lose the few precious yards of advantage that we had gained by hauling the boats up stream. For a moment the current did swing the stern of the *Coronado* around and I found myself looking directly down stream, with the rocks on shore flashing by as the current swept us toward the rapids.

"Back water, McGregory," I shouted. "Back water, Weatherhead. Pull hard, Carey, hard"—and the boat swung around again into proper position. The whole passage, from the instant we shoved off on the right bank until we landed at the head of the rapids on the left, must not have taken three minutes and in that time we crossed 150 feet of swift river, and were swept 600 feet down stream. There were other times on the river when individuals and individual boats were in grave danger but I doubt if there ever was a time when the entire expedition was so near disaster as it was in those three minutes, making a crossing above the mile long rapids in Cataract Canyon.

After a leisurely lunch period, devoted in part to seeking shelter from the fierce midday sun, we let the boats down a quarter or half a mile and made camp on a narrow, rocky bar, barely out of reach of the foaming water. I was pleased to notice during the afternoon that the level of water in the river was dropping steadily. Once, when we left the *Coronado* pulled up among the rocks while we lined the *Powell* down part way, we came back in an hour, to find the *Coronado* half out of the water and had trouble getting her afloat again. We were in water up to our waists most of the afternoon and the air was so cool by six o'clock that I was glad to change into dry clothing. Rain threatened and we put up both the tents, using oars as tent poles and storing our provisions carefully under shelter.

The men were cheerful that night, but were clearly tired after spending part of the morning and all afternoon portaging duffel and letting the boats down along the shore. Our hands were blistered from rowing and practically every man in the party came to me during the afternoon for applications of mercurochrome to big and little injuries sustained while scrambling about on the rocks.

That night, in my diary, I again expressed appreciation of Galloway and his work as navigating officer. I commented also on Bradley's good work as photographer and expressed regret at the prospect of losing him at Lee's Ferry. I noted the fact that I was hungry for candy, that I craved sweets and was rationing a five-cent package of licorice flavored mints that I had got from a slot machine in Greenriver. "Candy," I wrote, "is the only food I crave—that and a drink of nice, clear water."

Most of the men had crowded into one of the tents and the supplies occupied a large part of the space in the other. I slept out and was more nearly comfortable so far as my bed was concerned than I had been before, sleeping with nothing between me and the ground but a poncho and a blanket. My hips were getting hardened to it. Presently rain began to fall. The fire sputtered and went out. The raindrops splashed in my face, then found their way into my poncho, my blanket was wet along the edges and at the top around my head and shoulders. I had gone to bed fully clothed, except for my shoes which I hoped were keeping dry in the tent with the provisions, but a cold, mist-laden wind blew strongly up the canyon and I was wet and uncomfortable. I needed no prodding from my mental watchman to awaken me every two hours to look at the boats, I doubt if I slept that much all night.

Rain was falling when I aroused the camp on the morning of July fourth and Carey has since told me that he hated me sincerely when I routed him out that dismal dawn with my unwelcome call to "rise and shine." My river clothes, lying on a nearby rock, looked altogether too wet and cold to put on before breakfast and, hurriedly placing my blanket in my duffel bag, I threw the poncho over my shoulders and kept on the fairly dry clothes that I had slept in. All the men moved slowly and were so evidently disinclined to break camp that I regretted the necessity for moving on in the rain. I kept on my dry clothes until after breakfast, then packed them away in my duffel bag and changed into the water soaked, cold and uncomfortable trousers, shirt, hat and shoes that I wore during the day. I shaved and was ready for what proved to be my unhappiest day on the river.

One of the axes could not be found after breakfast and it soon became apparent to us that the water in the river had risen enough during the night to cover it, so effectively that we never saw it again. Rain fell intermittently and the younger men, especially, were gloomy, showing little enthusiasm for the difficult work they had to do. Galloway and the members of his crew began lining the *Dellenbaugh* down around the rapids and I followed with the other men, letting down the *Powell*, holding her close to shore by the lines at her bow and stern, floating her with the current around the rocks along the edge of the rapids.

Part way down we came to a "hole" into which the *Powell* was swept by the resistless power of the rising river. There is no way properly to describe a "hole." A "hole" in Rapids No. 22 is pictured on another page but even that picture is inadequate. The muddy water sweeping down stream pours over a great bowlder in the channel. There is a "hump" in the river where the bowlder rests and that hump, called a "pour," is all there is to warn the navigator of the terrible menace in his way. Then, with a roar, the water plunges down into the "hole" and woe betide the man whose boat is caught in its frightful vortex. One navigator on the river, swept toward a "hole" and unable to pull away from it, turned his boat stern first and—resigned himself to fate. The stern of his eighteen foot boat swept over the "pour," dropped down into the "hole" and the boat turned over from end to end on the unfortunate explorer. A "hole" is a miniature waterfall and a man caught under its drop is trapped and held there, battered to pieces, smothered by the cruel, muddy river. After seeing one or two "holes"—there are hundreds of them on the river—the men needed no further evidence of the advisability of clinging to the boats in the event of an upset in the river. A boat might stagger through such a place, a man with nothing better than a life preserver certainly would be drawn under and drowned. "Holes" to me were the most dreadful of the many dangers on the river. Rocks can be seen and they strike you clean and honest blows. Whirlpools are quiet and their dangers lie hidden below the swirling surface of the turbid stream. The possibility of being struck by falling rocks is remote. A "hole" may be hidden anywhere below an innocent looking "hump" in the surface of the water and the churning fury of its vortex—the eddying turmoil of its roaring, foaming water—brings swift death to any man thrown into it. His puny effort is hopeless, struggling vainly against the current which inevitably sweeps him under the "pour," battering him against the rocks until he is dead. I have seen great logs caught in a "hole" and held there for hours, plunged repeatedly under the drop of the water, battered and smashed against the rocks.

We came to such a "hole" on the morning of the Glorious Fourth and our very efforts to avoid it may have had something to do with the events that followed. We were letting the boat down stern first when, just above the "hole" the keel struck a rock and, in that unfortunate moment, the bow line slackened. The boat turned broadside in the river, the current caught it up and swept it over the "pour" into the "hole," where it promptly capsized. There was nothing to do but secure the stern line and let go forward, trusting to the current to sweep her out of the "hole" and swing her against the rocks below. I gave orders accordingly. The boat swept clear, came to the end of her tether and, bottom side up, swung into shore below. We righted her but in striking the rocks one of her hatches was broken and everything inside the cabin was flooded with muddy water. Two oars and a life preserver were torn loose and floated away. We unloaded the boat and learned that Bradley had been the principal sufferer. His motion picture equipment was wet and it looked as if we had lost all or most of our motion picture film, exposed and unexposed. Callaway fished his duffel bag out of the water-filled compartment, hastily unpacked it and lamented loudly when he reached his can of cigars and found it partly filled with water.

Rain was falling in torrents but there was need to unload the *Powell*, which we did, laboriously transporting all her cargo to the foot of the rapids. Then, for safety's sake, we unloaded the *Coronado* as well and portaged her duffel down. We spent several weary hours at that, carrying on our shoulders, over the wet and slippery rocks, hundreds of pounds of duffel, food, blankets and equipment. We lined the boats and were no wetter in the river than out of it. Constant urging was required to keep some of the younger men on the move back and forth along the shore. I learned that two of the men had discussed with Bradley the possibility of deserting the expedition and endeavoring to find their way back up stream to the head of Cataract and out, following Chaffin's trail to Greenriver, but I doubted if they would go and said nothing to them about it. Galloway, Adger, Seager, McGregory and Bradley were little affected by the turn events had taken. The older men as a rule bore up better than the younger ones and I realized that work not worry was largely responsible for the slump in our morale. But we still had 700 miles to go and if a majority of the men were unwilling, or unable, to work I knew that we could not hope to fight our way through to Needles.

We had a cold lunch, with hot coffee, in the rain and after we had finished we sat around on the rocks and rested. The younger men had discarded most of their clothing and few of them wore more than athletic underwear, trousers cut off above their knees and shoes. Few of them had hats. The older men were more completely clothed and all of us sat in the pouring rain, soaked to the skin, cold and uncomfortable. Given time to think, I felt active resentment toward the younger members of the party and all but hated them individually and collectively because they so clearly could not, or would not, beat the river. I resented Bartl's sitting on the lee side of a great rock with the rain dripping unheeded off his hat and down upon his unprotected shoulders—resented his sitting there looking glumly out across the roaring river when I wanted him to smile and simulate a cheerfulness that none of us could feel. I resented Holt and Callaway, Carey, Felton, Marshall, Weatherhead—all of them, because they needed driving when nothing more formidable confronted them than a day of labor in the rain. I was forced to the unwelcome realization that my untrained crew probably was unequal to the task that I had set for it and seriously considered the advisability of abandoning the effort and trying to find our way out of the canyon across the desert to some settlement. I considered this possibility but continued with the work of lining the boats around the mile-long cataract that roared and thundered in the mist and rain. As we came nearer the completion of the task my spirits rose. I saw that we were able after all to make progress against the obstacles that hindered us—my crew, unaccustomed to physical labor, merely needed to learn how to work.

The skies cleared early in the afternoon, there was brilliant sunshine again to cheer us and we got as dry as we could, working in and out of the water lining the boats. We brought the boats finally to a place where we believed it would be safe to launch them again in the rapids and loaded the duffel. Bradley had his camera in working order by that time and expressed a wish to stay ashore and photograph the boats running through.

Weatherhead shoved the *Coronado* off and as he started to hop into the boat he stepped off into deep water. He grasped the gunwale but his life preserver got in his way and prevented his climbing in. Meantime the current had caught us and we were entering the rapids with Weatherhead in grave danger of being carried away. Then Carey dropped his oar, reached over and hauled his companion in beside him. The swift current seized the boat and in the next five minutes we smashed through one great wave after another, some of them so high that they splashed over our heads. One of them struck me in the face and nearly strangled me. The boat, partly filled with water, was unmanageable and neither my crew nor that of the *Powell*, which was duplicating our experience behind us, found it possible to pull ashore as we had planned and I looked up in a moment to see my boat being swept around a bend in the river. What was awaiting us around that bend I did not know. Fortunately it was not another rapids but a backwater instead and we ran ashore on a sand bar on the bank opposite the one on which we had intended to land. The crew of the *Dellenbaugh* had better luck than we and managed to get ashore and pick up our badly frightened camera man. In constant danger every minute he was afloat, he was in only less peril when ashore. Surely this crazy river was no place for a camera man!

We camped on the sand bar and spread out to dry the onions, potatoes, corn meal, flour—everything that had got wet in the upset of the *Powell*. The cork came out of a bottle of catsup and the thick fluid poured over the rocks, whereupon three or four of the men hurried over and lapped it up, smacking their lips over the unexpected treat. Carey found a small rubber ball in a pile of driftwood and he and Felton played catch with it. After supper Holt and I, with mock ceremony, fired our pistols in celebration of the Fourth, while Bradley burned some film and flares that had been damaged in the *Powell*.

I planned to stay in camp until noon the following day and a smooth stretch of river ahead made me hopeful that some fast going was in store for us. From the top of a bowlder just above our camp we could look up stream to our camp site of the previous night. We had covered not more than three-quarters of a mile for the day.

"To-night," I wrote in my diary, "we all have a wholesome respect for the river. She is a mean old devil. My hands are blistered and I have a blister on my ankle. My back aches, my muscles are tired, it has been a hard day's work. Probably shall move on about noon to-morrow. I have added respect for Powell and Dellenbaugh and the others—and wonder if I did not make a mistake in selecting this season of high water for my river trip."

CHAPTER VII

The "Hole" in Rapids No. 22— The Flood—High Water and Morale— Plans for Lee's Ferry.

*T*here was bright sunshine on the morning of the fifth of July and in its grateful warmth we completed the drying out of our provisions and equipment. Bradley spent hours drying, oiling and polishing his motion picture paraphernalia and I was pleased when he reported to me that only a few hundred feet of film had been lost in the upset of the *Powell*. Galloway and McGregory repaired a hole in the *Coronado*. Adger and Seager, after placing their own equipment on the rocks to dry, again spread the bags of corn meal, potatoes, onions, prunes—everything that had been wet—on canvas tent floors laid down on the sand and spent the morning salvaging what they could of our food supply. Taking a bucket of paint and a brush I climbed up the slope above camp and painted the name of the expedition on a huge bowlder. I did that once again, in Narrow Canyon, but did not do it later when we were passing through Grand Canyon. It seemed somehow a presumptuous thing to do, to write our names on the walls of living rock that rose 6000 feet above the river.

Marshall, badly sunburned, found shelter from the heat under an overhanging ledge of rock and was a sorry sight, the inflamed skin on his arms and shoulders glowing through a thick application of boric acid ointment. Felton's pipe tobacco gave him much concern and Callaway, with his cigars spread out before him on a rock, carefully dried them out, turning them over again and again so that they would have the full benefit of the morning sun. The narrow sand bar for a time was littered with our equipment, but everything was dried and stowed away by noon and I announced that we would get under way again immediately after lunch.

We ran without difficulty through a small rapids just below our camp site and landed at the head of an ugly looking cataract that I later identified as No. 22. The rapids, at the prevailing level of water, clearly could not be run and we unpacked the boats for another arduous portage and let-down. I had with me copies of photographs made by Emery Kolb at Rapids No. 22 and was amazed to see the difference in the level of the water and the appearance of the rapids. A huge bowlder in mid-channel which raised its ugly head fifteen or twenty feet above the foam and spray at low water was completely hidden from our sight, while another great rock, which at low water was high and dry, now was twenty feet from shore with the tawny flood pouring over it, forming on its down stream side a deadly looking "hole."

The afternoon was spent lining the *Coronado* and the *Powell* around No. 22, and each time when we came to the "hole" there was a period of suspense while we worked the boat around it. It was necessary for us to bring the boat down to the "hole" and snub it there, holding it with our bodies away from the rocks. Then Galloway would pass the stern line out around a bowlder that barred the way, clamber down below and at his signal we would push the boat out around the rock where for a few anxious seconds it was practically at the mercy of the current. Of course, we retained our hold on the bow line and Galloway and the others hauled in from below, but the slightest miscalculation would have resulted in the boat being drawn into the seething maelstrom below the rock where it inevitably would have been ground to pieces. While lining the second boat Galloway suffered a hard fall which I feared for a moment had broken one of his legs but in spite of that he worked on and did not permit me to bandage his wound until both large boats were safely down. Darkness came before we could line the *Dellenbaugh* and, for the second time since entering Cataract Canyon, we made camp with part of our equipment below and part of it above a rapids, half a mile up stream. Rapids No. 23 roared threateningly below us.

The shore at No. 22 was lined with enormous bowlders and getting two boats and part of the equipment down had been a heavy task. It had been a hard day and, spreading our blankets out on a narrow shelf of sand hardly wide enough to hold us, we went to bed early. As usual I slept at the river's edge and lay for a long time watching the dying embers of the camp fire.

I was drifting off to sleep when suddenly, above the roar of the rapids, I heard a rumble like thunder close at hand and sat up instantly to listen. The stars were gleaming brightly overhead and a chill of apprehension swept over me as I remembered the possibility of sudden flood. Was there a wall of muddy, foaming water rushing in the darkness down the narrow canyon to engulf us? While I sat there listening the terrifying sound was repeated and, that time, I located it in the stream itself sweeping furiously by our camp. Rocks were being torn loose from the bowlder bank that formed the rapids above us and the powerful current was rolling them along the river's rocky bed. Reassured, I lay down again and was soon asleep though, had I known more about the river and its ways I should have read a warning in the roar of the rolling bowlders.

It was perhaps an hour later when I awoke with the feeling that some one was tugging at my leg. I lay for a moment half-asleep and then, realizing what it meant, I sat upright. The river was rising and the muddy water already was sweeping over my feet and legs. I found my flashlight and swung its beam around the camp. Our kitchen equipment was floating away. The boats were pounding on the rocks. The narrow sand bar was washing away from under us.

I jumped to my feet and sounded the alarm. My whistle shrilled in the darkness. The men tumbled out of their blankets and, first rescuing what remained of our kitchen utensils, we threw our blankets up on the rocks and followed with the rest of our food and equipment. Then the *Powell* and *Coronado* were hurriedly hauled up high and dry and we started back up stream in the darkness to save the *Dellenbaugh*.

It was nearly midnight when the rising water awakened me and between that time and dawn, with the river following after us inch by inch, we hauled 3000 pounds of boats and as many of equipment, up, up, up the steep talus slope to the very foot of the sheer cliff where further retreat was impossible. We made trip after trip by sputtering candle light along the bowlder-strewn shore to the *Dellenbaugh* and back. We crawled, slipped and fell, pulling at ropes, carrying boxes and bags of food and camp equipment. There was no rest for any of us until nearly morning when, with our equipment hauled as high as we could get it, we stood in a group listening to the rush and sweep of the water which filled the canyon from wall to wall, a booming, roaring flood.

The plunging river swept by in the darkness and I remembered what I had read of the flood of 1884. Such a flood I knew would destroy us. A few feet more would raise the water level to the base of the cliffs whose talus slope was our final refuge. How much higher would the river rise? The flood already was of unusual proportions. Were we in danger of destruction by a deluge of unprecedented violence on the Colorado? The night wore on and the river came no higher. An hour before dawn, Seager prepared hot coffee for all of us. Morning found the water falling. Our boats were high and dry a dozen feet above the torrent, thirty feet above the rocks to which they had been moored the afternoon before. Weary with a night of toil and terror we welcomed the dawn.

The flood that night raised the level of the water from ten to fifty feet in the narrow canyons. The gauging station at Lee's Ferry recorded 119,000 second feet, the highest water in many years. Harry Howland, back in Greenriver, watching the water rise steadily at the railroad bridge, attempted to warn us by placing messages in bottles and tossing them into the river which he hoped would float them down to us. One such message read, "River 10.48 at 8:30 A.M. and still rising. Look for rise on the Colorado about July 7th or 8th. Salt Lake City papers report that at Greenriver, Wyoming, on July 1st river was highest in nine years, caused by heavy rain and melting snow." That message traveled 700 miles through the canyons and was found ten feet above the normal level of the river at Katherine Mine, near Kingman, Arizona, in December and was forwarded to my home in New York.

The men that morning were surly, silent, or merely quiet, according to their several temperaments. Six of them were thoroughly disheartened and six were fine and cheerful. Most of them made no effort to recover their personal belongings. After breakfast I walked with Galloway, Adger, Seager and McGregory down along the shore as far as we could go. We examined the rapids and I found opportunity to talk alone with each of the men, except Galloway. Seager had overheard a conversation during the night which made it seem likely that three men at least would go out with Bradley when we reached Lee's Ferry. He expressed his own intention of going on. McGregory was uncommunicative and I was uncertain about how much I could depend upon him.

In my talk with Adger I told him it looked as if we were going to lose so many men at Lee's Ferry that we might have to abandon one of the boats. I reminded him that the necessity of doing that would seriously cut down our margin of safety and asked him if he would go on with me and a reduced number of men in the two remaining boats.

We were standing at the foot of a cliff two thousand feet high in the depths of a deep and narrow canyon from which escape would be impossible if we should lose our boats. Adger was worn and tired after the long night spent hauling our boats and cargo out of reach of the rising river. Our lives had been endangered by the greatest flood of water that had swept down the river in years. We were still in the steep central section of Cataract Canyon, where the declivity of the river is thirty feet per mile, shouting to each other to make our voices heard above the roar of the foaming waves. Adger, twenty-three years old, with promise of life opening before him, confronted with the threat of terrible death in the river, stood for a moment looking out over the swollen current and then leaning toward me said, "Sure, I'll go as long as you've got anything that floats."

A long time after we had got back to our homes I asked Adger to write me fully his impressions of the journey and he, who never at any time showed the slightest fear of the river, admitted frankly his constant fear of it. "I was afraid at every rapids," he wrote me, "so you see I was afraid most of the time."

We returned to camp at ten o'clock. Bradley had finished collecting his equipment and was sitting forlornly on a rock, his elbows on his knees and his hands cupped over his ears to shut out the roar of the rapids. I was reminded again of the stories Kolb has hold concerning "Jimmie" and his uncontrollable fear of falling rocks. I remembered having heard that one of the men in the government expedition in 1923 finally got so he could not sleep with the roar of a rapids pounding in his ears and, when the party camped at night near a rapids, he gathered up his own equipment and carried it back up stream, or down, or up a friendly side canyon out of earshot of the tumbling water. The Colorado is likely to bring out some unexpected response of that kind. Bradley clearly did not enjoy the river journey but he never openly showed fear of any of its many dangers. He made pictures while his boat plunged into one of the worst rapids in Cataract Canyon. He was reasonably cheerful during the long, hard portage of the fourth of July, when most of the younger men apparently sounded the very depths of despair. But, seated in safety on the shore, he could not tolerate the never ceasing roar of the rapids.

Not more than half of the other men had recovered from the hard blow the river had struck us during the night. They sat about morosely or worked in a desultory fashion, collecting their personal equipment and taking stock of their losses. Their muscles still ached from the previous day's grueling let-down, and from the night of toil among the rocks. They were tired and sore and sleepy. I was reassured when, toward noon, I saw Weatherhead trailing off by himself, interested again in the scenery, intent upon exploring a side canyon.

After lunch I reviewed Dellenbaugh's account of Powell's expeditions and concluded that we were almost through the worst part of Cataract and that, once through the rapids that roared just below our camp, and the mile or more of turbulent river that we had examined during the morning, we could expect easier going. I reported my conclusions to the men and left the book out for them to read, which several of them did. Others slept through the fierce heat of the short siesta period after lunch and peace and quiet descended upon our little camp.

A few minutes after two the shadow of the canyon wall brought us relief from the heat of the sun and, though some of the men still responded unwillingly and seemed to resent having to work at all, we let the *Coronado* and the *Powell* down below Rapids No. 23 and hauled them on skids completely out of the water, high and dry among the rocks. It was a big job but it went nicely. It was nearly dark when we finished and the *Dellenbaugh* was left where we had hauled her during the night, thirty feet or more above the rapidly receding water at the head of Rapids No. 22, three-quarters of a mile up stream. We would have to bring her down in the morning.

That night we slept crowded together on a strip of sand barely large enough to hold us all. The gayety of youth, crushed momentarily in some of the men by the threatened disaster of the night, again manifested itself in varying degrees in all of them and they were almost cheerful. The two big boats were safe below the rapids and the level of water in the river was falling noticeably from hour to hour. Our morale had improved vastly since breakfast and the men gave promise of being equal again to anything that might befall us. But things had happened during the past two trying days, and one still more trying night, that led me to believe that certain changes in our personnel would occur when we reached Lee's Ferry. The river, how-ever, was not through with us. Before reaching the Ferry other tests were to be made, tests that were to lift some of the apparently weaker men up into the class with the strong ones and hammer at least one of the stronger ones down—and out of the expedition, away from the river entirely.

I went to sleep early, listening to the roar of the river, aware that a pale crescent moon had raised itself above the canyon walls and was peering down upon us.

CHAPTER VIII

Travel Day—The *Coronado* in a "Hole"—Dark Canyon Rapids— Safe Through Cataract.

*T*he sound of my whistle aroused the camp at five as usual on the morning of July seventh and after breakfast we lined the *Dellenbaugh* down around Rapids 22 and 23, noting in passing how much the water had fallen during the night. At one place where we had run the two big boats in a narrow channel of water between a great rock and the shore there was no water at all and the *Dellenbaugh* was lined cautiously out around the bowlder where ten hours earlier a boat would have been upset, or snatched away by the swift stream. The topography, the very nature of a rapids will change almost from hour to hour and for that reason no adequate instruction ever can be given by one canyon voyager to another who may follow him. A rapids may be described as "bad" or "easy" and directions may be given in advance to land on the right or the left bank above it but its navigability varies enormously at different levels of water. Later, I shall tell how we ran in two minutes through a rapids at high water in July which, on my second journey at low water level in December, required three days to line the boats around.

We completed the loading of the boats at nine o'clock and were off again on the river. In my diary I described Thursday, July the seventh, as Travel Day. We covered ten miles and ran through every rapids that we came to. Time after time we ran ashore at the head of a rapids, selected a channel and went crashing through. The subsiding flood had left pools of water among the rocks. This water had settled overnight and we drank enormous quantities of it while examining the rapids. We stopped for lunch just above Gypsum Canyon and welcomed the break in the walls which indicated we were safely through the steep central part of Cataract.

As I have said before, rapids usually occur where side canyons enter the main one and are formed by great bowlders that have been carried down by tributary torrents and dumped into the river channel. Those bowlders partly dam the stream, the water backs up a few hundred feet, gathers its tremendous strength and sweeps over the obstruction with an awe-inspiring roar, throwing its weight furiously against the rocks that bar its way, churning its water into foam, dropping as much as twenty to thirty feet in a few hundred turbulent yards.

We learned finally to judge by its voice something concerning the character of a rapids and, as we drifted down toward it between the high walls, listened intently wondering if the approaching test would be a relatively safe or a perilous one. Long before our journey ended at Needles we came to dread the thunder that announced another rapids and listened anxiously for the sound like the crash of musketry which told us so many times that we were coming to a dangerous cataract.

We did not depend alone upon our ears to judge the fury of the rapids. As our boats swept down upon them, we looked eagerly down stream to see if it was a "bad" or an "easy" one and to determine whether or not it would be advisable for us to run through without first going ashore for careful examination. In many places the declivity of the river was so great that we could not see down through the rapids and Galloway, Adger and I would stand up in our several boats. If, then, we could not see the river where it plunged over the rocks we stood high on the decks of the boats. If, even then, we could not see down through the rapids, if the river simply dropped from sight, as it did in many places, we knew that the fall was a sharp one and pulled our boats ashore—unless, as happened at Gypsum Canyon, an untimely accident to our gear resulted in our being swept over the fall in spite of our efforts at the oars.

A large side canyon usually means a large tributary, a large deposit of bowlders in the stream, and a bad rapids. Gypsum is one of the largest canyons entering Cataract and, although the main canyon is fairly wide at that point permitting the river to widen to 250 feet, I had reason to believe that the rapids we heard roaring ahead of us was a bad one and we approached its head with caution.

A glance down stream from the deck of the boat assured me that it would not do to run through the rapids without further examination from the shore and, following Galloway's lead, I pointed the bow of the *Coronado* toward the left bank, signaling Adger a hundred yards up stream to follow me. We threw our weight on the oars and I heard a row-lock snap behind me. There was a feverish struggle to get the oar in action again, the boat swung around in the current and I realized that we had missed our chance to get ashore. I stood up in the boat, looked intently down stream and hurriedly put on my life preserver. The others followed my example. Then, with one oar out of commission, we turned the stern of the boat down stream and at ever increasing speed were swept smoothly down into the tongue of the rapids. We maneuvered the boat as best we could and though we were helpless to avoid the line of waves into which the swift current thrust us, we at least struck them squarely with our stern and avoided an upset. The waves rolled over the deck of the boat and the water poured into the cockpit where "Mac" and I were sitting. Other waves broke over the sides of the boat and flooded the forward compartment. Weatherhead told me later that the bear, sleeping in the bottom of the boat, was literally buried in the muddy water and clambered quickly to the deck where he stood with his feet braced to save himself from being swept into the river. We struggled to hold our position, to keep the boat from turning broadside in the current, to pull away from rocks that threatened our destruction. One by one the river thrust us through the long line of reverse waves that marked the apex of the current but we were through at last and, hurriedly bailing the boat, pulled ashore in a backwater on the right. I walked as quickly as I could back along the shore to let the others know what had happened. On the way I saw circling around and around in a backwater, two oars and a life preserver that had been torn loose from the *Powell* when she was upset in Fourth of July Rapids and before going on we salvaged this equipment. I reached a point of rock presently from which it was possible for me to signal the others and after examining the rapids and selecting a channel close to shore, Galloway and Adger ran their boats safely through.

That was a day of action, speed and dangerous going. All three boats needed bailing below Gypsum Canyon and after that was done about half of us walked for more than a mile along the shore, leaving the others smoking, chatting and loafing in the boats. The canyon opened out considerably and there was ample room for us to follow the talus slopes of the cliffs that towered perhaps a thousand feet above us. There were two or three bad places in the section of river that we examined but nothing looked particularly dangerous, nothing that we could not run without reasonable assurance of getting through. We returned to the boats, put on our life preservers and pushed the boats into the current.

That may simply have been a bad day for the *Coronado*. Possibly our rowing was at fault, or it may have been that broken row-lock. At any rate we had been under way only a few minutes when we again skirted close to disaster. We had just gone through a small rapids and were floating along stern first ready for the next one when suddenly I saw directly in our path a "hump" in the water and realized that we were headed for a "hole."

"Back water, 'Mac.' Pull, Carey," I shouted and, for a moment, the boat seemed to be moving away from the submerged bowlder almost as rapidly as the current was carrying us down upon it. Then the crazy river caught us with one of its million cross currents, swung us completely around, turned our bow down stream, and thrust us toward the rock and the seething "hole" that boiled and foamed below it. With the boat going bow first, our oars were almost useless and we could not see where we were going. At least we were not broadside in the channel and, knowing that we could not better our position in the fraction of a minute that remained to us, I called out to "Let her go." Would the keel of our boat touch the rock, and tip the boat enough to dump us all into the river? Would the boat upset in the "hole"? Not long did we have to wait for the answers to those questions.

I do not know precisely what happened except that the boat dropped suddenly down into the "hole," plunged her bow beneath the churning waves, and the rest of the boat went diving after. I heard the men behind me gasp and then the water struck me in the back and for a moment the boat was running all submerged. But it did not tip and throw us out. Thanks to its beam it kept an even keel. Thanks to its length it escaped being whirled around and carried back into the vortex. Thanks to its closed compartments it staggered through and remained afloat, with both cockpits level full of water.

"Bail for your lives," I shouted. Our bailing cans had floated away so we bailed with our hands and our hats, striving desperately to empty the water out of the boat that we might handle her to advantage in the rapids below us and into which the current threatened to carry our water-filled, unwieldy craft. Then "Mac" and Weatherhead bailed while Carey and I tugged at the oars and we managed finally to run the boat ashore. Even then so much water remained in our cockpits that the gunwales were awash and the bow of the boat was practically submerged. We looked back up stream and I wondered that none of us had seen the "hole" when we walked down along the shore. It was one of the largest that I saw anywhere on the river and how we failed to see it before I do not know. The boat was bailed and we resumed our interrupted voyage.

The walls began closing in again a short distance below Gypsum Canyon but there were few rapids and we moved along at a good pace. At only one place were we in much danger and that was where, just above Clearwater Canyon, a sharp bend in the river deflected the current so suddenly that it set in fiercely against the opposite wall and we had to pull with all our strength to avoid being swept against the cliff. We had covered ten miles during the day and in that distance had run fourteen bad rapids. Camp was made on a high ledge of rock between sheer walls opposite Clearwater Canyon and while I did not much like the camp site, because a rise of twenty or thirty feet would have flooded us out and the steep wall back of us would have cut off our escape, there was risk, too, in running any later in the gathering twilight and I concluded that, camping in a "boxed-in" canyon was merely one more risk that we should have to take.

The younger men without exception were in good spirits after the hazardous day. They were gay enough and worked with a will at unloading the boats and establishing camp on the ledge above the river. But, McGregory was in distress. He would eat no supper and sat by himself, silent and sullen.

I joined him presently.

"What is the matter, 'Mac,'" I asked him, "are you sick?"

"No," he answered without looking up.

"Well," I persisted, thinking one of the younger men had offended him unintentionally, "has anybody said anything to hurt your feelings?"

And again, without looking up, he grunted, "No."

I urged him to come and eat and when he lapsed into silence I thought I knew what the matter was and left him. I believed then and still believe that "Mac," accustomed to hard work, withstood better than the other men the severe buffeting of July fourth, fifth and sixth, when most of the time we were reasonably safe on shore and that the danger beat him down when we were swept through Gypsum Canyon Rapids and into the "hole" below that on the seventh. That was not McGregory's last bad day on the river and the time came finally when I asked him another question.

That night before going to bed I asked Bartl to watch the lines while I crawled into the cabin of one of the boats to load some photographic plate holders, closing the hatch after me to insure total darkness. The boat tugged at its lines and rose and fell with the waves. It was as if I were actually afloat, alone and in the dark on the treacherous river—which may account for the dreams I had that night of being swept, helpless under the battened hatch, down the river into Dark Canyon Rapids which I knew was roaring its defiance a few miles below us.

We got away at seven the next morning and ran through one small rapids after another until about eleven o'clock when we came to a fall which at first glance seemed impossible to run, but which we decided finally presented no more serious difficulties than several that we had come through successfully. A stream entering from a side canyon on the left had dumped a fan-shaped pile of bowlders into the river and in the course of ages the river had cut away the cliffs on its right bank, apparently finding it easier to do that than to clear its channel of the bowlders which were continually being added to by the side stream at flood times. The result was a bend in the river like a great letter "C." Bowlders, spread out fan-wise, formed the area partly enclosed by the bend and the river, tumbling furiously over the rocks in its bed, swept against the sheer walls that formed the outer line of the "C."

We examined the rapids and Bradley said he would like to remain ashore and make motion pictures of the boats going through.

Callaway volunteered to assist Bradley and, because the volunteer assistant was not needed in the *Dellenbaugh*, I agreed to his staying ashore. The rest of us then returned to the boats and, with Galloway in the lead, swept down toward the rapids.

The boats went through, one after another, and Bradley made some magnificent pictures which show the *Dellenbaugh* entering the rapids properly at the left of the point of the "V" and pulling away from the great waves along the base of the cliff. The *Coronado* is shown answering sluggishly to our tugging at the oars but holding her position fairly well in the channel and escaping the worst of the waves. He caught the *Powell* as she entered the rapids perhaps fifteen feet too far out toward the middle of the river and swept down through the worst of the waves, out of control, turning all the way around before plunging, fortunately stern first, into a wave that swept completely over the boat, all but burying it from sight. But luck was with them and the big boat carried them through.

After bailing the boats we dropped cautiously down to the head of Dark Canyon Rapids, hugging the shore and landing, finally, at the upper end of a mass of bowlders which partly dammed the river and produced one of the worst rapids in Cataract Canyon. The river here is about 200 feet wide and steep cliffs of limestone and sandstone rise 2000 feet above the water's edge.

The channel at Dark Canyon is shaped like the letter "S." The current enters the "S" at its upper end, as illustrated in Fig. 1 on page 48; is deflected sharply against its right bank, which is a sheer wall; rushes furiously along the base of the cliff; sweeps diagonally across the river, as shown in the illustration; and piles up against another wall of rock on the left. The pile of bowlders which have been brought down from Dark Canyon produces a rapids which we decided could not be run. We found clear if somewhat metallic tasting water in Dark Canyon and rested there an hour after lunch during the intense heat of midday. Peanut butter was on the menu and Marshall was so enthusiastic in expressing his liking for it that he precipitated a hot discussion concerning food, one of many that we had on the subject. Callaway, smoking one of his salvaged cigars which he had bandaged with a piece of paper, held forth loudly for beefsteak, so loudly in fact that he won the day. I looked to Carey to

High-water mark after the flood in Cataract Canyon.

A side channel offered passage for the boats at Dark Canyon Rapids. A few seconds after this picture was taken the river snatched the boat away from the men and swept it out into the raging river.

out-shout him, but either Carey also favored beefsteak or he was too uncomfortable in the heat to take part in the discussion.

After lunch we found a place where the river had cleared a side channel for itself through the bowlder heap that formed the rapids. This side channel, illustrated in Fig. 1, was deep enough to float the boats except in a few places where rocks obstructed the channel and we decided to line the boats that way instead of taking them out around, along the edge of the rapids. Marshall was so badly sunburned that I told him to stay out of the water and set him to carrying duffel down along the shore. The rest of us brought down the *Powell* and tied her securely in the backwater at the lower end of the pile of bowlders, just above the point where the river swept against the wall that forms the perimeter of the lower curve of the "S."

Next, we unloaded the *Coronado* and after seeing her started I took my camera and set it up at the lower end of the channel through which we were lining the boats, intent upon getting some photographs as the men brought her through.

Seager, Carey, Holt and Adger were pushing, tugging and hauling at the boat. Galloway and the others were holding to the bow line, letting the boat down, holding it against the pull of the river. When part way down, the stern of the boat jammed against a rock and, while the men who held the line waited, the men near the boat began to lift it over the obstruction. Suddenly the boat slipped over the rock, the current caught it up and hurled it down stream, snatching it away from Galloway and the others caught momentarily off their guard. Carey, Holt and Adger, helpless to hold the boat, saw it dart away from them. I saw that much of the action in the ground glass of my camera but before I could throw the focusing cloth off my head and reach the edge of the water the boat had swept by me, rushing headlong toward the main body of the river. As she passed me I saw a man's arm curled up over the opposite gunwale and the fingers of his other hand clutching at the life line for support. He got his head up presently and I saw that it was Seager. A boat was adrift in the river, but that was nothing—a man was clinging to that boat in imminent peril of his life.

At that instant Marshall took a hand. Dropping a bag of duffel he had just brought down, he clambered over some bowlders that stood in his way and made a flying leap into the river. I visualized two men drowned instead of one and when, with a few quick strokes he reached the line dragging behind the boat, I called out to him to climb aboard quickly and break out the oars. Seager, meantime, had pulled himself in and while he worked desperately to get the oars into play before the river could sweep them into the cliff below, Marshall struck out for shore, towing the line after him. Then, as quickly as she had snatched them away, the capricious river gave my men and my boat back to me. The backwater swung them toward the shore. I snatched up a long piece of driftwood, waded out, handed the other end to Marshall and hauled him up beside me. Then we made the boat secure. The party was still intact, but it had been a narrow squeak.

We resumed the interrupted lining and started on the *Dellenbaugh*. Again Adger, Holt and Carey were with the boat. Galloway and the others were handling the line, Marshall was portaging duffel and I was making pictures, with Seager standing by my side. The two larger boats were down and the small one should have made little trouble. But we had still to learn that lining sometimes is as dangerous as the apparently more hazardous business of running through a rapids. For the second time within half an hour the river snatched a boat away from the men who had the line and I looked up to see the *Dellenbaugh* rushing past me down the narrow, rock strewn channel, with Holt and Adger clinging to it, in danger of being crushed against the rocks, being carried toward the river—and the line of cliffs below.

I reached the water's edge a moment after the boat passed and when the foaming stream tossed one of the boat's lines within my reach, I grabbed it thankfully and passed it quickly around a bowlder. Seager joined me and when the line straightened out with the weight of the boat we held her firm. I stood up and looked down stream. Holt was still in the water, between me and the boat but there was Adger, safe on shore, *calling frantically for us to let go the line*. I could see no reason why we should let go and there were many reasons why we should hold fast but I had no cause to doubt Adger's judgment. We let go instantly and rushed down to see what was the matter.

Adger, after helping Holt out of the water, made the line of the *Dellenbaugh* fast and she was safe in the backwater. Holt sat on a nearby bowlder still gasping painfully for breath, holding his hands to his throat. The line had wound itself around his neck on the wild ride down the channel and when we made it fast above and the boat reached the end of its tether we came near strangling him.

What a river she is! How many different kinds of traps she sets to catch the voyager upon her troubled waters!

We were below the rapids but still had to pass the cliff on the left. Close to shore was the friendly backwater that had saved Marshall and Seager and the *Powell*. Thirty feet from shore as shown in Fig. 1, the apex of the current swept by like a living wall, rushing diagonally across the river, headed pell-mell for the cliffs below. To avoid being swept against the rocks on the left it would be necessary for us to ride the backwater up stream as far as we could go, then to pull into the current—and across the apex before the river could dash us against the cliffs.

Galloway went first with Seager, Holt and Callaway in the *Dellen-baugh*. They pulled into the current, part way across it, and were carried swiftly past the threatening line of cliffs and out of sight around a bend in the river. I followed with McGregory, Carey and Weatherhead in the *Coronado*. At least, I tried to follow. The back-water carried us up stream as we had planned and then we tried to pull into the current. I have said that the current was like a wall of water, moving down stream with tremendous velocity. With four of us tugging at the oars we found we could not get into the current. The edge of it swept us rapidly down stream, turned us toward shore and pushed us off into the backwater again. Where sometimes we could not get out of the current, here we could not force the boats into it. Adger and his crew in the *Powell* had a similar experience, joined us in the backwater and we started again. That time the *Powell* got far enough across the apex of the current to avoid being carried into the backwater but not far enough to escape serious risk of being swept against the rocks and when they passed us the men were pulling fran-tically at their oars trying to get the boat farther away from shore.

Again we tried, and failed. "What kind of a river is this?" I thought. "When you are in the current you cannot get out and when you are out you cannot get in." Then I glanced down stream and, in the gathering dusk, saw something that looked like a white boat piled up against the cliff half way around the bend in the river. I had not seen it there before. I thought it was the *Powell*, smashed against the rocks. I pointed the object out to McGregory and he, too, thought it was the other boat.

If the *Powell* had been wrecked the men would be in need of instant help and the roaring river, while holding us shore-bound in the backwater, seemed to be shouting to me, "Hurry! Hurry! Hurry!" The situation demanded speed, and justified unusual risk. I instructed Weatherhead to get ashore with the bow line and push the boat along stern first down stream past the backwater, to the upper end of the line of cliffs. He was then to shove her bow out, hop into the boat and, as she swung into the stream, we were all to pull her clear of the cliffs if we could. McGregory, using his oar as a pole, kept the stern of the boat clear of the shore and Carey and I waited with our oars poised for the moment when we should have to pit our strength against the fury of the river. We reached the end of the beach. Weatherhead pushed the boat out and jumped aboard. The current swung the bow away from shore and Carey and I bent to our oars. With not more than a foot to spare we cleared the cliff at the head of the bend and, while Carey and I pulled with every ounce of our strength on our oars, and McGregory and Weatherhead backed water most of the time with theirs to keep the bow of the boat pointed away from the rocks, we were swept rapidly down stream. We reached the place where I thought I had seen the *Powell* stranded and as we flashed by I was relieved to see that it was only a log lodged among the rocks. We came presently to ledges jutting out from the cliff and perched on them were Galloway, Adger and the others, shouting directions that we could not hear. Below the rapids we saw their boats pulled up against the shore and ran in, making camp for the night on a rocky ledge sprinkled over with sand where Powell had camped on his second trip through Cataract in 1872.

We soon had a fire going and Seager and Adger, assisted by Galloway, prepared supper. Rain threatened and the tents were put up although most of us laid our blankets out in convenient shelters under overhanging ledges of rock. Rain began falling and the food cooked slowly over the sputtering fire. It was after dark, and rain was falling steadily when supper finally was ready for us to "come and get it."

The shelter that I had selected under a ledge was large enough for only the upper part of my body and I went to sleep with the rain beating steadily on the end of my poncho that covered my feet and legs. When I awakened at ten-thirty to look at the boats the water had seeped in under the ledge and was dropping on my face and head. Also, by that time the rain had found its way into my poncho and my feet were wet. After examining the boats I lay awake for a long time too uncomfortable to sleep, but happy in the realization that we were safe through Cataract. Later in the night I heard some one moving about and my flashlight disclosed Weatherhead dragging the protesting bear gently by the scruff of its neck back toward the boat, from which it had escaped apparently intent upon joining us in the comparative comfort of the sheltering ledge.

Cataract Canyon with its forty perilous miles was behind us. In that distance the river had lost 415 feet in altitude, most of it in a series of fifty-four bad rapids, all but four of which we had run success-fully. We had come safely through a section of the river that had wit-nessed many fatalities. We had survived a flood of unusual proportions, had learned many lessons, and I felt that we were in better rather than worse condition than when we left Greenriver. I knew the mettle of the men, the merits of the equipment, and faced the future with rea-sonable confidence. I knew that Lee's Ferry with the opportunity that it offered to escape the river might yet wreck the expedition but was hopeful that enough of us would get over that barrier to navigate the boats through the Grand Canyon and on to Needles.

CHAPTER IX

The Lonely Prospector—
Glen Canyon—A Sand Storm—
Lee's Ferry at Last.

*T*here was no need to hurry on the morning of the ninth of July. We were safely through all but six miles of Cataract Canyon and unless unexpected difficulties were encountered we had food enough to take us to Lee's Ferry. According to my itinerary we should reach the abandoned town of Hite, Utah, twenty miles down stream, at the end of our twelfth day on the river. With reasonable luck we would reach that point within a few hours of the time that I had set, leaving us six days for the journey through Glen Canyon to Lee's Ferry.

Adger and Seager were up at four-thirty and I aroused the others at five as usual, but I endeavored to soften somewhat the shrill sound of my whistle and tried to let them know by the way I called out, "Up all hammocks," that they might if they wished lie abed a few minutes later than usual, leaving the loading of the boats until after break-fast. The rain had ceased falling but pools of water glistened on the uneven surface of the rocky ledge and the men enjoyed clinging for a few added minutes to whatever comfort they could find wrapped in their damp ponchos and blankets spread out on the rocks.

Bartl and Carey were sleeping together and though both of them had their heads covered, I knew they were awake. One of them rolled over presently and dragged the blanket and the wet, glistening poncho with him. There was violent tugging for a moment and then a noisy quarrel broke out between them.

"Stop pulling that cover," shouted Bartl, his voice muffled in the blankets.

"Go on," retorted Carey. "You've had the blankets all night and I've been out in the rain."

So it went, back and forth they tugged at the blankets and called out to each other. Presently there was unusual commotion for a moment as if the men had come to blows. The movement centered near the head of the improvised bed—and Rags emerged, stretched himself calmly and trotted off to look for the bear.

There had been little time for me to watch Rags and the bear while we were going through Cataract Canyon but I knew that after a few days spent in getting acquainted the animals had become fast friends. The bear was kept tied—chiefly to keep him from getting into the food supply—and the dog was free to wander where he chose. Rags was a thoroughly discouraged dog when he joined us at Greenriver. He had spent several days in the Salt Lake City dog pound and cowered about as if he was accustomed only to rough treatment. Some time passed before he knew just how to accept our friendly overtures and when the bear playfully tumbled him over, he was crushed.

Before many days had passed, however, Rags knew that he was one of us. Before we left Greenriver he had learned to know each member of the expedition by sight, could distinguish all thirteen of us from the villagers and, judging by his behavior, was ready at any instant to sell his life dearly in defense of the camp we had pitched down by the river. By the time we had been on our way a week he had overcome his fear of the bear and had learned that he actually could beat his roly-poly companion in a friendly tussle.

The bear, on the contrary, still lived in a world by himself—aloof from us, a separate entity. He was friendly enough and wanted to play all the time but always he was a bear and we were men. I suspect that Rags decided before we had gone very far that he was a man with the rest of us. The bear was friendly and playful, but he was impersonal and detached.

One of the bear's favorite games was to withdraw to the far end of his leash and hide behind a rock. He would permit us to walk unmolested back and forth in front of him for a long time, until he thought he had our suspicions lulled. Suddenly like a furry little thunderbolt, he would rush out, wrap his forepaws around the nearest knee of his victim, and bite him, growling noisily the while. He meant it all in the best of fun but his teeth were sharp as needles and the boys' legs showed many scars of his playful forays. He liked the fun to go his way and was easily aroused to anger when the men were too rough with him. When this happened there was nothing to do but hold his head until his temper cooled, or push him away and get out of his reach. He would tolerate very little rough and tumble play from the men without showing anger but never once did I hear him growl at Rags—and Rags used to maul him around until even the bear had more than enough of playing. Rags shared our meals. The bear was fed principally on boiled rice, pancakes and evaporated milk though he learned finally to eat practically anything that came his way—and everything else that he could steal.

I took time after breakfast to scald out my canteen. We had been using evaporated milk to settle the muddy water and my canteen had gone sour. The men who were doing kitchen police for the day finally got the pots and pans properly scoured, the boats were loaded and we got away at eight o'clock. In the next five miles we ran successfully through five rapids, in only one of which we shipped any water, and at nine-fifteen arrived at Mille Crag Bend which marks the end of Cataract Canyon. The river at this point makes a great bend and turns almost directly west through Narrow Canyon whose walls, narrow and rising in most places sheer from the river's edge, are from 500 to 1000 feet high. But there are no rapids in the seven miles of Narrow Canyon and we floated peacefully along, using our oars occasionally to steer clear of the rocks along the shore. The men shouted now and then at each other and "Hey, Ruth" again awakened the wilderness echoes. We stopped part way through the canyon, climbed the cliff and painted the name of the expedition and our own names, on the wall.

At twelve o'clock we reached the mouth of Frémont River, coming in from the right. Major Powell tells how, when his expedition reached this point in 1869, the pilot boat was run up into the river a few yards and a man in one of the following boats called out to inquire what kind of stream it was, fresh or clear. Investigation showed that the water in the smaller stream was even muddier and more alkaline than that in the Colorado and the man in the first boat answered, disgustedly, "Oh, she's a dirty devil." Whereupon Powell applied that name to the river. The stream later was named the Frémont River but to this day it is known locally as the Dirty Devil.

We landed and while Adger and Seager, assisted by the kitchen police prepared lunch, I set up my camera and made some photographs. Weatherhead, Bradley, Carey and one or two others set out to climb a high, barren knob of rock back of the camp and Callaway, who had discovered a duck in the river a short distance down stream, amused himself—and apparently the duck—by banging away at it with the same ineffective looking pocket pistol that had shattered the solitude of Stillwater Canyon. And, as in Stillwater, the intended victim grew weary of the noise after a while and flew away. I found shelter from the sun under an overhanging ledge and was gazing idly across the river when to my surprise I saw a man emerge from the water on the opposite shore. I looked closely, and was annoyed to discover that it was Holt. Unknown to the rest of us he had entered the river near our camp and had swum across, the swift current carrying him a quarter of a mile down stream. He had shown signs before of being headstrong and I felt that he had deliberately slipped away from camp and started without my knowledge, knowing that I would have opposed the venture. I was vexed that he would risk his life unnecessarily. He was painfully picking his way back up stream along the rocky shore and I decided, rather than send a boat over to pick him up, to let him have his walk as punishment for his insubordination. Then I asked Galloway to stand by in the *Dellenbaugh* and we watched him swim back. Long afterward Holt wrote me, "You never knew how close you came to losing a member of the expedition the day we stopped for lunch at the mouth of the Dirty Devil and I attempted to swim across the Colorado and back again. The river, as you remember, was four or five hundred feet wide. When about half way across I was caught in a huge whirlpool and found it impossible to make any headway and it was only after I was nearly exhausted that I managed to climb up on the other side of the river." Neither did Holt know how nearly that swim came to costing him his position in the expedition. It was only because he possessed the very courage that led him to attempt the crossing that I did not ask him to leave at Lee's Ferry—that and the fact that he was so tremendously valuable when lining the boats. Holt's strength and courage made him one of the three or four most valuable men in the party, but he did want to do things his way.

After lunch we drifted on down the widening river between walls much broken down and at two o'clock, came to the ruins of Hite. Only one house remained of the little group that was erected twenty years before when gold was discovered on the river. Below that, however, we saw half a dozen abandoned houses and many piles of earth, mine dumps that represented the fruitless toil of men who had tried vainly to wrest fortunes from the inhospitable rocks.

Each cabin as we passed it, deserted and in ruins, was a fresh disappointment. We had been twelve days on the way and were eager to get in touch again with civilization. Then, in a grove of cottonwoods on the left bank of the river, we saw a cabin with smoke curling lazily from its chimney. We shouted and a man emerged from the door, stood for a moment bewildered, and then waved to us in friendly greeting. We waved in turn and ran the boats ashore, making a landing only with considerable difficulty. The river flowed swiftly between steep walls of sand, fifteen or twenty feet in height. To get ashore and secure the boats it was necessary for us to select a place where a cottonwood grew close to the brink of the sandy wall. We then ran the boat in, Carey took the bow line and scrambled up the steep bank while Weatherhead held the bow of the boat against the shore, changing his position constantly to avoid being engulfed in quicksand. McGregory and I meantime were pulling at our oars, helping Weatherhead keep the bow inshore until Carey could take a turn around the tree with the bow line.

Waiting for us on shore we found a gray-haired old man, who welcomed us to his lonely home. We hauled our duffel up the steep bank and soon had a fire going, with Adger and Seager busy preparing the evening meal which I invited our host to share with us. He was a man of few words but he told us in reply to our questions that the nearest town, Hanksville, was seventy-two miles away, that the nearest point on the railroad was sixty-five miles beyond that, and that there was no way to get supplies in except on the backs of pack animals. He said that he had been alone on the river since his dog had died two years before, that he had been there six years "doing a little mining," and that he rarely got even to Hanksville oftener than once every three months.

He was a man of evident refinement, his tousled gray hair and unkempt beard failing to disguise the fine, clear cut features of his unusual face. His keen gray eyes were intelligent and friendly. Untrue to the popular idea of a hermit's reticence, he answered my questions almost eagerly and when I ventured to ask him his name he told me readily enough, William Carpenter. He was born and had spent the early years of his life in Glen Cove, twenty miles from my home on Long Island. He described to me wistfully the New York he had known and when I asked him if he did not want to visit his boyhood home and the members of his family "back east," he said he would like nothing better but that he wanted first to go to Old Mexico.

"There's gold down there," he assured me, "if you could only get it out."

Two years later, after a lecture in New York City, a man came to me and told me his name was William Carpenter and that he, too, lived in Glen Cove, Long Island. He said he had often heard of this other William Carpenter but the family had long believed him dead. So the old man had not got home in those two years at least. I wonder if he is still there on the river, or did he follow his will-o'-the-wisp into Mexico?

We left him the next morning, standing almost where we had seen him first, waving us farewell. A sudden torrent of men trailing after them the echoes of sounds that he had known in the world outside had swept unexpectedly down the canyon, breaking in upon his solitude, doubtless recalling to his mind half forgotten memories of long gone years, re-awakening, perhaps, desires he thought had died. And then, with life and the world before them, his visitors had departed, leaving him alone again. I often think of him standing solitary by his little cabin under the cottonwoods, alone through the years, the roaring Colorado his only companion.

We said good-by to Mr. Carpenter at eight o'clock Sunday morning, July tenth, and during the day we rowed and drifted with the current thirty-seven miles between the monotonous red sandstone walls of Glen Canyon. The country on top is a great flat table-land, the smooth, naked rock stretching out for miles in every direction. Through this plateau the brooks, the torrents, the tributaries all have cut their tortuous channels leading to the central canyon itself where the Colorado flows between sheer walls from 100 to 800 feet beneath the level of the land on top.

During the day we passed five or six abandoned dredges and saw many other relics of the gold rush on the river. At one place, where there was a break in the cliffs, we saw a small herd of cattle and Callaway suggested that he be permitted to bag one with his pistol.

"Beefsteak and onions would go good," he said, "even without the onions."

At no place did we see any sign of human life. In mid-afternoon we passed Hall's Crossing where once a cable was swung across the river to aid the miners in their search for gold. At six o'clock I saw some likely-looking cliff dwellings in the face of a cliff on the left and gave the signal to run ashore. After exploring the caves and finding nothing, we made camp for the night. Seager was too ill to help prepare supper and went to bed early after taking a dose of medicine that I prepared for him.

After supper I had a long talk with Galloway. Arrangements had been made for him to go with us only as far as Lee's Ferry and I believed that the time had come for me to propose to him that he continue with us all the way to Needles. I told him of Adger's determination to go all the way through and named the other men upon whom I thought I could depend. I discussed with him the proved excellence of our boats and pointed out to him how much better equipped we were in experience than we had been when we left Greenriver. Then I named the amount that I could pay and he accepted my offer with alacrity. I believe he would have been glad to go without remuneration although he could have ill afforded it. As a result of my late talk that night with Galloway I slept badly—because I had no opportunity to fix my bed properly and every time I turned over I rolled down the hill. I had much time for that reason to admire the moon that flooded the canyon with its soft light.

We were up at five as usual on the morning of the eleventh of July and got away at seven. There are no bad rapids in Glen Canyon but we splashed through a number of riffles during the day and, in one of them, even shipped a little water. We passed the mouth of the Escalante River at ten-thirty and, at twelve-fifteen, stopped at the mouth of the San Juan for lunch. No one complained openly to me but some of the men betrayed in many ways resentment at the long, hard grind at the oars during the morning. The fierce midday heat discouraged activity and we did not move on again until after two. Weatherhead and Carey had spent a large part of the morning arguing the relative merits of lives devoted to art and business but had little to say as we drifted down stream in the intense heat of early afternoon. I rode along suffering from indigestion, thinking how delightful it would be to have an orange to eat, or a grapefruit—but most of all I wanted a glass of clear, cold water. I had lost a filling from a tooth and wondered if I could have it replaced at Kanab.

The course of the river in Glen Canyon, as in Labyrinth and Stillwater, is tortuous. There are great bends where fan-shaped, willow fringed, flood plains extend far out across the floor of the canyon, thrusting the river against the outer rim of the curve—an outer rim of orange colored sandstone that rises magnificently 100 to 800 feet sheer from the water's edge. We landed at five-thirty on the right bank of the river, on a willow fringed peninsula, running the bows of the boats far up on the sand. We knew before we stepped out of the boats that the beach was quicksand but good camp sites are difficult to find in Glen Canyon; a thunder shower threatened and we could not risk searching for a better place in the gathering dusk.

By working fast, and cutting willows to spread underfoot, we managed finally to get the boats unloaded but by the time we had finished, the beach was a veritable quagmire into which we sank ankle deep at every step, making it extremely difficult if not actually dangerous to get the heavy bags and boxes ashore. I was in so much distress with indigestion I did not realize until the meal was nearly over that McGregory had not joined the others when the food was served. I went to him then and asked him if he was ill. He answered me as he had before in Cataract Canyon. Again he was surly and sullen and I was too ill myself to care much what he did when we reached Lee's Ferry. I set him down as company for Bradley and left him to his gloomy thoughts.

Supper fortunately was over when a terrific wind and rain storm struck. There actually was only a spatter of rain but the wind, shrieking and howling as it swept through the narrow canyon, carried with it clouds of fine sand which sifted into everything. My symptoms of indigestion had become acute and, seeking relief, I fought my way through the storm to where the boats had been moored in the quicksand and wondered as I searched for medicine if I should have to start through the Grand Canyon on a diet of evaporated milk and sodium bicarbonate. Then I returned to where I had spread my blankets on the ground, weighted with rocks to keep them from blowing away, and tried to sleep, with my head covered. But I could not stand that for long and went to sleep finally with the sand drifting over me driving in on my ear drums, sifting into everything, filling my eye sockets so that I had to dig the sand out before I could open my eyes in the morning.

Tuesday, July twelfth, was another Travel Day. Between seven in the morning and six-fifteen at night we covered sixty-one miles, and completed the first lap of our journey—from Greenriver to Lee's Ferry—two and a half days ahead of schedule. We stopped at noon at the point where the river crosses into Arizona and by mid-afternoon the walls had run up again to a thousand feet or more in height. I had not expected that and grew more and more concerned. Had we passed Lee's Ferry without knowing it? Were we already in Marble Gorge with no place nearer than Bright Angel Trail to renew our dwindling supply of provisions? I felt unaccountably depressed and was fearful that the other men would notice it. I eagerly scanned the river ahead. Steep sandstone walls rose a thousand feet above us. It was after six o'clock and darkness comes early in the narrow canyons. Should we press on or run ashore and complete the journey in the morning? I had about decided on the latter course when the river turned sharply to the right and the country opened out ahead of us. Five minutes later our boats were drawn up on the beach at Lee's Ferry and I had gone off to find Jerry Johnson, the ferryman, to make arrangements for transportation the next day to Kanab, ninety miles across the desert.

I had that night none of the fruit I craved but I did have clear and relatively cool water to drink and was feeling better. After supper I had a long talk with Marshall and he agreed with me that his sunburn was so serious that it would not be wise for him to go on with us into the lower canyons. Felton had come with Marshall on the expedition and decided to go out with him. Bradley was happily engaged in packing up for his journey back to Hollywood.

Several of the men had expressed having a desire to go with me to Kanab and I lay awake a long time deciding who should go. They all wanted—some of them needed and others deserved—a vacation away from the river. I finally settled upon Adger, Seager, Galloway and Carey, leaving Weatherhead, Bartl, Holt, Callaway and McGregory to endure the monotony while we were gone. I made the selection after long and careful consideration and later events convinced me that had I made any other grouping of the men we might never have got away from Lee's Ferry. Galloway, Adger, Seager and Carey with me. Weatherhead, Bartl, Holt, Callaway and McGregory at the Ferry. I'll venture that every man of them knows now why he was selected to go, or stay.

We planned to start the next morning a little after five, hoping to reach the Buckskin Mountains before noon, escaping the midday heat on the intervening desert.

CHAPTER X

To Kanab for Provisions—
Three Men Leave the Expedition—
Holt and Bartl Lost—
The "Miracle in the Desert."

$\mathcal{W}$e were up at four on the morning of July thirteenth and two hours later were ready to start on the ninety mile ride to Kanab. Most of us had clung tenaciously to such odds and ends of excess equipment as books, extra blankets and clothing, and all of this material, tied in bundles, was thrown into the truck to be shipped home from Kanab. Felton and Marshall added their duffel bags to the load and Bradley stowed away his motion picture equipment, films and personal belongings. Then nine of us and the driver, Jerry Johnson, climbed in and we were off, over what surely must have been the worst road on the North American continent.

First, there was the Paria River which we forded. Then the road struggled for miles along the base of the magnificent Vermilion Cliffs through House Rock Valley toward the Buckskin Mountains. The road dipped into bottomless ravines, crossed meager streams of water and climbed painfully out on the other side. We ran almost constantly in low or second gear and, time after time, it was necessary for all of us to get out and push the car up a hill or through a long stretch of sand where the wheels sank nearly to their hubs. The heat was almost intolerable and we had to stop repeatedly to replenish, from cans tied to the running board, the supply of water, boiling excitedly in the radiator. It was nearly noon when we reached the foot of the Buckskins and, after practically carrying the panting truck up the first rise in the foothills, found easier going among the scattered pine and cedar trees.

I talked to Jerry Johnson and learned that his father had succeeded John D. Lee, who was executed for his part in the Mountain Meadows Massacre, as ferryman at Lee's Ferry and that he, Jerry, remembered Frank M. Brown who with two members of his party was drowned in Marble Gorge, a few miles below the Ferry in 1889. He remembered Robert Brewster Stanton and Nims, the photographer with the Brown-Stanton expedition, who broke his leg and was hauled out on ropes over the steep canyon walls. He told me that he was an elder in the Mormon Church, the oldest of three brothers living at the Ferry. Later I counted thirty Johnson children and learned that the state of Arizona furnishes a teacher and a one room school house for the Johnson brood. The Mountain Meadows Massacre occurred in 1857 when a party of emigrants passing through Utah on their way to California were attacked by Indians or by Mormons or by both at Mountain Meadows and were killed to the last man, woman and child. Lee was declared guilty of leading the attack and was executed seven years later for his part in the crime.

There is much dispute concerning the guilt of John D. Lee, who fled to the river with one of his wives in 1871 and established a desultory ferry business. I was shown his lookout, a cone shaped hill near the Ferry where it is reported that he spent much of his time guarding against surprise by federal authorities. I have talked with his descendants who still protest his innocence and tell pitiful stories of the struggles of his faithful wife, Emma, who with a half-grown boy, continued to operate the ferry after the long arm of the law reached out and took Lee away to die before a firing squad on the scene of the massacre. I must leave discussion of his innocence and guilt to others but as I rode and walked that day up through the gullies and gulches of the Buckskin Mountains, I thought of the tragedy of Lee's life— and of the remarkable vitality of the church that had sent its sons and daughters out to conquer, cultivate and people this arid land.

I questioned Johnson about the flood that had swept through the canyons while we were in Cataract and he said the gauge at the Ferry had registered the highest water in many years. I found later that the peak of the flood measured 119,000 second feet and that when we were there the level had dropped to 40,000, which still was twice the average flow of the river. He confirmed the report I had heard that a motion picture company was planning to launch an expedition on the river in August or September and I was glad that I had started ahead of them. How remote from my mind was the thought that I should be a member of the party when the motion picture company's expedition entered the Grand Canyon five months later, in December!

Even a ninety mile ride through the heat and sand of a western desert must come to an end at last and at five o'clock, we drew up in front of the drug store in Kanab. This settlement, located 135 miles from the nearest point on a railroad, is no metropolis but there was a soda fountain in the drug store and leaving the men there, where they soon were engaged in testing their ultimate capacities for ice cream soda, I hurried off to the telegraph office where I found awaiting me a telegram in reply to the one I had sent out by Chaffin at the head of Cataract Canyon. The message read:

Sorry in view of report from Bradley cannot possibly ask another man to make trip with you. I have no authority to ask men to risk their lives. You must remember that all the camera man gets out of this trip is his salary. We recently lost valued staff man and we are under no circumstances deliberately to put man where his life is in danger. Sorry necessary take this stand but no court or law would countenance any other course.

Addressed to Bradley there was one which read:

Act on your own judgment. Do not want you take any chances you consider dangerous. Please tell Eddy impossible send substitute camera man if you consider this trip too risky.

I was not satisfied that Bradley had been quite fair with me. I felt that he had magnified the dangers, and I wired to New York:

Bradley says he was not given choice in matter of going on trip. He has family and is not strong. We came safely through flood waters in most dangerous part and have excellent start on feature film. Need camera man and five thousand feet of film in water-proof duffel bags at Grand Canyon Station. Will make it through from there in less than three weeks. Have man join us there July twenty-four. Trip not more dangerous than I outlined to you.

There was nothing more I could do but wait for an answer to my telegram and, after seeing that the men all had places to sleep and eat at the town's only hotel, I took Galloway with me to buy bolts, nuts, nails and other hardware necessary to make our boats proof against the further buffeting that was in store for them. Oranges and grapefruit were not on the dinner menu that night but, at sixty cents per plate, we enjoyed roast beef, potatoes, corn, string beans, bread, butter, apple pie, cheese and some other delightful dishes whose names I do not now remember.

I lay awake for a long time that night, between sheets in a real bed, wondering what answer I would have to my telegram but resolved to push the expedition through whether I had a camera man or not. I felt that every day we spent at Lee's Ferry added to the possibility of losing more of the men and was eager to get back on the river. The town's electric light plant consists of an automobile tractor engine hitched to a dynamo and electricity is furnished only until eleven or twelve o'clock. The noise of the engine had ceased, the last light had flickered out before I fell asleep.

Next morning I had the following answer to my telegram:

Trying to get volunteer to replace Bradley. So far impossible as Bradley has reputation for plenty of nerve and fact that he gave up discourages others. Willing to loan you negative and camera if you think you can make your own pictures.

I wired to New York for legal advice and had an answer before noon, telling me that my contract with the news film organization was useless in the circumstances. Realizing that I had to make my own pictures or do without them entirely, I accepted the offer and resigned myself to having nothing better than a still picture record of the journey from Lee's Ferry to the foot of Bright Angel Trail. But my faith in the intrepidity of newsreel camera men was forever shattered.

The morning in Kanab was spent getting together our store of provisions and other material needed for the next lap of the journey.

Seager had a boil on his face and we found a doctor who opened it. There was no dentist in town and my tooth went unattended. It was noon before we were ready to start and we stayed over for another meal. Then in the heat of the afternoon, and the succeeding cool of the evening, we jolted our way back over the ninety hot, rough and dusty miles to Lee's Ferry.

When we reached there long after dark I found Holt and Bartl missing and was told that they had started toward Kanab a few minutes after we left, hoping to hitch rides on the infrequent automobiles that passed along the lonely road. Again, I was annoyed at Holt for his unwillingness to abide by the rules of the game—and at Bartl for playing truant with him.

Early the next morning, Friday, July fifteenth, we hauled the *Coronado* and the *Powell* up on the beach, turned them over and examined their planking carefully. The heavy mahogany boards were badly scraped and battered and it was necessary to patch them in several places. Then they were painted and left exposed to the sun to dry. As the day wore on and Holt and Bartl did not return I began to wonder if I was going to have to go after them.

There was no shade where we were working and the cliffs, rising more than a thousand feet above our camp, reflected the fierce heat of the desert sun. At eleven o'clock a thermometer in one of the tents registered 111 degrees F. and I called a halt for lunch. A hot wind blew in from the Painted Desert and fine, dry sand sifted into everything. Some candles in our equipment melted and ran away. The varnish on my still camera was sticky with the heat and the lens scraped and scratched with the sand that had blown into it.

During the noon siesta I found shelter in a shed near Johnson's cabin and re-read the report of the government expedition of 1923, studied the maps and decided that we probably would have relatively easy going through the eighty-nine miles of canyon between Lee's Ferry and Bright Angel Trail. The level of water continued to drop in the river and I was hopeful of a fine, fast trip to Needles. In the late afternoon the air grew cooler, the wind died down and we stirred into activity. Weatherhead went away with D. C. "Buck" Lowrey, the local Indian trader, to buy souvenirs and canned chili con carne. Adger and Seager looked over the stores that we had brought with us from Kanab. Galloway worked on the boats. The bear sucked his paw hungrily, hummed softly to himself and watched eagerly every movement of the men around the kitchen. Rags sauntered off to see if he cared, after all, to make friends with Jerry Johnson's dogs. We planned to put splash boards on the boats the next day and in my diary that night I wrote optimistically concerning the prospects for the future, "The boats will be better than ever and the crews light and snappy."

Saturday, July sixteenth, was a long, hot day. We hauled the *Dellenbaugh* out of the water, repaired several breaks in her planking and gave her a coat of paint. Then we nailed splash boards on all three boats and were ready to resume our journey, but for the fact that Holt and Bartl still were missing. I had decided to postpone final repairs on the oar locks until we were down in the canyons where we would all be together, with no chance for any one either to desert or play truant.

McGregory ate no breakfast and, after working in a half-hearted way for a few minutes, trailed off to Johnson's shed and sat in the truck looking gloomily out across the desert. I followed him a little later and found him in a mood identical with the one he had been in the night we camped on the high ledge opposite Clearwater Canyon and also on our last night in Glen Canyon. Again I asked him if he was ill or if any one had offended him and again he answered "No," to both my questions. And so I asked him another.

"What is the matter, Mac," I said, "do you want to leave the expedition?"

And his answer came back very faintly, "No." Nor would he explain the reason for his sulkiness. I saw that there was little I could do and after urging him either to cheer up or explain his behavior I left him. But even then I began to figure what we should have to do if he decided, after all, to leave us before we could get away from the Ferry. Two men who had applied to join my expedition lived in Dallas, Texas. It would take ten days for them to reach us and in that time almost anything might happen. If Holt and Bartl had been there we would have started early the next morning on our journey through Marble Gorge.

Not more than half a dozen automobiles crossed the Ferry, in either direction, during the day and Holt and Bartl were in none of those that came from the direction of Kanab. Adger, Seager, Galloway and McGregory went over to the trading post late in the afternoon to buy themselves a supper of crackers and canned chili con carne and the rest of us prepared a bizarre meal of bread, corned beef, pancakes with syrup, canned grapefruit, rice pudding and coffee. After supper I arranged with Johnson to take me back to Kanab to look for the missing men.

I awakened at three-twenty the next morning, aroused Callaway who had expressed a desire to go, and called Johnson. Callaway and I had cold coffee, canned grapefruit and rice pudding for breakfast—all left over from the evening before. The food satisfied our immediate needs but it is not a breakfast that I should recommend.

With the first blush of dawn flooding the sky, its hues reflected upon the colorful walls of the Vermilion Cliffs, we set off for the second time through the lonely length of House Rock Valley toward the cedar tufted Buckskin Mountains. Again the engine raced in low and second gears, again the radiator boiled, again we jumped out in the sand and helped the weary truck drag its burden up the steep slopes. We reached the half way point at Jacob's Lake about ten-thirty and I was disappointed at not finding the men there. I found a fire warden's telephone, however, and telephoned to Kanab only to learn that two men answering the descriptions that I gave of Holt and Bartl had started toward Lee's Ferry two days before.

At Johnson's suggestion I hailed a cowboy passing by in a truck—cowboys in that country now drive trucks almost as much as they ride horses and are romantic looking figures in their sombreros and high heeled boots jolting over the roads in their heavy cars—and he reported that he had seen two men riding in a truck headed for the V. T. Ranch the afternoon before. Then, having played his part in the "miracle" he drove on.

I telephoned to the V. T. Ranch and was overjoyed to learn that Holt and Bartl had spent the night there and had started that morning to walk thirty miles back to Jacob's Lake. We drove off in the direction of the V. T. Ranch, keeping a sharp lookout for the missing men. Mile after mile we rode, passing through a great, unexpected forest of cedar, pine and fir trees until, five miles from the ranch, I saw the missing members of my party trudging along toward us and with them was a third man, carrying what seemed at first glance to be a small suit case.

We stopped beside them and both Holt and Bartl hastened to express regret for the delay that they had caused. Then they told me what had happened and introduced their companion. They had hitch-hiked their way to Kanab, arriving there a few minutes after we left at noon on the fourteenth. They started back on the fifteenth, got as far as Jacob's Lake where they slept under the trees, and on the sixteenth climbed aboard a truck which they thought was going to Lee's Ferry but which took them to V. T. Ranch instead. That evening they were telling a group of visitors at the ranch who they were, where they had been, and where they were going. Among other things they described Bradley's desertion and brought out the fact that the expedition probably would have to go the rest of the way without a motion picture camera man. The "miracle"—which began to happen when they left Lee's Ferry, gained momentum when at Jacob's Lake they got on a truck which was headed in the wrong direction, and accelerated its pace considerably when I accosted the truck-driving cowboy that morning—got under full way about that time and one of their listeners, Oscar Jaeger, of Dubuque, Iowa, spoke up and said he was an amateur motion picture photographer; that he had a camera and some film with him; and that he would like to take Bradley's position in the expedition. They invited him to join them, agreeing to conduct him to Lee's Ferry where he could discuss the matter with me.

If this was a story instead of a recital of real events Jaeger would have turned out to be an excellent camera man and the "miracle" would have been complete. But he was only an amateur and his work of course did not measure up to Bradley's fine performance. Still, he did join us, made the best pictures he knew how to make, and completed as well as he could the picture record that Bradley had begun.

We returned to Lee's Ferry, reaching there late in the afternoon and I had a restful night—which I needed—happy in the knowledge that the expedition would get under way again in the morning.

CHAPTER XI

McGregory Gives Up—
First Through Soap Creek Rapids—
Mouth of the Little Colorado.

"This has been a glorious day," is how I described July eighteenth when I began listing its events that evening in my diary.

The camp was astir at four forty-five and, at seven, having bade farewell to Jerry Johnson and his flock of shy youngsters, we shoved our boats away from shore, on a river carrying 40,000 second feet of water. Losing Marshall and Felton had made it necessary for me to rearrange the boat crews and, having demonstrated sufficiently my ability and willingness to pull an oar, I decided to make the rest of the journey in the pilot boat with Galloway. Adger continued in charge of the *Powell*, with Bartl, Carey and Seager for his crew. Jaeger sat on the cabin hatch amidships and Rags stood on the after deck, ready to jump down into the cockpit when we came to a rapids. I placed Holt in charge of the *Coronado*, with McGregory, Callaway and Weatherhead for a crew. The bear rode with them, at Weatherhead's feet in the forward compartment. A bucket of partly cooked beans intended for our lunch rode with us, tucked away under the deck of the *Dellenbaugh*.

We were entering the Grand Canyon where in 285 tumultuous miles the river falls 1540 feet. Perhaps the best way to understand the Grand Canyon is to visualize the plateau of northern Arizona as a great topographic step which rises at the Grand Wash Cliffs abruptly from the coastal plain and extends hundreds of miles to the north. At

Lee's Ferry the Vermilion Cliffs rise sharply a thousand feet to form another step which, in turn, slopes back toward the north until it is surmounted by another step, and another plateau, in the vicinity of Cataract Canyon. The Kaibab Plateau of northern Arizona, therefore, is a flat table-land and the sedimentary surface rock which is at the river level at Lee's Ferry, appears on the rim of a high cliff where the river emerges on the coastal plain. If the Colorado River had been content to meander out across the plateau and plunge over its edge onto the plain below there would have been a magnificent waterfall at Grand Wash Cliffs but it chose instead to cut its way through the step and the Grand Canyon is the result—a rock-walled, steep-sided valley 285 miles long, thirteen miles wide in places and more than a mile deep.

I have said that the river at Lee's Ferry flows on the surface of the limestone which forms the top of the plateau. But that does not continue long. Within a few miles it has cut its way through the limestone stratum and into the sandstone, shale and other strata that lie below. In Fig. 3 I have attempted to show how the river has cut its bed through the succeeding strata. This drawing also shows how a "U" shaped canyon usually is formed in sedimentary rock except in the Redwall Limestone, and sometimes in the sandstone where sheer wall canyons are produced. On a later page is illustrated the "V" shaped canyon that results when the river cuts its way into the underlying granite. With this picture before us we are ready to enter Marble Gorge, the sixty mile section of Grand Canyon extending from Lee's Ferry to the mouth of the Little Colorado.

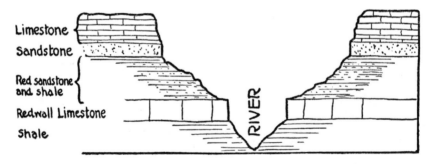

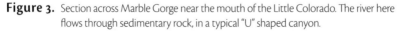

Figure 3. Section across Marble Gorge near the mouth of the Little Colorado. The river here flows through sedimentary rock, in a typical "U" shaped canyon.

Galloway and I led in the *Dellenbaugh*, the *Powell* was second in line and the *Coronado* third. Just below Lee's Ferry, where the Paria River enters from the right, there are some riffles and we splashed through them gayly. Sheer walls rose 500 feet on the left and we floated rapidly down toward Marble Gorge, where high cliffs presently would close in on both sides of the river. We were safely away from Lee's Ferry, with the crew practically intact—three stout boats, eleven men, a bear and a dog. Another half mile and there would be no turning back for any of us.

Then McGregory's spirit broke. I heard him shout, "Run ashore, I'm leaving"; and turned to see the *Coronado* headed for a pile of bowlders and a break in the wall on the right. We turned the *Dellenbaugh* toward shore and the *Powell* followed. "What," I wondered, "is the matter with Mac?" But I believed that I knew.

The *Coronado*, farther up stream when we turned toward shore, had less trouble than we did with the swift current and made a landing several minutes ahead of us. When we got there McGregory had gone. The moment the bow of the *Coronado* touched the bank he had leaped out of the boat and started climbing up the cliff.

Then I saw him and called out to him to stop. He stopped but refused to come back to the boat and I went nearer to talk to him. I asked him what was the matter and he said that he was unwilling to risk his life in the rapids with Holt in charge of the boat. I offered to transfer him to the *Powell*. He refused to make the change and the truth came out. McGregory wanted to quit. I talked with him for several minutes, pointing out to him why I believed that we would encounter no worse dangers below than we had come safely through in the canyons above Lee's Ferry. I urged him to go even as far as Bright Angel Trail, explaining to him the difficulty of getting out to Kanab. But while I talked to him, he edged away. He acted as if he were fearful that I might convince him against his better judgment and turned suddenly and resumed his scramble up the cliff.

"Come on back and get your duffel bag," I called after him.

And without so much as turning around he answered, "I don't want it."

That was the last we ever saw of McGregory. We placed his duffel bag on the beach and called out to him that it was there. Then I examined the cliff carefully and saw that he would have no trouble getting out. Then, after waiting a few minutes to make certain he was not coming back, we went on without him. Jaeger volunteered to pull oar in the *Coronado* and alternated between rowing and picture taking from that time on. I wakened at night many times during the remaining weeks we spent on the river wondering if McGregory found his way out but was always able to visualize the place where he left us, and to assure myself that twenty minutes of easy walking would have brought him to the road to Kanab along the base of the Vermilion Cliffs. Or, on that side of the canyon, he could have worked his way without difficulty back along the edge of the river to Lee's Ferry.

"Then," as I wrote in my diary, "the day began." The walls closed in, the river narrowed and we ran through two small rapids. The only maps I had of this section of the river were the ones made by Major Powell and they showed little detail of either the river or the canyons. But I knew that we should reach Soap Creek Rapids within a few miles and was on the alert for it. I sat in the stern of the boat, which was floating stern first down the river, with my hands resting on the splash boards thoroughly enjoying the panorama of river, cliffs and sky as it unfolded before me. No dream I ever had equaled this reality, either in beauty or in danger. We splashed through a riffle which I thought was Badger Creek Rapids and, at nine o'clock, there came to our ears the familiar roar of tumbling water which I decided was the warning voice of Soap Creek, in which Brown lost his life in 1889 and which no one ever had run through successfully. In eight miles the river had cut its way through the upper strata of limestone and sandstone into the shale and the steep walls towered 800 feet above the water's edge.

We floated cautiously down to the head of the rapids and ran ashore on the right. Then we clambered down over the bowlders and examined the worst 800 yards of river that we had yet encountered. Yes, undoubtedly this was Soap Creek and, like the other successful navigators of the river, we would line our boats around it. Galloway looked longingly at the rock-strewn waste of furious water and, eager to be the first one to run the rapids, suggested that he would like to try to get through alone in the *Dellenbaugh* but I discouraged him. I doubt if any boat in the world could have run through successfully at the level of water prevailing at the time. We rowed to the other side and spent two hours lining the boats a hundred yards along the shore to escape the upper end of the rapids and ran through the rest of the way.

Then we dropped down the river three miles to another bad one. Rain had begun to fall and the wind was blowing strongly up stream. The wind might add to the difficulty of keeping the sterns of our boats pointed properly down stream but the rapids looked as if it might be run successfully in spite of that and we returned to the boats, removed our shoes, adjusted our life preservers and were off.

Leaving the navigation of the boat to Galloway I permitted myself to enjoy the thrill of the wild and dangerous ride. A few swift strokes at the oars placed the boat almost in the middle of the river, the stern swung around so that we were facing directly down stream and we seemed at first scarcely to be moving. As we drifted down into the head of the rapids our pace increased until, with a last burst of speed, the swift current thrust us into the waves, ten to fifteen feet high from trough to crest, tumbling over backward, dropping on the deck of the boat, pouring over the splash board, sweeping over us, wetting us from head to foot, half filling our boat with water. The rain almost blinded us and the wind, whipping off the tops of the curling waves, flung the muddy water furiously into our faces. Sky and earth and water were arrayed against us, and I found unexpected joy in the unequal conflict. I swore each time I threw the weight of my body to one side or the other to meet the crazy lurches of the boat and the river became a living thing, a monster clutching with dripping fingers to snatch away our lives. I ducked my head when the turbid, snarling waves broke over me, pouring off my hat brim, half stran-gling me, and held my body rigid against the blows the river struck when the waves swept over my chest and shoulders. I remember yet the feel of the water in the boat splashing about my ankles, how the waves looked rising and falling ahead of us, the muddy water blend-ing with the rocky walls and they, in turn, lost in the leaden sky.

The river was always alive to me but never more so than that morning. Why I so enjoyed the battle I do not precisely know. I am certain that I would be described by any competent observer as a mild mannered man but there I was cursing the dragon in his very lair, defying him to do his worst. The dragon, in turn, tossed our boats about, splashed them almost full of muddy water, ruined our pot of half-cooked beans, but permitted us to make the run successfully. We plunged through and ran ashore below to bail the boats. Galloway reported the loss of his second hat, and borrowed one from Carey.

This happened at eleven o'clock on the morning of July eighteenth, and it was not until five months later, when I went a second time through Marble Gorge, that I learned we had been mistaken on my first trip in the matter of geography. We had run successfully through Soap Creek Rapids without knowing it. The cataract we had lined around three miles above was Badger Creek and, with the rain blowing in our faces and the waves threatening to swamp our boats, we had run through Soap Creek—the only ones who had ever done it successfully. Parley Galloway had his wish after all. He piloted the first boat that ever ran successfully through Soap Creek Rapids.

At twelve-fifteen we reached a place where a rock as large as a two-story house had fallen into the river, partly blocking the channel. We stopped there for lunch. I was interested in seeing how the men reacted to the danger. We all felt again as we had felt the first days in Cataract. The three day rest at Lee's Ferry had made the journey again a picnic. While bailing the boats below the rapids the men talked about the "big ones" that had nearly got them. Seager said something at noon about not having ever again to seek the thrill of a scenic railway and Adger remarked upon the relative calm of flood times on the Mississippi River.

I was pleased to find that the rapids were not so numerous as they had been in the central section of Cataract and while there was considerable fall in some of them the drop was short and sharp and few of the rapids presented serious difficulties at the high level of water then prevailing. We continued on in the afternoon, running every rapids we came to. We came at one place to a rapids between sheer walls. Vertical cliffs rose directly from the water's edge. We could not examine the rapids adequately. But we had found before that sheer wall rapids usually are clear of rocks and we splashed through without serious misgiving. Galloway agreed with me that high water has its advantages, certainly it makes for easier going. We camped that night under a ledge of rock thirty feet above the river.

I decided, on July nineteenth, to keep a detailed record of events and my diary shows a typical day of rapids running in a relatively easy section of the river.

"Up at five, breakfast, shave and away at seven-thirty. Passed high rock almost blocking the river. This rock leaves not more than thirty feet of channel on the side where the boats were run and the water sweeps through at tremendous speed. Landed at eight-five and studied a rapids—ran through, shipped a great deal of water. Dropped down into the trough of one wave so far and so fast that it tickled the pit of my stomach, like a roller-coaster. At eight-thirty we ran in and looked over a rapids—ran it—ran three smaller ones without stopping to examine them from shore. When a rapids drops ten feet or more you cannot see from above where the river goes; it drops out of sight and you know it is a bad one. If by standing up in the boat you can look down stream and see where the river goes, it is not so bad.

"Landed again at nine to look over a rapids. Found three rapids in a row and ran them all. At nine-twenty went through another without stopping to look at it very closely, and it was a big one. Boats half-filled with water. Landed at nine-thirty to look. I decided to photograph the boats going through but the run was rather tame. This took until ten-thirty. Back on the river. Ran two without looking them over from shore. Shipped water in the second one.

"The river in less than thirty miles has cut through 400 feet of limestone and sandstone and another 1300 feet through the red sandstone and shale, down to the marble stratum which begins here to show at the water's edge. Three more rapids, between rising walls of Redwall Limestone, nothing to do but run them. At ten-fifty a rapids which we ran without looking at from shore, shipped water. I ride in stern facing forward, stern first, making it bow. When we ship water I duck my head, water hits me on hat, down back of neck. At eleven-thirty we stopped to examine a rapids, found pool of water up a side canyon and stopped for lunch. Away again at one-thirty. Ran rapids below lunch place. At one-forty ran rapids after looking down through it from deck of boat. At two-thirty came to side canyon coming in from right. Decided to stop on sand bar to make long needed repairs to row locks on *Coronado* and *Powell*. The others went exploring some Indian cliff dwellings while Galloway and I sawed out part of the gunwale, bolted the new oar locks into place and the boats were as good as new. Adger brought back from cliff dwellings a pair of rope moccasins—probably worn five thousand years ago by some member of a vanished Indian tribe. All the men found pieces of pottery, arrow heads and many corn cobs. This apparently was a center of life centuries ago, there must be a way out somewhere along here to the rim."

The river here flows between nearly vertical walls of Redwall Limestone 300 feet in height. Above the limestone rise other walls of sandstone, shale and limestone to a total height of 2500 feet. The river, in thirty miles, has cut its canyon to that depth beneath the floor of the Painted Desert. The upper strata are gray, pink, saffron and other colors and rise sublimely overhead. Marble Gorge, because of its palisades of limestone, stained red by seepage from the overlying beds of red sandstone and shale, is one of the most impressive of the Colorado River canyons. It is colorful and awe inspiring beyond description.

"Off again at four-thirty," continues my diary. "Turned a bend in the river and there, on the right, was a spring of clear water gushing out of the face of the cliff forty feet above the river. Clear water! We wanted some and tried to pull ashore but the current was too swift and we could not make it. There were ferns and other green plants around the spring. It was Vasey's Paradise, so named by Powell, thirty-two miles below Lee's Ferry. Ran two rapids below Vasey's Paradise at five o'clock. Ran on until six, running several small ones. Then came to larger one. Good place to stop and we camped above it. Now the rapids are roaring directly in front of me. A nice place to camp. Even have a spring, and there is sand on the rock ledges for us to sleep on.

"Have made thirty-five miles in two days, thought we had done better. May make it to Little Colorado to-morrow but doubtful as there is a bad stretch of river ahead. Apparently we take a lot of time looking the rapids over. Good speed on the river, current is swift and the rapids are swifter. Must press on, should like to make it to Bright Angel Trail in six days but Upper Granite Gorge may hold us up. Drank less of this frightful water to-day, chewed gum instead.

"Found my canteen had gone sour again from use of evaporated milk in settling water. Longed all day for ice water, milk—ah, milk!—and grapefruit. Feel better now that row locks are fixed. If they hold out until we reach Bright Angel, they will last to Needles and we shall not have to wait for new ones to come from Los Angeles. Threatening rain again to-night but the boats are tied high. It would take a big rise to get them.

"This is a delightful camp. My bed is just at edge of the water but our kitchen is up a side canyon and going to it is almost like a vacation away from the river. The walls rise sheer above us on both sides of the river. The roar of the rapids reverberates in our ears. A great ledge below camp affords a view of the river down stream for half a mile to a bend in the canyon. A quiet, restful camp—the expedition a unit again, dependent upon itself, sufficient within itself, centered upon the river, with no thought but getting through."

That was one of the best camps we had on the river and I slept reasonably well except for waking up several times to flash my light on a bowlder which I had previously selected as a water gauge. I was little worried, almost secure in the knowledge that nothing less than a deluge could endanger the boats. There was a sprinkle of rain during the night but I was much less disturbed by that than by the fact that my rock ledge sloped toward the river and every time I turned over I came near rolling off into the water.

We got away at seven as usual on the morning of the twentieth of July, and in the next few hours passed through some of the grandest canyons anywhere on the river or, for that matter, anywhere in the world. Gorgeously colored palisades of Redwall Limestone towered 500 feet above us and the unbroken face of the wall was carried another 1500 feet into the sky by cliffs of other stone. The total depth of the canyon is 3400 feet and the strip of blue that can be seen from the bottom of the river trench seems very far away indeed. The walls have been sculptured by erosion, and by the fall of great masses of rock, into many marvelous forms. Caves were numerous and we passed some gigantic arches, high above us in the limestone cliff, which we recognized as the Royal Arches.

For long distances the walls were sheer on both sides of the stream and the river hurried along through narrow, winding canyons that were scarcely wider at the top than at the bottom. Rapids occurred between sheer walls. The swift stream hurled its tremendous volume of water first against one side wall and then another, and we were hard put at times to prevent our boats being piled up against the rocks. High water made for fast and dangerous going. There were many dreadful looking whirlpools and although I believed there was little danger running through them, so long as we were not tipped out of the boats, I never failed to be impressed by their mighty power.

Even in our twenty-two foot boats, with four men pulling at the oars, there were many whirls that we could not pull directly through. They almost always were strong enough to turn the boats around several times before we could get clear of them. I would look over the sides of the boat, down into the vortex of the whirls as we went along and think what such whirlpools do to men—how they catch them, whirl them around and around their fatal circles, draw them in toward the terrible center, suck them down and crush their bodies against the rocky bed of the river. Then I would remind the men again to cling to the boats in the event of an upset in the river. Traveling whirlpools swept across the stream, turned our boats around in mid-channel and moved away, leaving us thrilled by their mighty display of dreadful power.

Below the whirlpools were "boils"—sudden miniature geysers in the river where the water which had been drawn down in the whirls found its way again to the surface. These "boils" usually appeared suddenly and formed boiling mounds of water that rose two or three feet above the surface.

At nine o'clock we reached Bowlder Rapids where a great rock partly blocking the river left us little choice of channels through the turbulent stretch of water. I thought that running through this rapids would make a good motion picture and took Jaeger's place in the *Coronado* while he photographed us running through. At ten-five we passed Triple Alcoves and, by eleven, had completed the run through the narrower part of Marble Gorge and were in the relatively open section near Nankoweap. Here the river flows through shale. There were sloping banks on either side and the Redwall Limestone formed a stratum in the cliff above us, as shown in Fig. 3. Again there were talus slopes on one side of the river or the other and there were bushes along the shore. In one or two places there were half a dozen stunted cottonwood trees. Back of the narrow shore, and the fringe of shrubs, the walls rose 3000 feet or more but they rose less abruptly, in a series of receding walls with narrow talus slopes between.

We ran through Nankoweap Rapids and, at twelve, reached Kwagunt Canyon, Creek—and Rapids. There were trees on the fan-shaped pile of débris that Kwagunt Creek has dumped into Marble Gorge and, best of all, there was clear water in the little stream. We stopped for lunch and I enjoyed as much water as I could drink. While Adger and Seager were cooking I went swimming in a quiet stretch of water above the rapids. Galloway and Holt, armed with pistols, went deer hunting and though there were many tracks, the hunters returned empty handed.

We got away again at two and, after running through two bad and half a dozen easy rapids, arrived at three-fifteen at the mouth of the Little Colorado. Rain was falling when we landed but the sun was soon shining again. I had planned to stop there for an entire day to give the men a badly needed rest but said nothing about it at the time, concluding that an afternoon and evening probably would be enough for all of us.

We soon had our camp established. I made individual photographs of all the men and then they wandered away or lay around resting. Weatherhead took his camera and climbed the cliff above us as high as he could go. Galloway and Holt took the *Dellenbaugh* and rowed across the river to explore some likely looking caves that they thought might have been cliff dwellings. The other men read, talked and rested. I hauled out my maps again and tried to determine what kind of going we could expect on the rest of the run to Bright Angel Trail.

We had voyaged sixty-one miles through Marble Gorge, with its twenty-seven bad rapids, in less than three days and with reasonable luck should go the rest of the way, twenty-eight miles to Bright Angel Trail, in three more. But a few miles below us was Hance Rapids, the Sockdolager and the Upper Granite Gorge—what effect those obstacles would have upon our progress I did not know.

CHAPTER XII

Unkar Creek—
How We Ran Hance Rapids—
The Sockdolager—
Trapped Under the *Dellenbaugh.*

*W*hen we left our pleasant camp at the mouth of the Little Colorado on the morning of July twenty-first, we entered upon a new phase of our adventure. In Cataract Canyon the river, aided by heavy rains, had struck us so suddenly and hard that we barely escaped disaster before our voyage was fairly begun—a relentless attack that played havoc with our morale, and defeated four men of the thirteen who started. There was time as we floated through Glen Canyon for some of our wounds to heal and while there were rapids in Marble Gorge as dangerous as any on the river, there were occasional stretches of smooth flowing river and we had made a quick, successful passage through. The journey had been almost equally divided between difficult and easy going and at least a few of its picnic aspects lingered with us still. But from that time there were few rest periods. Never below the mouth of the Little Colorado, until we emerged at last from the Grand Canyon 224 miles below, did the tireless river rest for long in its efforts to destroy us.

We got away at seven o'clock, just when the canyon is most beautiful. The summer sun had found its way to the bottom of the narrow gorge and the brilliant colors of the rocks stood boldly forth. Cliffs of gray limestone and sandstone, more than 1000 feet in height, formed the rim of the canyon that blended with the sky almost a mile above us. Beneath that wall of harder rock was a red or red-brown talus slope, a band of softer shale and sandstone 1100 feet in total thickness. Everywhere below the red beds extended magnificent cliffs of Redwall Limestone, 500 feet in height. Finally, at the river's edge there were talus slopes of shale, green in color, contrasting strongly with the murky tones of the river water.

The clear light of early morning brought out in bold relief towers and cliffs and battlements that disappear at noon when the sun is directly overhead, to reappear at sunset when the shadows stretch their lengths from the canyon walls. Many artists have attempted to reproduce, interpret or suggest the majestic proportions and indescribable colors of the Grand Canyon. They usually paint from the rim or near it, looking across the mighty chasm. Of the canvasses I have seen, many are harsh and some untrue because of the vastness of the scene, the constantly changing light or the limitations of the palette. A few of them are beautiful but none succeed in capturing the iridescent, majestic splendor of the canyons.

Cape Solitude towered 3000 feet above us at the junction of the rivers. Chuar Butte stood high above the river on the right. Comanche Point, Navajo Point, Grandview Point—a dozen landmarks along the rim of the Painted Desert, 4000 feet above us—came into view as we floated down the river. I glanced up stream toward Marble Gorge and up the narrow canyon of the Little Colorado and, finally, back upon the cliffs directly over us and everywhere the rocks reflected the ruddy glow of the rising sun, its colors augmenting and blending with their own brilliant hues. Red is the predominating color in the Canyon, perhaps the color-echo of a million roseate dawns.

There was little time, however, to marvel at the beauties of the canyon. At seven-twenty we ran a fair-sized rapids and, ten minutes later, one in which we shipped a little water. At eight o'clock we came to Lava Canyon Rapids. Galloway and I stood up in the *Dellenbaugh*, looked down through the racing waves and decided that the run promised a thrill without great danger. We ran swiftly through and as the other boats started to follow, I looked back up stream and saw, almost directly in their path, a foam-flecked bowlder

Lining Badger Creek Rapids, inhospitable gateway to the Grand Canyon. Here is one of the two large boats, outfitted with everything that years of planning could provide for the thousand hazards of the river trip. Note the water-tight compartments forward, amidships and aft.

Sockdolager Rapids—with is sheer walls, rocks, 20-foot waves and furious current flowing 30 miles an hour—guards the gateway to the mile-deep Granite Gorges.

that threatened disaster. I stood up and signaled Adger to run his boat to one side and he pulled away. Then he relayed my signal to Holt in the *Coronado* and both boats got safely by. But I was struck again by the cruel cunning of the river. She is relentless in her efforts and the only chance for safety lies in constant vigilance.

The gorge opened out below Lava Canyon Rapids and one by one we recognized Vishnu Temple and other familiar peaks which comprise the imprisoned mountain range laid out before the startled gaze of the tourist to Grand Canyon. There was a fringe of cotton-woods and lesser shrubs at the river's edges and we surprised half a dozen wild burros along the shore. These burros are a remnant of the herd that formerly carried tourists up and down Bright Angel Trail.

"If we had a gun," said Callaway, "we would have some burro meat for supper."

Dried beef was spoken of thereafter as burro meat and Adger and Seager were asked many times why they had selected the oldest and toughest animals in the flock.

At nine-forty we reached Unkar Creek Rapids. At Unkar Creek there is a fan-shaped peninsula on the right and a sheer wall curved like the letter "C" on the left. The current sets against the outer curve of the "C" and the channel is strewn with bowlders. We walked down stream a long way to examine the rapids and decided it could be run. Then Galloway pointed out to the men in the other boats a partly submerged rock that we should have to avoid running into while getting out into the channel and we shoved off in the *Dellenbaugh*. I was seated at the stern as usual, with my hands resting on the splash board. The boat was running stern first with the current. How fast we were going I cannot say but the rapids was not a bad one and our rate of speed did not seem excessive. But apparently we were traveling with greater rapidity than I thought. The keel of the boat hit squarely against the rock that we had picked out so carefully and we were going so fast that I was thrown forward across the deck, breaking off the half-inch oak splash board with my hands and wrists. Fortunately, the boat slipped over or around the rock and, sprawled across the deck, I reached over into the water and salvaged the splash board which was nailed back into place during the noon halt. It has been estimated that the water flows through the rapids at a speed of thirty miles per hour and I am quite ready to believe it. I have scars yet on my wrists from the gashes I received that morning when I broke off the splash board of the *Dellenbaugh*.

We ran through four bad rapids and several easy ones before eleven-thirty. Lava Canyon, Tanner Canyon and Unkar Creek all were negotiated successfully and then we came to Seventy-five Mile Rapids which, fourteen miles below the junction of the two rivers, actually marks the end of the more or less open canyon through which we had been traveling and is one of the worst rapids at fairly high water anywhere above the Granite Gorge. We ran it, but it required hard pulling to keep the boats from being dashed against the cliff on the right. At eleven-forty we were swept around a sharp bend in the river. The stream turned suddenly to the north and we ran ashore above Hance Rapids, where the river drops twenty feet in a few hundred yards.

The stream at Hance Rapids is 250 feet wide; there is an unusually large, fan-shaped pile of débris where the side canyon comes in on the left, and the channel of the river is dotted with rocks. We walked down along the shore and decided that the rapids could not be run. Then I concluded it was time for lunch and Adger and Seager, assisted by the kitchen police, began preparing the meal. I got out the still camera to make some pictures of the rapids; most of the men found such shelter as they could from the heat of the noonday sun, and Galloway walked down stream again to re-examine the cataract. It was almost intolerably hot and we made no effort to get started again until after one o'clock.

Then, as happened many times, we looked at the rapids again and, perhaps because we had just been fortified with dried beef and rice pudding, the fall looked less threatening and we decided it could be run. Galloway and I were to go first in the *Dellenbaugh*, take our chance of getting out below if our boat was wrecked, and the others were to follow unless we had great difficulty getting through.

The men ranged themselves along the shore to watch our progress and we shoved off in the little boat. We had planned to pull well away from the shore and out around a big rock at the head of the rapids, then pull back toward shore to avoid a "hole" and then out again to escape some rocks close to shore at the foot of the rapids. We started away properly enough but the current was strong and swept us into the rapids thirty feet from the place we had selected. Then the stern struck a rock a glancing blow, the bow swung around and, to avoid capsizing, Galloway pulled the boat toward the middle of the stream directly toward the "hole" we had been so intent upon avoiding. He cleared the rock and turned the bow toward shore again and pulled at his oars. But the current outpulled him and I saw that we were being swept helplessly toward what I believed to be the most dangerous part of the rapids. Nearer and nearer we came to the "hole." I could see the "pour" above it, the "hump" in the water that showed the location of the rock. Then I could see the "hole" itself and realized that we were drifting into it. I braced myself and watched the stern of the boat sweep into the outer rim of the churning chaos of water, hesitate a second as if undecided whether to plunge into the maelstrom under the rock or go on. Then she swept by and we were through.

But I had looked over the side of the boat into the whirling, churning water and knew that I had looked into the face of the death that I most feared on the river. I can see the vortex yet when I close my eyes, and do see it sometimes in my dreams. But we swept on, shipping half a boat load of water in the high waves at the end of the rapids. I reached for a bailing can, grateful for something to do, but before I could bail the boat and Galloway could pull her ashore the current had swept us three-quarters of a mile down stream and sheer walls prevented our getting back to warn the men or to help them with their boats.

We climbed the cliff and found a place finally from which we could see the foot of the rapids but that was as far as we could go. We could do nothing else but wait and as I waited I hoped fervently that the men would be content to line the boats. They must have seen the difficulties we encountered and would not attempt to run the rapids. This was the only time while we were on the river when I was separated from the men, and Galloway was with me. The younger men were quite alone.

I had felt constantly the heavy responsibility that rested upon me to get those fine, young men safely through the canyons but I never felt it so keenly as I did at Hance Rapids when neither Galloway nor I could aid them in any way. It is not certain that either of us could have helped—and surely the sleepless hours that I endured during the journey accomplished nothing toward shielding them from the dangers of the river—but so long as I was with them, actually sharing their risks, I felt that I might somehow help them if they needed it. But I was three-quarters of a mile away, and Galloway was with me. Would they line their boats as I had told them to if Galloway and I had trouble, or did they know how near we had come to being wrecked? I knew that Adger would decide and knew he appreciated the danger but he was only twenty-three and a youthful commander might conceivably throw away his life at such a time rather than display caution which might be mistaken for cowardice.

We waited perhaps for twenty minutes and I had begun to think that they had considered discretion the better part of valor and were unloading the boats and portaging the duffel, when suddenly one of the boats came into view plunging through the waves near the foot of the rapids and, presently, the other one appeared behind it. They both were through and I stepped back of Galloway because I did not want him to see that there were tears in my eyes. I realize that nothing can be achieved without risk and I know there always will be young men who are eager to gamble their lives against the vagaries of air currents, the whims of a river, or the chances of death on mountain heights but that day I came near resolving that when I go adventuring again I shall take with me old men with whiskers down to their waists and if they get killed it will be their own responsibility. The crews of the *Powell* and the *Coronado* joined us, the boats were bailed and we proceeded on our way.

We were entering the Upper Granite Gorge. Here the river has cut its way through five thousand feet of sedimentary rock and another thousand of granite, the earth's foundation stone. This section of the Grand Canyon is more than a mile in depth. Granite resists the force and fury of the water and the bed of the river is narrow. Practically everywhere the walls rise eight hundred to a thousand feet sheer from the water's edge. There are no talus slopes, no friendly shores upon which to land the boats—nothing but turbulent, muddy water, flowing between black granite walls. In many places, as shown in Fig. 4, nothing can be seen from the river but the "V" shaped granite gorge and it is difficult to realize that there are other, brighter colored cliffs above the dismal granite walls that hem the river in.

There are three granite gorges in the Grand Canyon: Granite Gorge, Middle Granite Gorge and Lower Granite Gorge. Granite Gorge, which is forty-one miles long, begins within a mile below Hance Rapids. Middle Granite Gorge is four miles long and begins

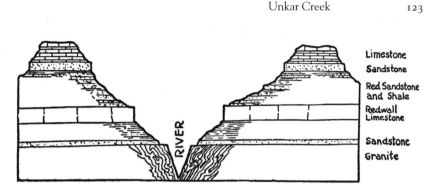

Figure 4. Section across Grand Canyon near Sockdolager Rapids. Here the river has penetrated the granite and flows in a gloomy "V" shaped trench 6000 feet below the surface of the Kaibab Plateau.

eight miles below Granite Gorge. Lower Granite Gorge is about fifty miles long and begins a few miles above Diamond Creek.

The mighty river falls 465 feet in the forty-one miles of Upper Granite Gorge. There are a hundred bad rapids. The canyon is narrow and the heavy, hurrying water flows with incredible velocity between its dismal shores. Here, concentrated in every mile, are dangerous rapids, "holes," whirlpools, tumbling waves, furious water, rocks—every kind of danger that we had encountered in the five hundred miles that we had come. And as a gateway to this series of canyons stands the great Sockdolager Rapids.

When Major Powell arrived at this rapids in 1869 he stood on a projecting spur of rock, gazed down through the tumbling mass of water and said, "There is the Sockdolager of the world." By that he meant that he had come to what he considered the worst rapids on any river anywhere upon the face of the earth. We knew its approximate location and, when its roar came thundering to us up the canyon, we ran our boats close to shore and approached it cautiously.

Edging our way as close to the head of the rapids as we dared, we ran ashore. One man from each boat leaped upon the rocks and held the boats secure, there being nothing there to tie them to. The others of us climbed up to see as much as we could of the Sockdolager. Granite walls rose so steeply from the water's edge that we could not find our way down along the rapids and, from where we stood, only the upper portion of it could be seen. What lay beyond the narrow gateway we could only guess.

Before us was a river of turbulent water, white with plunging waves from shore to shore. We could not line our boats around, we had to run them through. There was no climbing out, no going back, no walking around—nothing to do but run the rapids, and at the prevailing stage of water, it looked as if that was an impossible thing to do.

The height of the river's fall in the Sockdolager has been variously estimated by canyon voyagers. Powell recorded a drop of seventy-five or eighty feet in one-third of a mile. The fall actually amounts to only twenty feet, but most of it occurs in the first hundred yards and, having seen the mighty cataract, I can understand Powell's miscalculation. The waves have been described as thirty feet high but Major Birdseye's expedition measured their height, at relatively low water, and the government later published a pamphlet in which it was announced that they "measured in fact only about twenty feet from trough to crest." Only about twenty feet from trough to crest! And the *Dellenbaugh* was sixteen feet long.

I wondered what happens when a current flowing thirty miles per hour picks up a boat sixteen feet long and thrusts it truculently through waves twenty feet in height from trough to crest.

It was necessary for us all to go through and I directed that the boats be run fairly close together, so that we might help each other if there was need for it. The apex of the current was not clearly marked and after picking a channel down the middle of the river away from the rocks on either shore, we returned to the boats. As usual, we removed our shoes, tying them to the cleats of the boats, and adjusted our life preservers. Galloway and I shoved off in the *Dellenbaugh*. Adger followed in the *Powell*, and Holt in the *Coronado*, came third. As a last precaution I slipped a string that was attached to my hat under a strap on my life preserver and tied it there. I did not want to lose my hat, and the protection it gave me from the rays of the sun.

Once away from shore the current carried us at steadily increasing speed down into the rapids. We dropped into the trough of the first great wave and the muddy water boiled over the deck, over the splash boards and into the cockpit. The wave broke over us as the river forced us through but we staggered over its crest and down, down, down again into the trough. The boat bobbed about like a cork when it finally reached the crests of the waves and dropped into the troughs as if it were loaded with lead.

Each time it seemed impossible that we could climb up the next wave. The muddy, tumbling water threatened to swamp the boat. The very bottom of the river seemed to drop from under us. I expected momentarily to feel the boat strike a rock. I thought of "holes" and whirlpools and tightened my grip on the life line, remembering my own instructions to the men, "Cling to the boat whatever happens." There were seconds, while the boat floundered in the troughs of the waves, when there was nothing in sight but walls of water and the blue sky far overhead. I ventured to look back and saw the *Powell* close behind, all four oars helpless for the moment, two of them fanning the air as the boat rose to the crest of a wave and the other two buried deep in the surging water. But the Sockdolager was mostly "big water," our boats were seaworthy and we made it through. We swept around a bend in the river into relatively calm water and I hastily bailed the boat.

Attached to the side of the boat was a waterproof pocket in which I kept my watch, compass, maps, diary and pencil. I took out the map and a pencil and leaned over to note the hour in which we had come safely through the Sockdolager. Galloway at the same moment began to roll a cigarette. For a second we were both off guard. Less than twenty miles down stream was Hermit Falls where I had said to my wife eight years before, "There's my river." Perhaps the river remembered and, looking at me, may have muttered to itself, "There's my man." I felt the boat tip suddenly and before I could throw my weight to either side she was flipped completely over, with Galloway and me trapped under her, struggling for our lives. After allowing us to run one of the greatest of her rapids the erratic river had upset our boat in relatively calm water, so unexpectedly that neither of us knows to this day what did it.

It flashed into my mind to wonder how long it would take me to get out from under the boat but I wasted no time toying with the thought. I thrust my arm out and my hand touched the gunwale. I pushed my head and body under it and reaching my hand up, grasped the life line strung to the side—without ever once losing hold of the boat. In another second I was on the surface.

I straddled the keel and looked for Galloway. He had not come up and I had started to slide back into the water when suddenly he bobbed up at my side. He had been a little longer getting clear of the boat but when he was clear his life preserver shot him to the top in a hurry. Then, directing the *Coronado* to salvage our oars, I called the *Powell* to our rescue. As she drew alongside I removed from my mouth the pencil with which I had been writing at the time of the upset and carefully handed it to Seager. That was the first moment I realized I had clung to it at all. "Strange," I wrote later in my diary, "what we do in sudden emergencies of that kind. Better not have anything heavy in my hands when the boat is upset."

Before getting into the *Powell* we righted the *Dellenbaugh* and then began a struggle to get the water-filled boat ashore. The line had become tangled in some way and only a few feet of it was clear. We made repeated efforts to get the *Powell* ashore but, each time, the current caught the *Dellenbaugh* and we were powerless to pull against it. Meantime we were floating rapidly down stream toward Grapevine Rapids and I saw it would be nip and tuck if we made it. Time after time the bow of the *Powell* came almost near enough to shore for one of us to leap to the rocks with her bow line, only to be hauled to midstream again by the current tugging at the water-filled *Dellenbaugh*. We were drifting down toward the rapids and the battle seemed hopeless when, with a final effort, the crew of the *Powell* got her bow near enough for Carey to leap ashore. There was barely room for him to stand but he found a knob of rock around which he snubbed the line and we had won.

I had planned to go on down the river to Bright Angel Trail that day but by the time we were ready to travel again it was getting late and two of us at least had had enough of running rapids for one day. We came at five o'clock to an unexpected shelf of rock on the left bank of the river above Grapevine Rapids and I gave the signal to run ashore.

That was another pleasant camp. After we were settled for the night Galloway reported that he had lost his hat, the third since leaving Greenriver, and expressed surprise that I still had mine. Then I showed him the string with which I attached it to my life preserver and he appeared later in the evening wearing his third borrowed hat, no less collegiate than the others had been. We had for dinner that night ham, potatoes and gravy, camp bread, rice pudding, dill pickles and cocoa. We were jolly enough, our morale was fine. I was pleased with the way the men had handled the boats and looked forward with reasonable confidence to the battle that was ahead of us below Bright Angel Trail. I had little reason to fear any more desertions and

believed that the party would be intact when we left our next stopping place for the final lap of the journey.

My bed was spread that night as usual near the water. Weatherhead
was off at the opposite end of the rocky ledge and the others were
grouped around the kitchen fire, back against the cliff. The black granite walls hemmed us in. I waxed poetic and set down in my diary:

> To-night is very lovely,
> The river swirling by,
> And high above the canyon walls
> A cloud-flecked, sunset sky.

I may have meant by that simply that I was glad to be on shore,
safe momentarily from the dangers of the river.

CHAPTER XIII

Bright Angel Trail— Out at Grand Canyon— Horn Creek Rapids— Overnight at Hermit Falls.

*T*here was no need to hurry on the morning of July twenty-second and we slept a few minutes later than usual, or at least we kept very still wrapped in our blankets enjoying the luxury of not having to "rise and shine" while the shadows of night still lingered in the depths of the canyon. After a lavish breakfast of stewed prunes, cereal with evaporated milk, flapjacks and coffee, we clambered down over the rocks to look at Grapevine Rapids whose roar had filled our ears all night.

The river in this section has carved a "V" shaped trench through the Archean schist and granite. There is no shore line in the season of high water at Grapevine Rapids and, to select a possible channel, it was necessary for us to climb 200 feet or more along the smooth-faced cliff, far above the muddy, tumbling water that filled the bottom of the gorge from shore to shore. Below us swept a cataract in which the river dropped seventeen feet in a few hundred yards. The channel was dotted with rocks and I clung to the rocky wall following with my eye pieces of driftwood that floated through the rapids. I could see that the slightest miscalculation on our part would result in shipwreck and smiled a little to myself when Galloway said, as he had said so many times before, "Well, I don't see nothin' there."

Grapevine was kind to us and although the muddy water poured over the splash boards into the *Dellenbaugh*, and waves broke in places over my head and shoulders, we ran through without mishap and bailed the boats below without running them ashore.

I was more alert than I had been the day before. I watched the riffles as well as the rapids and realized that the tip-over below the Sockdolager had shaken my confidence in the seaworthiness of the *Dellenbaugh*. But in the Granite Gorges it was necessary for us to be on the alert anyhow. The river is narrow and swift, the current flows with great velocity and rapids are frequent. For an hour we ran swiftly through one riffle after another with an occasional rapids thrown in for good measure. Then we came to calmer water and, at nine-thirty, passed under the footbridge swung across the river on cables at the mouth of Bright Angel Creek and ran ashore. From there we walked half a mile up the side canyon to Phantom Ranch.

Again I was in touch with civilization and its attendant worries. Would there be a camera man to join us at the head of Bright Angel Trail or, failing that, had the newsreel organization sent me the promised camera and film? Were my provisions there? I telephoned to the rim but could learn nothing from that distance.

I delayed our departure from Phantom Ranch until eleven-thirty to give the "trail party" from the hotel time to reach the river at the foot of the trail. Then we shoved off, hoping to sweep in upon the startled tourists in a manner calculated to give them something to talk about the rest of their lives. We plunged through the rapids at the mouth of Bright Angel Creek, floated swiftly around a bend in the river and, with our flags proudly flying from the bows of our boats, ran in at the foot of the trail—and found there to greet us not the hundred or more awe-stricken tourists whom I had hoped to find but, instead, four nonchalant young fellows who were mildly interested but clearly did not know what it was all about.

We had completed the run of eighty-nine miles from Lee's Ferry in five and a half days instead of eight as I had planned. We were twenty-four days out of Greenriver, Utah, and my original schedule had allowed me twenty-six. We had covered a total distance of 421 miles and still had 367 to go to Needles, 189 of them through the mile deep gorges of the Grand Canyon.

Leaving Bartl and Carey to guard the boats the rest of us followed the "trail party," riding on mule-back, to the rim. The distance from the river to the rim is seven miles and the difference in altitude between the two points is 4466 feet, almost a mile. By walking fast we were able to keep up with the mules but the day was hot and I was glad the trail was no longer.

We were ahead of our schedule and there were no telegrams for me. Also, there was no camera man, no camera, no films—nothing but my provisions, which had arrived together with a letter from my father, the first I had received since he learned that I was starting through the canyons. In it he wondered if I would "ever grow up."

"Well, maybe not," I wrote that night in my diary, "but I believe now that I shall, even to the extent of fixing on a new dream, a dream in which money and comforts figure largely. That seems to constitute growing up, the crowding out of romance and settling down to work and golf. But it will suit me to do that, at least it seems to me now that it will. I must realize that this is my big adventure and that now I must be content to work, and earn and save. It still is too soon to define the new dream but it probably will take the form of comforts at home, security, automobiles, money, a trip to Europe sometime, or even a journey around the world when I am old."

I sent a long night letter to New York and had for dinner two pieces of the best peach pie that I have ever eaten. In the evening Galloway and I had a long visit with Emery Kolb, veteran of two canyon voyages and he very generously went over our maps with us, describing in detail the worst of the many cataracts that we had still to pass. The character of a rapids changes from season to season and from year to year, but it was comforting to receive from Kolb directions to "land on the right above the rapids" or "watch out for 'holes' in this rapids, it is full of them." Of the 190 bad rapids in the 189 miles between the foot of Bright Angel Trail and the Grand Wash Cliffs, which mark the end of the Grand Canyon, Kolb said that fourteen were especially dangerous and told us as nearly as he could how we might know when we were approaching them.

I had not met Kolb before and was interested in seeing that he was a small man. Courage, of course, is no more dependent upon a man's height than it is upon tough whiskers and other spectacular physical characteristics but we have been taught so well to associate one with the other that it comes as something of a shock to most of us to find men of small stature performing deeds of heroic proportions. I remember my first meeting with Lieutenant, now Major, G. A. Vaughn who shot down thirteen enemy planes during the World War. I had pictured him a tall, handsome knight. Actually he is less than average height and close study of his keen, intelligent eyes, and the set of his lips, is needed to disclose the qualities that make him an outstanding figure in a group of giants. Dellenbaugh is less than five feet six inches tall, while Galloway and Dodge are only slightly taller. Adger, on the contrary tops six feet and so does Holt. All of which proves nothing at all perhaps except that the size of the man has nothing to do with his willingness to face unusual hazards.

During the evening the boys wandered about. Word got around that they were members of an expedition going down the river and I was gratified to see that they attracted attention because of it. Even Galloway and I came in for a little glory but I became discouraged and went to bed when an old lady to whom we were talking admitted that she had not even known before that there was a river at the bottom of the canyon.

Saturday, July twenty-third, passed with no word from New York. Holt and Callaway went back to the river to watch the boats and Bartl and Carey joined us on the rim. I had slept badly the night before and was eager to resume our journey, to get away from Bright Angel because of the possibility that more of the men might decide to abandon the expedition. Late in the afternoon a camera and 2000 feet of film were delivered to me and I needed no other reply to my telegram. I arranged for a mule train to pack our supplies down to the river and planned to get away the next afternoon.

After lunch on Sunday—I noted in my diary that the dessert consisted of peach pie and ice cream—we started down the trail toward the river. The party was intact and I did not know until long afterward how thoroughly our stop had proved me right in placing confidence in Weatherhead's ability to fight his way through to Needles. At the time of the flood in Cataract Canyon, Howland, in Greenriver, had written a letter to Weatherhead's father which convinced him that he had better write to his son and tell him to leave the expedition.

Weatherhead received that letter when we reached Grand Canyon. He could have withdrawn had he wanted to. His family, through his father, urged him to do so and be it said to his credit he wired to them that he intended to stay with us. Before we reached the river we met Holt on his way to the rim. He had left Callaway alone to guard the boats and was on his way to join us. Holt, as I have said before, was a valuable member of the party but there are certain rules and regulations which must be adhered to by armies and expeditions alike and one of those rules, perhaps the first of them, is that the individual must submerge his own wishes in the interests of the group as a whole and this, Holt never quite learned to do. He may even have thought that I was easy to impose upon. Perhaps I was but in my fashion I chose to lead the expedition, not to drive it.

We reached the river at six and before the mules were unpacked rain began to fall. Our spirits, dampened by the rain and doubtless affected by the prospect of the dangerous journey that lay ahead, reflected the gloom of the canyons. We had late supper and hurried to spread our ponchos and blankets on the wet sand and rocks. Our morale was at low ebb. The men moved sluggishly. Our provisions were piled on the beach, the more perishable of the supplies having been stowed away in the boats to protect them from the weather. Just as I was preparing to slide in between my blankets Weatherhead reported to me that he had found a cave large enough for two of us and I joined him. Our feet protruded from the inadequate shelter and the rain pattered all night on our ponchos but the upper parts of our bodies were dry and I avoided having to endure another of my pet abominations—rain spattering in my face when I am trying to sleep. I felt a little guilty about the men being out in it but decided finally that there was little choice between my fairly rainless cave with its uneven, rocky floor and the drizzle on the beach, with relatively soft sand to sleep upon.

We were up at five as usual on the morning of July twenty-fifth. The men moved slowly and I did not feel energetic enough myself to hurry them. Also, there was a new supply of provisions to stow away and it was twenty minutes after eight when we started. We ran quickly through an easy rapids just below our camp and, at nine o'clock, ran ashore on the right at the head of Horn Creek Rapids.

The sky was overcast and more rain threatened. Two men have since been drowned in Horn Creek Rapids and its reputation as a "killer" is established, but it needed no such tag that morning to tell us that it was a dangerous thousand yards of river. There were several "holes" on either side of the stream near the head of the rapids and there were many rocks whose ugly heads were raised above the surface of the water. Half way down the rapids a dike of granite projected from the rocky wall twenty feet or more into the river and the force of the current swept against it furiously, hurling spray high into the air. If we entered the rapids near the left shore we would be in danger of dropping into any one of half a dozen "holes." If we could avoid the rocks near the head of the rapids on the right, and the "holes" below them, there still would be danger of crashing into the granite ledge below. A dozen dangers threatened and we studied the rapids thoughtfully for many minutes. Taking Galloway and Adger with me, I crawled out as far as I could on the granite ledge and between us we decided finally that our best chance lay in running close to the shore, and to the granite ledge, on the right.

Galloway and I went first in the *Dellenbaugh*. We ran dangerously close to the bad "hole" on the right, pulled far inshore to avoid a rock and then quickly out again to avoid being carried against the ledge below. There had been rapids in Marble Gorge where our boat seemed to glide along with the waves, here it was literally picked up and tossed about. A wave struck the bow of the boat on the left and poured over me, striking so high that it strangled me for a moment and filled my left ear with water. The force of its blow against the bow thrust our boat half way around, broadside in the tumbling water and, with Galloway tugging at his oars, carried us down toward the granite ledge. I glanced up stream and saw that the other boats had started through and noted that they were farther out and apparently in a better position than ours. Then I looked again toward the ledge with the water piling up against it and though I know how undependable such estimates are I would swear that we missed it by not more than half a dozen inches. The other boats followed and a few minutes later we were bailing out below.

It was about nine-thirty when we ran through Horn Creek and an hour later, after running Salt Creek Rapids and a number of riffles, we came to Granite Falls, three and a half miles down stream. At Granite Falls there is a sheer cliff on the right against which the main body of the river is deflected by a pile of bowlders that has been dumped into the canyon by Monument Creek, entering through a gorge on the left. The sky had cleared and there was light enough to make motion pictures. I took Jaeger's place in the *Coronado* and watched Galloway drop down toward the head of the rapids alone in the *Dellenbaugh*. We had intended running close to the cliff because the channel was on that side but Galloway went too close and while we were floating down toward the rapids I could see that he was having trouble keeping his boat from striking the rocky wall in a dozen places where ledges jutted out into the river. Then we had our own hands full keeping the *Coronado* clear and I could not see what had happened to Galloway. He made it through safely but told me afterward about the trouble he had had. Waves splashed into the *Coronado* at both her bow and stern and both cockpits were half filled with water. We waited for Jaeger to join us and hurried on after bailing the boats.

We reached Hermit Falls at one o'clock and even after lunch the rapids looked too dangerous to run. This rapids was run successfully at a lower level of water by Birdseye's expedition in 1923 and is not considered a particularly dangerous one. We might have run it successfully; certainly we ran many others on the river that looked as bad or worse, but the combination of waves at the top which would fill our boats and other waves at the bottom that might tip us over, looked too dangerous and because it was an easy rapids to line the boats around, I decided on the latter course. Then, as happened many times when lining the boats instead of running them through the rapids, we came near to losing a man in what would seem to be the safer operation. Carey slipped off a rock that he was standing on. His feet were swept from under him by the swift current and but for the fact that he brought up against another bowlder to which he clung until we could throw a line to him, would have been carried down into the rapids. He was without a life preserver and it is doubtful if he could have come through alive.

That night the *Powell* and the *Coronado* were resting half way out of the water on the rocks at the foot of the rapids and the *Dellenbaugh* was in a quiet haven above. "The men are tired," I wrote in my diary, "and a little grumpy. The strain tells and I shall be glad to reach Elves' Chasm or some such place, where we will be together again as a unit away from all contact with the world outside, and spend an entire day in camp. We need a good rest, all of us. The trip is long and hard and I'll be glad to have it finished."

The wind began to blow at sunset and fine, dry sand drifted into everything. We had unloaded the boats and the sand drifted like snow into and around our stock of provisions. There was a sprinkle of rain and I was forced finally to cover my face with my blanket but even then I could feel the sand as it sifted under my covers, into my hair, my ears, my eyes, down the back of my neck, everywhere.

There had been a day and a night of rain. I was on the alert for a rise in the river and was up a dozen times flashing my light on the *Powell* and *Coronado*, watching a rock that I had placed on another as a marker in the river. There was little sleep for any of us that night and I knew that the men would be tired in the morning. Our camp equipment and provisions were scattered about among the rocks, half buried in the drifting sand.

Our boats were separated, above and below the rapids. I felt that the expedition was dangerously disorganized and waited impatiently for morning and a chance to knit the loose ends together again.

CHAPTER XIV

Walthenberg Rapids— "By George, Mr. Eddy, We're Not Going to Make It!"—A Bath at Elves' Chasm.

The morning of July twenty-sixth was gray and dismal. The men were tired and displayed little enthusiasm for the work they had to do collecting the equipment scattered about on the beach. We found the *Powell*, which had been hauled up on the rocks below the rapids, nearly full of water as a result of waves having washed over it all night and Bartl slowly bailed her out. The *Dellenbaugh* was snug and secure in the sheltered cove above the rapids.

After we had shaken the sand out of our blankets and rolled them up preparatory to stowing them away for the day we collected our equipment and piled it neatly near the boats. Then we brought the *Dellenbaugh* down and hauled her up out of reach of the waves. The big boats were bailed and launched. While Weatherhead and Galloway held the *Coronado* away from the rocks the rest of us packed the duffel away in her compartments, the members of her crew took their places and we pushed the boat off. She floated swiftly down stream, clear of the rapids and the men landed there to wait for us. Next, the *Powell* was launched, loaded and shoved clear of the rocky shore and, finally, Galloway and I got away in the *Dellenbaugh*. That was one of the few times when we were forced to tie the boats overnight below a rapids. It is much better to secure them above, in the relatively calm space usually to be found there.

At Boucher Rapids, two miles below, we picked a channel close to the left shore and the *Dellenbaugh* would have gone through nicely if the *Powell*, running closer than we had intended, had not run into us. We were thrown off our course for a moment, the bow of the boat swung around, struck a rock, tilted and threatened for a second to tip over and to throw both of us into the river. Fortunately, however, we slid over the obstruction and came through, with our boat half filled with water. It would be more accurate to say the boat was half filled with muddy water and partly cooked beans because we were we carrying a bucket of beans stowed away under the after deck again that day and it was tipped over with the result that the projected principal lunch dish was splashing about in the bottom of the boat, irretrievably mixed with muddy water. I was wet from head to foot and would have welcomed sunshine enough to dry my clothes and drive the early morning chill from the air.

I have said little about Jaeger. He was with us, making pictures when I asked him to. But he was too economical with film. It was his theory that only a "flash" was needed and that when he exposed ten or fifteen feet of film on any subject he had done that subject full justice. It was only by actually standing over him that I could be certain of getting what I considered an adequate amount of footage.

The sun came out presently and we reached Crystal Rapids. I decided that we should have some pictures made from the boat as it plunged through. I took Jaeger's place and he perched himself on the deck of the stern compartment. We started off and Jaeger held his camera pointed toward the waves. Suddenly we dashed around a sharp bend in the river and ahead of us was the *Powell* sweeping down upon an unexpected rock that all but blocked the channel. It was a stirring spectacle. Adger and his crew were pulling at their oars. The swift current hurried them along and below them was the bowlder, thirty feet or more in width at its base and as many high— with the water dashing madly against it.

"Get that," I shouted to Jaeger and then turned my attention to the oars because we, too, were being carried toward the rock. We pulled clear of it and swept by with perhaps a dozen feet to spare. It had been a magnificent opportunity to make motion pictures and when I eagerly asked Jaeger afterward if he had got it, he told me sheepishly that he had only twenty feet of film in his camera when we started and that all of it had been used before we reached the bowlder and the fine picture it afforded.

We ran through four other rapids in quick succession and at twelve o'clock, although there was no rapids to stop us, I asked Galloway to run the boat ashore. I thought it would be pleasant to stop once for lunch out of sight and sound of a rapids. The canyon was narrow, the walls were steep and there was little firewood. We climbed about the rocks looking for sticks however large or small and I was amazed to find water-piled driftwood a hundred feet above the prevailing level of the river. A line of mud along the walls, from ten to fifty feet above the water level, marked the height reached by the river while we were going through Cataract Canyon but here was driftwood piled another fifty feet above that—probably deposited there by the great flood of 1884. Imagine those canyons with another hundred feet of rushing water piled on top of the river that even at a relatively low level required our utmost strength and skill—and luck—to navigate successfully.

We got away again at two but it was clear to see that all of us were weary of rapids running and wanted nothing so much as a little needed rest. We ran through half a dozen small rapids and, at four-ten, reached the one at the mouth of Ruby Canyon. Upon examination it looked worse to Galloway than it did to me. But he decided finally that it could be run and I went back to the boats to look at my maps. Galloway joined me presently and I was surprised when he told me he had gone back to his first opinion, that the rapids was too dangerous to run. He wanted to show me why and I went back with him along shore to the foot of the five hundred feet of wicked looking water. We examined the rapids together and he concluded again that it could be run successfully. Then we returned to the boats and I decided that we would do well to stop at Ruby Canyon for the night, which we did.

Neither at Ruby Canyon nor elsewhere did I ever differ with Galloway to the extent of insisting upon running through a rapids that he thought we should line around. In fact I never did question his judgment but once, when farther down the river at Bass Canyon

I told him I thought we ought to line the boats instead of attempting to run them through as he proposed we do. Even then I deferred to him—and we ran through successfully. But I knew at Ruby Canyon that he was tired and was not much surprised when he told me during the evening that he was suffering with a backache.

I believe that some of the men, Holt especially felt at times that I was over-cautious. We actually ran through all but ten of the rapids we encountered, a record unequaled by any other Colorado River expedition, but I suspect that some of the men were not satisfied with that accomplishment; they might have tried to run more of them than we did. The responsibility of deciding when to run and when to line is a heavy one with so many lives at stake and, at the risk of being called over-cautious, I never gave the word to run unless I felt reasonably certain that we had a fighting chance to finish at the bottom, right side up. There were many things to consider, not the least of which was what would happen to the boats if for one reason or another they became unmanageable. What would happen if they were picked up by the river and swept through the rapids out of control? What would happen to the men if they were thrown into the water? I studied the current, following pieces of driftwood through with my eyes, watched the waves, picked out the rocks, "holes" and whirlpools and when I finally said "Let's go," I said it with the full realization that a number of fine, young lives might end tragically if I had underestimated the dangers ahead of us. Because that responsibility was mine, instead of theirs, may explain why I sometimes seemed to them a little over-cautious.

Our camp at Ruby Canyon was a pleasant one. The sun was out again and, although we could see little but the thousand feet of granite wall that towered above us, there was clear sky overhead—with several hours of daylight remaining in which there was nothing much to do but rest. The boats were secured in a backwater above the rapids. Galloway had spread his blankets out and did not stir much during the afternoon—and when Galloway was not working either on the boats or around the fire helping with the cooking, I knew that he was tired indeed. Callaway was nursing an infected thumb which he declined to let me treat. Holt was engaged in reading from cover to cover a copy of the *Cosmopolitan* that had come his way during the stop at Grand Canyon. Bartl, whose turn it was to do kitchen police, helped prepare the evening meal. Carey apparently was tired out and had a nap before supper. Jaeger worked on his camera and film for a few minutes and then joined Bartl in his tasks. Adger and Seager, after spreading out their blankets for the night, turned their attention to preparing the evening meal. We had dumplings made of dried apples that night and although they were not quite successful, we enjoyed them none the less for that. Weatherhead as usual made his camp apart a little from the rest of us and spent an hour or more writing in his diary. We were a unit again, tired but apparently happy. There was a sprinkle of rain and a blow of sand just at bedtime but the storm passed over and we enjoyed a peaceful night.

The next day, Wednesday, July twenty-seventh, was a short day on the river and there was time that night to describe its events in some detail in my diary.

"Clear and hot," I wrote. "Got away from Ruby Canyon at seven. Ran the rapids below camp successfully. Missed the big waves but ran through enough of them to soak me from the chest down. Ran into a little one almost at once. It looked bad because the waves converged in a way which made it seem likely that they would tip us over, as they nearly did. It isn't always the big rapids that get you, it's the way the waves behave. Reached Bass Canyon Rapids at eight o'clock and spent a long time looking it over. Difficult to line but extremely dangerous to run. There was a bad looking 'hole' near the head of the rapids and a bad reverse wave at the right about half way down. How could we avoid both? I favored lining and Galloway was for going through. We studied it a long time and, still not quite convinced, I decided to accept his judgment. After all, we have to take some chances.

"We picked a channel just right of the center of the river, avoided the 'hole' and ran through beautifully. That is one thing about high water—you do it beautifully and in a hurry, or you don't do it at all. The other boats followed and I surely was relieved to see them come through. A dangerous rapids. In one place the *Dellenbaugh* rose high on a wave, met the reverse roll of water and hesitated for an instant as if undecided whether to drop back into the trough, roll over and over in the wave, or go on. Then she plunged through, but it was a bad second or two. The 'picnic' attitude toward running rapids has disappeared entirely. The nervous strain of risking our lives ten or fifteen times a day in bad rapids is beginning to tell. There is no longer any eagerness to run them. Where once there were evident signs of disappointment when the decision was to line the boats, now there are just as apparent signs of relief. We tire by noon or shortly after and I find it difficult, after a morning in the rapids, to go on after lunch to a long afternoon of dangerous going. The men welcome every opportunity to rest and either my 'Let's go' has lost some of its exciting quality, or the men are more difficult to move.

"An amusing thing happened between Bass Canyon and Shinumo Creek. Adger called out to me, 'Have you any checkers in the *Dellenbaugh?*' I had overheard some friendly arguments between Adger and Bartl in the stern of the *Powell*, and Seager and Carey in the bow, concerning which team was doing most of the work at the oars and I asked, in reply to Adger's question, 'Who for?' Each team instantly pointed to the other and, as if it had been rehearsed, all four men answered in unison, 'For them.' The big boats seem to float faster than the little one and for days, as they overtake us, the fellows have been yelling at Galloway and me to get that flivver out of the way.' They even call our boat the '*Dellenbarge.*'

"I find that Galloway shares my distrust of the *Dellenbaugh*. And, why not? When we go through rapids we bounce all over the place. Up high and down low with the boat tipping right and left, shipping water over both sides and both ends. The big boats plow through with less bobbing about. Of course they ship water but they do look safer at this stage of water. We go barefooted in the boats but tie our shoes to the cleats so they will not be lost if the boats are tipped over. We put our shoes on when we go ashore because the rocks are blistering hot. We go whole days without taking off our life preservers except at lunch time. I have abandoned underwear, easier to swim without it and less clothing to absorb this sandy water.

"At eight-fifty we ran ashore on the right and climbed high up above the river to examine Shinumo Rapids. There was a magnificent view looking down toward Powell Plateau, and the rapids was an easy one. We ran through Shinumo, and the next five mile stretch of river was one continuous riffle interspersed with rapids. In that distance the river drops seventy feet and flows with tremendous velocity over its rocky bed. We swept by Shinumo so fast that we could not get ashore. Just below that we saw a beautiful clear stream coming in from the right, probably it was Shinumo Creek and I remembered what Kolb had said about its being a dangerous place to camp. The creek, filled with clear water, invited us to stop but sheer granite walls and the bad stretch of river below make it an extremely dangerous camp site—a rise of even a few feet in the river would have flooded the narrow bar, leaving not even a ledge for us to stand on, and would have carried our boats away. It was early in the morning, we had no reason to stop even for a few minutes except to get some clear water to drink, so we hurried by.

"Stopped at Hakatai Rapids thinking it might be the dreaded Walthenberg about which Kolb had warned us. Then at ten-thirty we came to a big rock in the river and knew that we actually were approaching Walthenberg. We rowed down as close as possible and landed on the left.

"A bad one indeed. As Kolb said, it is full of 'holes.' The worst ones are on the left, the side we landed on. Looked as if we could make it if we ran close to the right. 'Let's go' before our courage oozes out. Back to boats and we led off. Could not make it as far to right as we wanted to and we shot in, with the current pulling us toward a fearful looking 'hole.' I tightened my grip on the splash board and glanced toward my feet to see that they were clear of the rope coiled in the bottom of the boat. Then I heard Galloway's voice behind me say, 'By George, Mr. Eddy, we're not going to make it!' The most nearly excited remark that I have heard him make in five weeks, since we left Greenriver. The current swept us so close to the 'hole' that the stern of the boat passed through a part of it, but we slid safely by. Then we rode her, high up and low down and shipping very little water. We couldn't stop for half a mile below but I saw the *Powell* come through finally and then the *Coronado*. It was not until later that I learned the *Powell* had been thrown against an overhanging ledge of rock so violently that a hole was smashed in her mahogany planking, fortunately above the water line.

"Adger declares that they ran the biggest waves in Walthenberg that they have run anywhere on the river. He said they were in the trough of one, in their twenty-two foot boat, looking up, and couldn't begin to see over. The waves must have been twenty to twenty-five feet high. The big boats shipped more water than we did. Just below the rapids we passed another enormous rock in the center of the river. Then we came to a more peaceful section and, at one o'clock, reached Elves' Chasm. Had lunch; I consulted maps, saw that we had covered twelve miles in which we had run thirteen bad rapids and had lost 130 feet of altitude. Decided to call it a day, with an afternoon to rest. A stratum of sedimentary rock is dipping down toward the river and I hope we will soon be out of the granite.

"There is fine, fresh water here and I had a real bath with soap in a pool, the first since I left New York. All of the men bathed, some shaved for the first time in days and others washed clothes. All rested and all are going around half naked. I am wearing no shirt, no socks, no underwear, but I cling to my hat and trousers. Weatherhead looked shocked when he saw me barefooted and shirtless. I remember he said a long time ago, the day he had the long argument with Carey in Glen Canyon, that he considers clothes a mark of civilization and that he did not intend to turn barbarian and discard his. So far as I know he is the only one now who clings to underwear and socks. I have warned him about the heavy Indian trinkets he is wearing on his hat, some he bought at the trading post at Lee's Ferry. To-day when landing he fell overboard and but for the fact that he had removed his shoes he might have been dragged under by the weight of his clothes—a sacrifice to his ideal of civilization."

After lunch Seager went geologizing and Weatherhead explored the Chasm. We found the names of three men marked on the rocks under an overhanging ledge, "Norman Oliver, R. L. Elliott, J. T. Steward—U. S. G. S. May 1905 and June 1907," and knew by this that there was a way in to this point from the country on top. The men apparently were members of a survey party connected with the United States Geological Survey and had visited the place twice according to the inscription on the wall.

In the afternoon I took a nap. "Guess I'm bilious," I wrote in my diary. "Eating too much. The gloomy granite gorge seems to be affecting me, or maybe it's my liver. Not downhearted but more aware of the danger. Am glad to have some of the worst of the bad rapids behind me. Dozed in the afternoon."

This was the rest and relaxation that I had been planning for days and all of us enjoyed it thoroughly.

CHAPTER XV

"Rags" Is Left Behind—
More Dismal Granite Gorges—
How the *Powell* Was Lost in Deubendorf.

$\mathcal{W}$e left Elves' Chasm Thursday morning, July twenty-eighth, at seven-fifteen. There was a small rapids just below our camp, with a submerged bowlder and a "hole" at the head of it. Galloway pulled the *Dellenbaugh* far enough out to avoid the rock and the *Powell* followed us in safety, but the crew of the *Coronado* was less successful. With the bow of the boat pointed toward the opposite bank the men pulled at their oars, trying to get out around the rock before the swift current could sweep them down upon it. Another thirty feet would have given victory to the men but they lacked that thirty feet and the river won. They saw too late that they had lost and then there was no time for them to straighten their boat around and approach the "hole" stern first. Broadside in the channel, they were carried down upon the bowlder. It became a question then whether or not the keel would strike the rock and tip the boat enough to toss the men over its side into the "hole" below. We were down stream with no chance to get back to rescue them from the whirlpools below the bowlder. We watched while they drifted down upon the rock, over it and into the "hole." Fortunately the boat was big enough to float through the whirl, and we turned our attention again to the river below us.

About a mile below Elves' Chasm the granite disappeared below the level of the water on the cliff at the right and we were again between walls of sedimentary rock. We were through the Upper Granite Gorge, where in forty tumultuous miles the river loses 465 feet in altitude. In those forty miles, between narrow walls of granite, we had successfully negotiated thirty-five bad rapids, beginning with the Sockdolager where the *Dellenbaugh* was upset and ending with the unnamed, easy rapids below Elves' Chasm where in a relatively insignificant "hole" the river came so near to trapping the crew of the *Coronado*.

Sedimentary rock makes for easier going and we ran quickly through one small rapids after another. The canyon opened out and the brilliantly colored Muav and Redwall Limestone cliffs towered above us. There were talus slopes near the river and we felt again that we had elbow room. But the river gave us little rest. We came presently to a place where three gravel bars extended into the river, the upper and lower ones from the right bank and the central one from the left. The channel of the river was shaped like the letter "S," with a "C" tacked on at the bottom of it. The inner curves of the three bends were formed by fan-shaped peninsulas of rock that had been dumped into the river from side canyons and the outer curves were sheer cliffs against which the obstructions threw the current, first on one side, then on the other, then back again to the first. Each bar produced a rapids which means there were three of them in quick succession.

In getting around the rocks in the first rapids we were forced to run close to the sheer wall on the left bank. To get safely through the second cataract we had to pull directly across the apex of the current close against the wall on the right as we had at Dark Canyon and finally, to negotiate the third one, we were compelled to pull again toward the left wall. All three boats got through with two minor mishaps. In the second rapids the current swept the *Coronado* against the cliff on the right and shattered an oar. In the third one, the *Dellenbaugh* brushed against the rocky wall on the right with sufficient force to scrape off both oar locks on that side of the boat. If the rapids had not been comparatively "easy" ones we might have found ourselves in serious difficulty but had they been "bad" ones, we would have lined the boats along the shore.

Just below that point cliffs of sandstone up to 150 feet in height occur on both sides of the river at water level and when we discovered a convenient ledge on the left, we ran ashore to make repairs.

Rags, as usual, went ashore with us and while Galloway and I worked on the oar locks the men spread themselves out on the ledge to rest and the dog wandered away and crawled under a bowlder to escape the heat. The repairs were soon completed and we resumed our interrupted journey. The boats were shoved off, the swift current seized them and then we heard a frantic bark from shore. Rags had looked up to find us gone. Standing with his front feet in the water, unwilling to plunge in, he seemed to realize his danger and with plaintive barks and whines he was pleading with us to come back for him. But the current was too strong for us to row against. He followed us along the shore a few yards until a projecting ledge of rock halted him, and there he stood while our boats were swept out of sight around a bend in the river.

The next half mile offered no landing place. Sheer walls of sandstone hemmed us in. When finally we got ashore again it seemed impossible that we could rescue Rags. Adger, Bartl and I climbed to the rim of the cliff overhanging the river and worked our way, finally, back to a point directly above the ledge of rock on which the dog was prisoner. We called him. A furious shower of excited barks answered us. He thought he had been saved. But 150 feet of perpendicular cliff still separated us!

I started back toward the boats to get some ropes with which one of us could be lowered down the side of the cliffs. Then Adger called out that he had found a ledge he might be able to descend.

Down the rocky wall he climbed, with Rags, Bartl and me watching him. When he dropped the last few feet to the narrow strip of shore Rags welcomed him with a series of happy barks and frenzied rushes that almost carried both of them into the river.

Then, lifting and pushing Rags before him, Adger climbed back up the face of the cliff. Twenty minutes later Rags was safe again. But if he had been left behind in any one of a thousand other places on the river where we had stopped for one reason or another, we could not possibly have got him out. By so narrow a margin did Rags achieve the distinction of being the only dog that ever has journeyed through the Grand Canyon.

On the way back to the boats I told Adger I thought he had done a fine thing.

"It was nothing," he replied. "I couldn't have slept nights if we had been forced to go on without the dog."

The morning was excessively hot, my canteen was soon empty and I was reduced to drinking the muddy river water. Leaning over the side of the boat I scooped up as much water as the smaller bailing can would hold and, after allowing it to settle for a few minutes as well as it could in the boat, I drank pint after pint of the murky stuff. But the water did not satisfy my thirst.

"Barrels and barrels of it," I wrote in my diary, "do not do the trick." It did, however, interfere with my digestion.

At eleven-fifteen we ran through Fossil Rapids and for the second time within a few hours the river hurled the *Dellenbaugh* against the sheer cliff that formed its bank. Galloway unshipped his oar in time to save it from being smashed against the rock and the only damage was done to the heavy oak covering board along the gunwale of the boat. A mile and a half below Fossil Rapids we entered Middle Granite Gorge and ran ashore at twelve-thirty, for lunch above the rapids at Specter Chasm.

The granite wall on the right side of the river at Specter Chasm, shown in the photograph on page 81, illustrates the character of the walls through the Granite Gorges. Here the walls rise nearly 200 feet above the river at the point where they are lowest. In many places the stream has cut its way through a thousand feet of this dark colored igneous rock and cliffs a thousand feet high occur on both sides of the river, rising abruptly from the water's edge. These granite walls are so high and rise so steeply that the voyager on the river cannot see over their tops to the other thousands of feet of sedimentary rock that rise above the granite. The canyon that the river has cut through the granite becomes an inner gorge—a narrow, dismal trench where a thousand dangers threaten and from which escape is impossible in case of shipwreck.

There was almost unbearable heat at Specter Chasm. The desert sun blazed directly overhead, the rocks were so hot that we could not bear to touch them with our hands and there was no shade anywhere. But in spite of that Adger and Seager started a fire and soon had huge flapjacks cooking for our midday meal. We explored the chasm and found a stream of water which was hot, alkaline and unfit to drink. We ate our lunch sitting in the water up to our necks and sat about afterward on the rocks and fairly cooked ourselves in the sun. At two-thirty we were glad to resume our voyage down the river and ran without mishap through Specter Chasm Rapids.

A short distance below the rapids we entered the narrowest part of Middle Granite Gorge, where the protesting river is crowded between high, steep walls less than a hundred feet apart. The current swept along smoothly but with great velocity and there were few places where we could land. The action of the water had carved the schist and granite into many fantastic forms. There were places where, in ages past when the bed of the river was much higher than it is now, great "pot holes" had been formed by the whirling action of backwaters in the river. Where a whirlpool persists in one place for a long time in a swift-flowing stream of this kind, it picks up rocks and sand which it whirls around until it has bored a hole in the rock which forms the river's bed. Along the walls in Middle Granite Gorge we found cross sections of "pot holes" thirty feet deep and five feet in diameter. Those "pot holes" had been at one time in the bottom of the river but years of erosion have lowered the bed until the walls of the ancient "pot holes" now form part of the canyon itself. We walked about in the "pot holes" and crawled from one to another through clefts in their walls. A few hundred yards down stream we passed out of Middle Granite Gorge and ran ashore above Bedrock Rapids.

Bedrock presented a problem. The water was high and a sheer cliff on the right made it impossible to line the boats along the shore. Near the foot of the rapids, close to the left wall which also rose steeply from the water's edge, was a small, rocky island. This island divided the current, most of it flowing to the right of the pile of rocks, and produced on its left, against the left bank, a smaller channel made impassable by rocks in the river's bed.

To enter the rapids at all it would be necessary for us to pull the boats well away from the rocks close to the shore on the right, permit them to run part way through the rapids, and then pull hard back toward the right bank to prevent their being swept against the island or, worse, carried down into the impassable left-hand channel. Almost anything might happen and I decided we should have motion pictures of the boats going through—first of two boats, taken from the cliff; then from one boat, taken while we were actually running the rapids.

Jaeger was stationed on the cliff and I took his place in the *Coronado*. Galloway in the *Dellenbaugh*, and Adger and his crew in the *Powell*, shoved off, running as close together as they could for safety's sake. The *Powell* plunged in, for once ahead of the *Dellenbaugh*, and started upon what was to be the last run of her short but spectacular career. The current carried her swiftly through the upper end of the rapids. Then the men turned her bow toward shore and pulled mightily on their oars. Every stroke brought the boat nearer shore and every second saw the current carry her nearer the rock against which the waves were plunging at the foot of the rapids. It was a question which would win. Then, watching from shore, I saw the boat pull away and in another moment she was rushing by the island, scarcely an oar's-length from the rocks. By that time Galloway in the *Dellenbaugh* had been carried down into the rapids and was bearing down upon the rock. We watched him while he too was swept within a dozen feet of the obstruction against which the muddy water plunged so furiously.

It had been my plan to have Jaeger make motion pictures showing the *Coronado* sweeping down upon the rock and it looked as if that picture, at least in the making, would be a thrilling one. We pulled the boat well out into the river, entered the rapids, permitted the current to carry us fifty yards or more down stream and then pulled for shore. Jaeger, kneeling on the deck of the middle compartment, held his camera pointed toward the rock and I could hear the hum of the camera motor above the roar of the rapids. But we ruined that picture, or at least we destroyed the thrill of it. We tugged too effectively on our oars and pulled the boat clear of the axis of the current, missing the rock by forty feet. Jaeger's picture shows madly-dancing waves, flashing oars and, at a safe distance, a great rock against which the water is flinging itself in futile fury.

Both the *Powell* and the *Dellenbaugh* had shipped some water and while the boats were being bailed I looked again at my maps and determined upon Tapeats Creek, three miles down stream, as our objective for the day. I understood that there was clear water in the creek and was eager to camp where we might have something more palatable to drink than the muddy river water. We shoved off and floated rapidly three-quarters of a mile down stream to the head of Deubendorf Rapids. I was aware of the evil reputation of this fall and perhaps committed a strategic error when I permitted the lure of clear water at Tapeats to tempt me into battle so late in the afternoon, with the men already tired from a long day on the river. It is easy, however, to see mistakes in retrospect and there was no way to foresee what was so soon to happen. We examined the rapids carefully from shore and determined upon a let-down.

Colonel Birdseye, in 1923, named this rapids in honor of S. S. Deubendorf, a member of Julius F. Stone's expedition, whose boat was wrecked there "for the second time" on November 8, 1909. I have already mentioned the Stone Expedition which was guided through the canyons by Nathan T. Galloway, father of Parley. The following excerpt from Mr. Stone's diary describes briefly the difficulties and dangers his party encountered running the rapids that now bears Deubendorf's name:

> Granite disappeared at ten-forty, off at one-five, running everything in good shape until three-fifteen when we reached one that looks pretty bad, having a narrow channel with very high waves for a long distance. However, we decide to try it and Galloway picks out his course along the right side where there are some rocks, but no big waves. He goes first, I next, then Deubendorff last. As I drop into the eddy below the first rock I see Galloway has been unable to follow the channel he decided upon and his boat strikes a partly submerged rock twenty feet from the place he tried to reach. Therefore, I at once decide to go into the heavy waves which turns out to be the proper thing, as I go through all right, but on looking around at the first place where I can safely do so, I see Deubendorff's boat on the crest of a big wave near the upper end of the rapids, then it goes out of sight and reappears in the act of turning over almost end on. It comes down among the waves bottom up, while now and then I get a glimpse of Deubendorff's head bobbing up a moment and then disappearing again, but out of sight the greater part of the time. I call to Galloway and try to catch the bow line of Deubendorff's boat as it reaches me. This I am unable to do because of the high canvas sides of my own, but Galloway slips

his line through the iron hand hold at its stern, takes a hitch around one leg and so tows the boat to the right bank before it reaches the next rapid.

I pick up the things that float down and then we set about righting the boat, which is soon done and the water bailed out. In the meantime Deubendorff who has so suddenly decided to run this rapid headfirst without a boat, and succeeded, has crawled out about three hundred yards below where the accident happened and has come down to help us. His head is pretty badly cut and he looks done in, but his first words are, "I'd like to try that again. I know I can run it." So do we, because we saw him do it. He doesn't seem to know how to get scared, but all's well that ends well and soon we cross to the left bank, build a fire, wood being a little scarce, he puts on dry clothing. I tinker up the cut on this head, the wet things are spread out to dry and but for a broken oar, there is little evidence of trouble. This rapids is in Conquistador Aisle, so named in the Shinumo Quadrangle of the Government map and whoever runs it successfully or otherwise will know they have tackled a real job.

We started with the *Dellenbaugh* and lined her down in a few minutes with little difficulty. At only one place did we have trouble. About half way down the rapids there was a group of submerged rocks over which we had literally to lift the boat. This necessitated our getting dangerously far out into the stream and entailed considerable effort but was, in the circumstances, the only thing that could be done with any degree of safety. To push the boats out beyond the rocks and endeavor then to haul them in would, I knew, be an undertaking in which there was considerable risk. We lined the *Dellenbaugh* and went back to get the *Powell*.

We made it a practice, when the operation promised to be unusually dangerous, to unload the boats before lining them down along the shore but getting the *Dellenbaugh* through had been comparatively easy and I thought it was not necessary to unload the *Powell*. I did, however, take out of her compartments all of the photographic equipment. I was eager to preserve my still and motion picture record of the journey and as films are easily destroyed by water I made it a practice to portage the camera and film every time we lined the boats.

Having my camera out I decided to photograph the men letting the *Powell* down and, leaving Galloway in charge of the operation, placed my camera on a rock overlooking the most difficult part of the rapids, where it was necessary for the men to lift the boat over the pile of partly submerged bowlders half way down. I made my set-up and was ready—but I made no photographs that day.

When the men and boat came within the camera's field I threw the focusing cloth over my head and shoulders and peered into the ground glass, just in time to see one of the men shove the stern of the boat far out in an effort to get it out around the pile of bowlders that obstructed the channel close to shore. I dropped the focusing cloth and shouted but the roar of the rapids drowned my voice and by the time I reached the men the damage was done. The *Powell*, caught broadside in the current, had been carried down against the outermost of the rocks thirty feet from shore and was wedged there, her stern submerged beneath the rushing water, her bow thrust high up in the air, with the weight of the river pouring into her open after compartment. And there she stayed, swaying in the current, resisting our united efforts to drag her off. We tugged and hauled in vain. The water surged over her, she was fast. We got out a block and tackle and threw our last ounce of strength upon her bow line but could not budge her an inch toward shore. Then darkness came and we were forced to stop for the day.

My diary tells what else we did that night, and some of the things I thought:

"On way back to camp I nearly stepped on a small rattlesnake. It crawled under a stone and then I could not find it in the gathering dusk. Carey killed it a few minutes later. But why go prodding around after snakes when so many other dangers threaten? Weatherhead was greatly excited and hopped about shouting, 'kill it,' as if his veneer of civilization had worn through in at least one place and he had reverted to the barbarian so far as snakes are concerned. Loaned Bartl my blanket and a suit of underwear and I shall sleep on the poncho.

"Dark before supper was finished. No spoons, no plates. Had bacon, camp bread and coffee. Some raisins, too. Fine. They seemed like dessert and to have something of that kind is almost as heartening as the harmonica music used to be during the war when some indefatigable doughboy got going just before bedtime after a long day in the mud."

The loss of the Powell seriously cut down the expedition's margin of safety. Four precious days were spent in fruitless efforts to haul the boat ashore and then, previsions running low, the men were forced to go on without it, under-provisioned and overcrowded in the two remaining boats.

No boat ever has run successfully through the fury of Lava Falls. Many rapids must be run because sheer walls prevent letting the boats down around them. Here it was necessary, and fortunately possible, to take the boats out of the water and slide them over the rocks along the shore.

I attempted to describe my feelings, with one of my precious boats apparently lost, wedged against a rock in the river.

"How do I feel to-night? Discouraged? Yes, almost so badly that I wonder why I ever selected such a hazardous undertaking. Am wondering about ways of getting some of the men out of the canyon if all of us cannot ride in the two remaining boats. It cuts down the margin of safety to lose one of the big boats but I think we can get through without it."

Far more important than what we say we think are the things we do.

"Slept near the *Coronado*," continues the diary, "and looked at her several times during the night. Had difficulty getting to sleep, could not keep my mind from dwelling on the dangers of the rapids yet to be passed. Not so much discouraged as I might be. Made some good movies of the wreck. Hope to get her off in the morning. Water unusually red, must be a flood from the Little Colorado. Difficult to make pictures and manage the expedition too."

I described in my diary several times on the journey the "wholesome respect" we all had for the river. It was more than that with me, I very frankly feared the mad, crazy stream. I doubt if any man could travel 500 miles through its rapids without recognizing its strength and cunning and being correspondingly afraid of it. The best I could hope to do was to keep that fear from becoming apparent to the others. That night at Deubendorf, while the muddy water surged over one of the boats that I had nursed so many miles through the narrow canyons, I undoubtedly feared the river but also knew I had "made some good movies of the wreck" and still hoped "to get her off in the morning." No, we were hard hit but very far from beaten when we divided our blankets and lay down to rest that first night at Deubendorf Rapids.

We spent all day, the twenty-ninth of July, at Deubendorf, trying vainly to wrench the *Powell* from the clutches of the river. There was ample time for me to describe the events of the day and perhaps no truer picture of what happened there, at least as I saw it, can be presented than by setting down here, verbatim, the major portion of my diary as I wrote it at the time.

"Discouraged by our inability to get the *Powell* out. Up early and worked hard at it until noon. Adger and Carey crawled out by way of the bow line and unloaded the forward and middle compartments and we hauled the stuff ashore. Salvaged as much of the food as we could. Impossible to get into the rear compartment on account of the water beating over the stern of the boat. Attached lines forward, amidships and aft and pulled from every possible angle. Could not budge the boat and to-night she is still jammed against the rock, held there by the sheer weight of the rushing water. Everything is lovely so long as the boats go along with the current but the instant an obstruction is struck and the boat is stopped, the river smashes it by its irresistible strength and the tremendous weight of its muddy water. The river is falling to-night and we may be able to do something to-morrow. Maybe we had better wait another day. If we cannot get the *Powell* out we shall have to strip down to absolute necessities and make it in two boats. In the afternoon we brought the *Coronado* down and drew her up on the beach beside the *Dellenbaugh*.

"After lunch I walked down to Stone Creek at the foot of the rapids and enjoyed the luxury of having all the clear, cool water I could drink. Then I worked on the maps. Among the bad rapids ahead, Upset, Lava Falls, Separation and Lava Cliff probably will be the worst. Two of them must be run. Lava Cliff must be lined, from the cliff. We shall be overcrowded and under-provisioned in two boats but I believe we can make it. If we cannot get the *Powell* off to-morrow we shall cut down to necessities and go through as fast as possible before our food gives out.

"Had a good dinner to-night—corn bread, ham, chocolate pudding and tea. Feeling more cheerful than at noon when I was alone, considering prospects for getting through. Feel better with the crowd, guess I am a fair weather sailor myself. Still, it is hard lines to lose a big boat with so many miles yet to go. Shall be glad to get away from the continual anxiety of the river.

"Slept fitfully. Awake every hour or so to flash my light on the boats. At two-thirty discovered the river was rising and that the *Coronado* was knocking on the rocks. Aroused the camp, excepting Adger, Weatherhead and Jaeger whom I could not find because they were spending the night up a side canyon sharing Weatherhead's blankets. After tightening up the bow line of the *Powell* we hauled the *Coronado* and the *Dellenbaugh* higher up on the beach. Fortunately we are in a good position if the river rises very high. Then off to bed again. It turned cool and I put on my shirt and trousers, Bartl has my blanket. The rise in the river looks bad for the *Powell*."

Saturday, July thirtieth, was little better, although by that time I was pretty well resigned to the loss of the boat.

"Up at five after a restless night," says my diary. "Water still up, higher than it was when we reached here. Worked on the *Powell* but could not move her. Cannot get out to the boat now to take out the duffel bags. The water is pouring over her so that we cannot reach the rear hatch. Hope to be able to do it late to-day. If everything else fails, we shall knock in the wall of the rear hatch and salvage as much material as we can. Food supplies are running low and we must get away to-morrow without fail. Spent an hour or more this morning with movies, doing some scenes that I had planned but had not completed. Shall do more this afternoon. Carey sick, Callaway not well. Took a short nap this morning in shade of the cliff over by the little creek. Awakened suddenly, startled, wondering what time it was and if the boats were safe. The anxiety is wearing, shall appreciate a day free from worry.

"Perhaps it is just as well that we have to wait here to-day, until the water goes down to normal level again. The river has risen steadily all day and to-night the muddy water is pouring over the upturned bow of the *Powell*, wedged in with her stern pinned against the rocks. Galloway told me to-day that he felt that the wreck was due to his carelessness in having permitted Holt to push the boat out when she should have been guided inside the rock against which she is jammed.

"Seager and Weatherhead spent most of the day geologizing and exploring. They climbed out along the creek bed below the camp. Carey is better to-night and Callaway apparently is well. May have to stay here another day, no use trying to go on while water is so high. Felt very gloomy and discouraged after lunch. That may have been because the rising water had just compelled us to haul the boats higher up on the beach. Maybe I only needed company because I felt better after finding Holt and Callaway (they were the only ones I could find, the others having gone off somewhere up the side canyon looking for shade) and talking with them for a while. Even borrowed Holt's *Cosmopolitan* to divert my thoughts from the river. Tried to sleep but could not get the river out of my mind. How pleasant it will be to sleep out of earshot of a rapids, away from the anxiety of the dangers yet to come.

"Only a few bad ones between here and Needles, with an average drop in the river of only six feet to the mile, as opposed to ten in the last hundred miles, and twenty-one feet to the mile for ten miles in the vicinity of Granite Falls. We still have Lower Granite Gorge to do, however, and that will make fifty miles of dangerous going. Feel reconciled to-night to the loss of the *Powell* and see no reason why we should not make it through nicely. At noon to-day, for about ten discouraged minutes, I was almost in favor of ending the trip at Kanab or at Diamond Creek, but I was tired, the sun was blistering hot and the river was rising. Actually, I believe I should go through with only one boat and two or three men to row it.

"A trip like this differs from almost any other kind—the danger is constant, the strain never lets up and time is a factor. Five or six weeks is a long time to battle with a river of this kind and there are few rest periods because time again enters in and you must get through on schedule or run the risk of starving to death. Last night when we had to pile out and pull the boats farther up on the beach, it was too much even for soft-spoken Parley Galloway, who said to me as we hauled away on the lines, 'Isn't she an old devil, though?'

"I agreed with him that she is.

"Night before last the water was red, apparently a flood running out of the Little Colorado. To-night, the water is brown. The flood evidently is running out and I doubt if there will be any further rise, but I shall be on the alert. Surely I am gathering material for a thousand anxiety dreams!

"Have talked privately with each of the men and believe they will hold together to the end. They admit that they are thoroughly fed up with the river but no one wants to quit. Carey said that the loss of the *Powell* has been a distinct shock to him.

"'I have known for a long time that there was a lot of power in the current,' he explained to me, 'but I had not realized that it would pin a boat against a rock like that.'

"If Galloway, Adger and Holt stand by me, we shall win—and in them I see no sign of weakening. We are lucky to have nice clear water in the nearby creek. Driftwood is floating down the river. The rise has been so gradual it seems unlikely that we shall have a big flood and if we do, we are in a good position to save the boats. I have had everything piled high on the rocks in case the water does come up. I wish that I had something very good to read, to distract my mind a little. I am sleepy but cannot sleep. I find myself longing for sleep, eager no doubt for the rest that it would give me from concern about the river. Most of all, I am eager to travel.

"Tried unsuccessfully again to-day to get the *Powell* out. Hoping now that the water will wash the boat off the rock but not much chance of that. Probably shall have to spend another day here, waiting for the flood to subside and trying to save the boat, or at least the duffel bags in her after compartment.

"Pleasant and cool for an hour or two in the morning. Then the sun strikes and it is hot. Beautiful light effects on cliff early in the morning. At noon it is almost unendurably hot and there is not much shade except under the scrub trees in the side canyon and very little there. Finally, the rocks get too hot to touch. Later, there is shade behind the rock ledges. Then the sun drops behind the opposite wall, the shade creeps across the river, the air cools perceptibly and we stir about. At twilight it is cooler and even the rocks are no longer very warm to the touch. Then, rapidly, darkness and off to bed—if you can call it that. I sleep in athletic underwear, which I do not wear during the day, on top of a folded poncho. In the early morning, if the air is cool, I put on a shirt and some trousers."

CHAPTER XVI

Overcrowded and Under-provisioned in Two Remaining Boats—Kanab Canyon— Indecision Rapids—Lava Falls.

*W*hen I got up to look at the boats a few minutes after midnight on the morning of July thirty-first, I was encouraged to see that the river was falling and by the time I called the men at five o'clock the water level was no higher than it had been when we reached Deubendorf on the afternoon of the twenty-eighth. I decided to make one more effort to haul the *Powell* off and, if we failed in that, to get as much duffel as we could out of her rear compartment and go on without her.

We made the trial immediately after breakfast. There was a three-quarter inch line attached to the stern of the boat and with the aid of a block and tackle we were able finally to break that heavy rope but the boat remained where she was. Adger and Carey then went, hand over hand on the tightly stretched bow line, out to the boat and using the rope as a trolley, we sent an ax out to them. I had decided to get the duffel out before making this last effort to save the boat. We might break the bow line as we had the one at the stern and then there would be no chance to salvage the material in her after cabin.

Adger, standing on the rock against which the boat was jammed, swung his ax and the wall of the compartment gave way. One by one he dragged out the thoroughly soaked bags of duffel and sacks of provisions. Carey attached a rope to them and they were hauled ashore. Water still was pouring over the stern of the boat and it was impossible to get everything out. The most serious loss appeared at the moment to be two dozen cans of evaporated milk, a sack of flour and half of our stock of vegetables. They had fallen into the bottom of the compartment and could not be reached. The salvaged duffel and provisions were spread out on the rocks to dry and the rest of the morning was spent in fruitless efforts to save the boat. It became clear to me finally that her keel was bent if not actually broken, and certainly many of her ribs were smashed. With a few more ounces of strength we might finally have broken the boat in two but her stern apparently was wedged behind a rock and we could not haul her an inch toward shore. We abandoned the effort and I asked Adger and Seager to have early lunch so that we could get away by one o'clock.

The equipment that had been rescued from the *Powell* dried in a few minutes, spread out on the rocks, and all of us had blankets and ponchos again. We found that our potatoes, onions and corn meal were ruined and dumped them out among the rocks. It was necessary now to get all of our duffel and food under the hatches of one boat and we abandoned as much equipment as we could spare. One of the tents was left behind. Extra clothing and blankets were piled high up among the rocks, out of reach of the water. I threw away some maps and the covers to my loose-leaf diary in order to save space in the boat. Practically every man in the party found something that he could add to the growing pile of equipment that we proposed to abandon. All of our food supply—and it had been seriously depleted by the loss of a sack of flour, and half of our total supply of potatoes, onions, evaporated milk and corn meal—was now in one boat. To lose that boat, as we had lost the *Powell*, would place us in peril of starvation.

There was need to rearrange the crews and I placed the *Coronado* in Adger's charge. Bartl sat with him in the stern of the boat and Carey and Callaway were in the bow. Weatherhead, Jaeger and Rags rode as passengers. Seager and Holt joined Galloway and me in the *Dellenbaugh* and, on account of the added weight, we unlimbered an extra pair of oars for them to use. The bear rode with us, comfortably settled on the after deck.

Overloaded in the two remaining boats, under-provisioned for the 300 mile journey that lay before us, compelled to entrust our food and most of our equipment to one boat, we started off. Our margin of safety had been dangerously cut down by the loss of the *Powell* and now, on account of the dwindling food supply, we were compelled to hurry when there was more need than ever that we proceed cautiously.

We got away a few minutes after one o'clock, both boats riding heavily under their increased loads. We ran through a riffle below Deubendorf and reached Tapeats Creek, and the rapids there, at one-thirty. The rapids were easy ones and a few minutes later we splashed through a whole series of riffles. For half a mile the river tumbled and foamed over its rocky bed and while the stretch could not properly be called a rapids, there were places which were extremely danger-ous. The river loses ten feet in altitude in less than a mile and most of that drop occurs in the half mile of riffles. Perhaps Birdseye and the Geological Survey were right, after all, in marking the stretch of river as a rapids.

A few minutes later we found ourselves again between narrow granite walls and heard a rapids roaring in the distance. Then we came suddenly upon a waterfall plunging into the canyon over the sheer wall on the right and ran ashore to examine it. I had heard of Deer Creek Falls but no description that I had read had quite prepared me for this beautiful little fall of clear, cold water plunging seventy-five feet through a cleft in the rock into the river bed below. We enjoyed the beauty of the scene, photographed it, drank our fill of clear, cold water, and then stood under an edge of the fall and bathed in the unaccustomed luxury of water free from mud and sand.

After half an hour at Deer Creek Falls we ran through the rap-ids whose roar we had heard before we landed. There was a wicked "hole" near the head of the rapids and we ran so close to it that I could look over the side of the boat into its muddy, churning mael-strom. I described the incident that night in my diary and added, "How I hate those 'holes.'" I have wondered since if it was hatred that I felt or merely fear.

There was fast water for several miles after leaving Deer Creek Falls but the granite gradually was replaced by sedimentary rock and below Fishtail Rapids the high, narrow walls fell away. The cliffs receded from the river's edge again in a series of walls and talus slopes. The "V" shaped walls of granite were replaced by "U" shaped walls of sandstone, limestone and shale. We could see the rim of the canyon again thousands of feet above us and, on top of that, was a welcome view of sky and clouds and desert sun. For three miles we ran along on a swift but peaceful stream, free from rapids. Two big-horn mountain sheep stood idly on a cliff and watched us pass. At five-fifteen we reached Kanab Canyon and ran our boats ashore on the right.

Kanab Creek enters from the right and a wide, low bar of rocks extends far out into the river from that side. The water still was trick-ling between the bowlders. Pools of water high up on many of the larger rocks showed clearly that the bar had been entirely under water during the flood that swept down the canyon while we were tied up at Deubendorf. The nearest dry sand was 200 yards away, at the foot of the cliff. We could not get the boats nearer shore on account of the bar and were compelled to tie them to bowlders and risk a rise in the river during the night. We found a place that was fairly dry and Adger and Seager started the evening meal while the other men picked their way across the bar to the sand where they spread out their blankets for the night. I decided to sleep near the boats, beside the bowlder to which the *Coronado* was secured.

We had the last of our ham that night, and the bear came near to getting that. I had noticed that he was unusually boisterous and ill-tempered during the afternoon and a few minutes after we landed he broke the rope with which he was tied and the familiar cry went up, "The bear's loose." We caught him easily enough but it was clear that he was restless and unhappy. Then the ham was put on to fry and the bear, sucking his paw, voiced his complaint in terms that I should have recognized at once if I had not been so much concerned with other things. Suddenly the whine ceased and the bear, loose again, made a dash for the kitchen. Before any one could get hold of his leash he had planted his paws in the frying pan and when Seager pulled at the rope the bear held fast to the pan and the bear, the pan and the ham were scattered in all directions among the rocks. Then I remembered that we had failed to feed him earlier in the day at Deubendorf. We secured the bear, collected the ham, wiped off the sand, and proceeded with our interrupted meal. Afterward I fed the animal. His complaining ceased and he submitted to being tied with a rope which he had twice demonstrated his ability to break. He escaped several times on the journey but never offered to go away from us. He would find Rags, stop there, and a friendly wrestling match would ensue, or he would get into the food supply and wait for us to come and drag him away. When the alarm was given that the bear was loose we all made a dash for the kitchen, and usually he was there ahead of us.

After supper the men went over to the ledges of sand along the base of the cliff and I was left alone on the bar.

"Kanab not a good camping place," I wrote in my diary. "Sand too far away, across a wide, rocky bar. Mud and pools of water among the rocks where we are camped to-night—at least where we are doing our cooking—show that the bar was under water during recent flood. Perhaps it is just as well that we were held up, these rapids would be bad at a higher level.

"Concerned about Upset Rapids five miles below here. It will require careful going with our overloaded boats. Bill says the *Coronado* is overloaded and rides so deep that she is difficult to handle. But the rapids may be mostly big waves. Have set out a marker, hope the water does not come up during the night. The walls through here are high and red and beautiful. Bright Angel shale crops out along the stream and at the base of the canyon walls. Above that is a stratum of the Muav Limestone on which rests a cliff of Redwall Limestone. Above that is the Supai formation, all topped with the gray walls of Kaibab Limestone along the distant rim. There is color again and I am glad to be out of the granite. Except for the fifty miles of Lower Granite Gorge the river below here averages a fall of only six feet per mile and that will be easy after what we have been through. Expect a fast trip from here to Needles. Shall try to make Lava Falls by tomorrow night, thirty-three miles.

"Feel better when I am on the move, and am glad to be away from Deubendorf, that rapids even sounds bad, nothing like Kanab. Looks like a bad night, the sand is so far away from the boats that I shall have to sleep on the wet rocks, but I have my blanket again and, with the poncho, shall make out."

And it was a bad night. I was uncomfortable and restless, wide awake at two o'clock worrying about Upset Rapids five miles below. I evidently had a bad dream because I wakened once, startled, and flashed the light on my marker to see how much the water had risen. I was relieved to learn that it had not come up at all. I looked out across the bar toward the river where, a hundred feet away, the rapids foamed and roared in the darkness. The thought came to me, "She is a wicked devil," and in the same instant I realized that I had personalized the river to such an extent that I might not have dared, there in the darkness and alone, to stand up and say aloud what I was thinking. I believe I knew in that instant why the Indians say of the Colorado, "The river is not good for Navajos," and sprinkle its water with sacred meal before they venture to cross it at Lee's Ferry. Even the educated mind is likely to revert to fear and superstition in times of stress and most of us are prone to placate demons and devils when we are threatened with dangers that we do not feel able, by our own efforts, to overcome.

I lay for a long time listening to the roar of the rapids, interested in having discovered that I would be unwilling to cast defiance in the river's teeth. It is much easier to be brave about such things in the day time when we are secure and no immediate danger threatens. I was able, finally, to argue down my own rising flood of primitive reactions to insecurity and grew interested in pondering upon the origin of superstition generally, but it was a revelation to me to see the response of one more or less cultured mind to the ceaseless battering of the relentless river.

We were up at five o'clock as usual on the morning of August first and got away at seven. In the next two hours we ran safely through six bad rapids, including the one at the mouth of Kanab Canyon and wallowed through five easy ones. At Kanab we failed to pull as far out into the current as we had planned and both boats came dangerously near to hitting a dozen rocks that jutted out from shore but we got through without mishap. Vicious cross waves threatened to tip the *Dellenbaugh* over in a small rapids just below Kanab and half filled the boat with water. The morning was cool and cloudy and the drenching we received was not a welcome one.

At nine-fifteen we arrived at Upset Rapids, five miles below Kanab. Kolb had warned us particularly of this one, and with good reason. When, in 1923, he had endeavored to run a boat through it he was drawn into a "hole." His boat turned upside down and Kolb disappeared. Frank Dodge, whom I was to meet later on my second canyon voyage, courageously plunged into the torrent and swam to the boat which, fortunately, had floated clear of the "hole." The boat had come up on the side of the river away from the others and it looked for several minutes as if Kolb had been drowned but Dodge found him, still partly stunned by a blow he had received on his head, but otherwise unharmed.

We landed on some rocks on the right and clambered down to examine the rapids. There was a bad rock thirty feet from shore on the right and to get out around that would place the boats where it would be almost impossible to avoid running into the "hole" which had capsized Kolb's boat. With the boats as heavily loaded as they were I was not certain they could be run through successfully. I was undecided, and so was Galloway. I was inclined toward running through and he was not. Then we looked at the rapids again and he thought he saw a way to get through and, meantime, I had changed my mind. I decided finally to line the *Dellenbaugh*, carry part of the duffel down below and run the *Coronado* through lightly loaded. We could then load the *Coronado*'s duffel—and her two passengers, Weatherhead and Jaeger—in the *Dellenbaugh* and transfer them back to the *Coronado* as soon as we could get together down below.

We lined the *Dellenbaugh* and carried the duffel down to the lower end of the rocky beach, where it ended abruptly against cliffs rising sheer from the water's edge. Then we returned to the head of the rapids and I realized for the first time that I was about to send a boat through a rapids after my own boat had been lined around it. I went to Adger and told him that I intended to take his place in the *Coronado*. He protested. I made the same proposal to Bartl and he, too, expressed his desire to go through with the boat. Carey was next and he was unwilling to relinquish his place in the *Coronado*. It began to look as if I might have to ride as a passenger. Then, I approached Callaway but before I had time to explain my plan to him and get his answer, Galloway joined us, after a last examination of the rapids, and announced the discovery of another rock, the hitherto unnoticed presence of which made it extremely doubtful if we could get through successfully. So, after all we lined the second boat, loaded her up at the foot of the rapids and were under way again at ten-thirty. Indecision Rapids is what I called it in my diary although the government map commemorates Kolb's adventure with the name "Upset" instead.

By the time we finished lining the boats I was wet to my shoulders and then the rain poured down and I was drenched from head to foot. It rained intermittently all that day and for several that followed. I realized it might be better to stop and wait for brighter days if for no other reason than that we could make better pictures, but our provisions were running low and we were far from our journey's end. We had lost so much food in the wreck of the *Powell* that there remained enough to last us not more than five or six days and we still had more than 300 miles to go, fifty of them through the furious miles of Lower Granite Gorge. Another delay, even for a day, would mean short rations and the chances were so great that we would be compelled to stop somewhere along the way for one reason or another that I did not dare stop to wait for the skies to clear. At that, there remained only a few hundred feet of unexposed motion picture film and I knew that I should have ample opportunity to use that before we arrived at Needles.

We ran—or, rather, plowed on account of our heavy loads— through one rapids after another during the morning and, at eleven-thirty, in a place where the stream flowed smoothly between high sheer walls of red limestone, came to a great rock in the river. The rock bore the semblance of the head of an enormous animal of some kind and stood, facing up stream, its great mouth open, threatening us—like Cerberus guarding the gates of hell.

"Now," I thought to myself, "if I were given to presentiments and forebodings of disaster, I should find it easy to see something in that ugly rock," and spent several minutes convincing myself that I actually did not. Our minds are such productive culture media for superstition, and all the other unreasoned responses that grow from fear, that I hope parents and teachers will some day cease to cultivate them in the eager, curious minds of growing boys and girls.

We reached Havasu Rapids at twelve-fifteen and although we managed to get ashore on a narrow ledge of rock below Havasu Canyon, we could find no place where the boats did not pound dangerously on the rocks and hurried on. The river for miles through this part of the canyon flows in a narrow, steep-sided gorge cut through the Muav Limestone. There are few places where it is possible to get the boats ashore and I began wondering early in the afternoon whether we could find a place where it would be safe to spend the night.

At one o'clock we came to an overhanging ledge of rock with a sloping bank below it wide enough for us to land upon and tie the boats. We ran ashore and had our lunch, crouching under the ledge which shielded us partly from the rain. We moved on again at three and as the boats were carried rapidly along between the steep, limestone walls I watched constantly for a break in the cliffs—for a talus slope upon which we might camp and up which it would be possible to haul the boats in case of flood.

At four o'clock we approached a rapids and, "Too late," says my diary, "we discovered a very sharp fall of ten feet or more at its head."

"We took her nicely," says my journal written that evening, "but, as evidence that the strain is beginning to tell, I felt a sudden quickening of my pulse when we dropped over the top of the wave and into the trough below—it could have been a 'hole' or almost anything. Guess I'm getting nervous about these rapids."

Half a mile below this cataract the stratum of limestone rose above the level of the river and as we ran again into the Bright Angel shale the canyon widened, there was a comfortable talus slope between the edge of the water and the limestone cliffs and I knew that we would have no difficulty finding a place to camp. There were occasional riffles but there were stretches of river between them where for the distance of a mile or more the stream swept peacefully along between its thousand foot walls of limestone at whose bases on each side of the river there were welcome talus slopes of the softer shale. There were bushes along the shore and infrequent stunted trees to vary the landscape of dripping glistening rocks.

It was still raining when we came to a sandbar on the left and ran ashore for the night. In landing I stepped out of the boat to make the line fast and found myself in a bed of quicksand. Then I moved over to a rock and, climbing about hauling the boat ashore, stepped off the edge of the rock into the water up to my neck. I had been wet all day and could get no wetter but it was cool and I was glad when the rain stopped a few minutes later and I was able to change into dry clothing.

"Am longing for clear water to drink," I wrote in my diary that night. "Do not get enough unbroken sleep, digestion bad—the strain begins to tell. Shall be awfully tired of this river before we reach Needles. Am glad there are only a few bad rapids below. Hoped to reach Lava Falls to-day.

"Seager has a bad toe, has stubbed the same toe three times. Looks infected, soaked it in mercurochrome and bandaged it up. This would be a bad place to fight infection. Wet sand to sleep on to-night. Sky looked clear toward sunset. Hope the river doesn't rise. Begin almost to dare to plan details of getting to Needles—and back to Long Island. River is so much milder than in the granite, but there is granite again at Separation Rapids and for fifty miles up and down the river above and below that. Feel stiff from being wet so much. I should sleep well to-night—no rapids roaring in my ears, a sandbar to sleep on, and a high talus slope as a refuge in case of a rise in the river."

Every one seemed a little unwilling to move on the morning of August second and it required a good deal of urging to get the boats loaded by seven o'clock. But there was less each day to pack away, only one boat to load and we were on the river again at the accostomed hour.

I have never been able to locate that camp exactly on the map and do not know precisely where the rapids is that gave us a bad five minutes just after we got under way. But, wherever it was, it had a dozen bad rocks at its head and many more at the bottom and we shipped half a boat load of water getting through. At eight-thirty we passed a great block of lava, thirty or forty feet wide at its base and extending at least as high into the air, and knew that we were approaching Lava Falls Rapids.

In this part of the canyon we saw the first of several large masses of lava which, sometime in the geologic past, flowed over the rim of the cliffs to the bottom of the canyon and thence along the bed of the river. Undoubtedly there was water in the river when that stream of molten rock crept across the plateau on top and plunged over the cliffs into the gorge below. What a magnificent spectacle that colossal encounter of fire and water must have made! In places the lava congealed in the position it assumed when it fell over the side of the canyon's rim and it is from such a phenomenon on an adjacent wall that Lava Falls Rapids derives its name. At one time the lava obstructed the river's bed to a height of hundreds of feet but the river had gradually cut it away until now the lava pinnacle and the rapids are all that remain of it. But that is enough. Lava Falls Rapids cannot possibly be run and a glance told me that we should have to lift the boats bodily out of the water and skid them fifty feet overland, over the great bowlders along the shore.

Four hours of tedious, back-breaking labor were required to lift the boats, first one and then the other, up out of the river onto the rocks and then to skid them down around the worst of the rapids. The big boat weighed 1200 pounds and there were only ten of us to get her ashore, lift her over the rocks and launch her again in the river. When we slid the *Coronado* into the water her stern caught for a second on a rock, her bow swung around into the current, the boat tilted dangerously and we came near to losing her. There was a brook filled with clear, sparkling water at Lava Falls Rapids and we gulped it down eagerly, only to find that it was charged with some chemical and was dreadful tasting stuff. We had lunch and got away at one-thirty.

There was fast going below Lava Falls. The rapids were relatively easy ones and there were long distances between them, with the water flowing along at a swift pace. There were some bad ones, too, and at three-fifteen we again skirted close to disaster.

We came to this rapids, ran ashore and noted a bad "hole" half way down. The water poured over a big rock, the "hump" that marked the rock was a high one and the "hole" below was horrible to look at even from shore. It boiled over backward and promised to engulf anything or anybody who came within its reach. We went in and drifted down toward the rock. The men began pulling hard to the right to get around the rock. The boat was broadside in the river— and that is how we were going when we came to the hump of water that marked the presence of the rock beneath. I waited for the keel of the boat to strike the rock, and the current to tip us into the "hole." I saw before we reached it what was likely to happen and braced my feet to be thrown clear of the boat, intending instantly to grab for a life line when we struck the water. But the boat cleared the rock, dropped down into the "hole"—and through it. I was trembling when we finished the run through the rapids and wrote in my diary again that night, "The strain begins to tell." The strain had been "telling" for days and weeks and I only flattered myself when I wrote that it began to tell in the unnamed rapids below Lava Falls.

And it told on the others too, in ways that I noted in my diary but shall not set down in my book. I shall let my own reactions stand as the reactions of all of us. I was tired of the journey before it was finished, and so were all the others. Bartl, for instance, told me before we reached Deubendorf that it was a wonderful experience—but that he would not repeat it for a million dollars. Galloway admitted to me frankly that he was tired of the river trip. Carey asked me many times during the last ten days how soon I hoped to be in Needles. There were unpleasant incidents, including one fist fight which flared up suddenly for no better reason than that the men were tired and their nerves on edge. There were even one or two sinister demonstrations of qualities that ordinarily do not show themselves except under unusual circumstances and fortunately not often even then. But, by and large, my own reactions I believe were more or less the reactions of all of us and if, at times, I may have been less heroic than some of the men, there were times when perhaps I was more so. At best our qualities vary from day to day and show themselves variously under different conditions. A drizzle of rain may depress one man and not another. Falling rocks, "holes," rapids, whirlpools—all the several dangers may produce unlike effects upon different men or a man's behavior on any given day may depend entirely upon so lowly a thing as the condition of his stomach or his liver, or how he has slept the previous night.

I treasure a letter I received from Adger months after the journey was completed. Written in response to a request of mine for the "real truth" about the trip he sets me up, and knocks me down, then sets me up again—meantime assuring me that he, who showed less fear than the doughty Galloway himself, was afraid of the river all the while.

"You have asked me to tell you the real truth about the expedition," he wrote. "I am afraid that I will be of little help to you but I will try to put in writing the things that I will always remember about the trip through the canyon, things that make it seem more like a dream than a reality . . .

"When you arrived in Greenriver I was disappointed in you (you asked for the truth); you did not seem to take the river seriously enough; you did not look to me like a man who had lived in the rough, one who could take things as they came. But later I learned to know you; at least I think I did. I found out that you hid your real feelings most of the time. Many times on the trip I think that you were afraid, but you did not show it before the men. I think there were times when you were sorry that you had ever started the trip; times when you thought that we would never get out; but at no time did you discourage the men by letting them see that you were worried and afraid. You never asked of the men anything that you were not willing to do yourself. I used to watch you on the river and in camp and I think I knew the thoughts that were going on within you. As I have said, on meeting you in Greenriver I was disappointed; when I left you at Needles, after being with you night and day for two months on the worst river in the world, you will remember that I asked you to let me know if you ever went on another expedition as I wanted to go with you—that is what the river did for my first impression of you. That desire to go with you still holds good.

"About Galloway, if it had not been for him we would all be in hell now. He showed us how to run the river and his example held the men together. He knew what to do and just when to do it. His quiet, easy ways made all of us admire and like him. He showed courage of the finest sort; he wanted to take the chances first to see if it would be safe for the rest of us. He always did more than his share of the work, never complaining, never discouraging . . .

"As for myself, I can say that there were many times when I wished that I had never started on the expedition, but at no time was I ready to leave it. I think this was about what all of us felt. If, at Lee's Ferry, you had suggested going we would have gone, every one of us, but as long as you stayed we all stayed. I was afraid at every rapids, so you see I was afraid most of the time. I was glad when it was all over and I think we all were. The hardest part of the trip to me, and I think to the rest of us, was the nervous strain of never knowing what was going to happen next. One rapids after another, never time to get over the one that we had just gone through. There were times when I thought that all of us would be drowned, and I have been swimming ever since I can remember. The Colorado is the only water that I was ever afraid of; that it is something to be afraid of only the few of us who have gone down it know. I was afraid; I think we were all afraid. Maybe I am wrong but I don't think so."

We made camp on the night of August second on a wide, rocky bar on the right bank of the river. A stream entered from a side canyon but the water was colored bright red with the sand and silt it carried and was unfit to drink.

"The walls are much lowered along here," I wrote in my diary. "Lava flows cover them in places. Occasional small trees and bushes along fringe of soil at river's edge. Willows. Hope to have shade at noon to-morrow. Sorry not to stop for more photographs but dare not until we have finished Lower Granite Gorge, the food is running out. We are camped at a wide, safe place in the river, and I shall try to sleep straight through to-night. Diamond Creek, Separation Rapids and Lava Cliff—three worst ones below here—hope to do Diamond Creek to-morrow. May be home in two weeks. How nice it will be to take Kathleen and Richard for a drive along the back roads on Kings Point, or out toward Oyster Bay."

CHAPTER XVII

Through Separation Rapids—
Distress at Spencer Canyon—
The Last Hurdle—Success in Sight.

$\mathcal{W}$hen it wasn't the river, it was something else. I probably could have slept fairly well on the night of August second because the gorge was 300 feet wide where we were camped and a pile of rocks at the mouth of the side canyon on the right offered a high, safe haven to which we could haul the boats in case of flood. But the bear was tied to the bow of the *Dellenbaugh* a few feet from where I had spread my blankets near the water's edge and he was restless because some wild animal, probably a deer or a mountain sheep, prowled around camp most of the night. Between the prowler and the bear on one side and the river on the other I got little sleep and, eager to cover as rapidly as possible the relatively quiet section of the river above the Lower Granite Gorge, sounded reveille at four forty-five. By getting our duffel bags stowed in the boat before breakfast we were able to get away from camp on the morning of August third at ten minutes after six.

For more than an hour we floated rapidly down stream, splashing through an occasional riffle but encountering no bad rapids. I did not know exactly where we were and began early in the day to look for Diamond Creek Canyon. At seven-forty we reached a rather formidable looking rapids at the mouth of a canyon entering on the left and I thought it might be Diamond Creek. We ran ashore hopefully but the trend of the canyon was not in the right direction and I knew that we were mistaken. "Looked rapids over," says my diary, "shot it, shipped water."

Then followed several miles of easy going and at ten-thirty, seeing another likely looking canyon entering on the left, we ran ashore to see if it was Diamond Creek. But again we were disappointed and, once more, shot a rapids and shipped half a boat load of muddy water. Then the search for Diamond Creek became a game, and jokes concerning its non-appearance flew thick and fast between the men. This game, however, did not continue long. At eleven o'clock the river narrowed, the pleasant talus slopes along the shore disappeared and the sandstone cliffs gave way at the river level to dark colored crystalline schist. We entered the Lower Granite Gorge. I knew that the steep, black walls extended practically to the Grand Wash Cliffs, at the lower end of Grand Canyon, and that if we survived the next fifty miles our chances of getting through to Needles would be very good indeed.

At eleven-thirty, with the "V" shaped walls of granite rising high above us, we ran ashore for lunch and I was interested in seeing how the granite had affected the spirits of the men. During the morning, floating along between the brightly colored walls of sedimentary rock, the men had been boisterous and full of cheer. Callaway had been especially appreciative of my failure to find Diamond Creek and suggested that we stop somewhere and ask a policeman. They joked with one another and had a gay time. Then, as the granite closed in about us, their spirits sagged. They settled down to grim battle with the river and the only sound to be heard above the ceaseless rush of the water was the noise the oars made in the row-locks. We ran dangerously through a long, hard rapids where in a few hundred yards the fall in the river was more than twenty feet and every one seemed pleased when I gave the signal, half a mile below, to run ashore for lunch.

We got away again at one-fifteen and, at two-forty, came finally to Diamond Creek—thirty-five and one-half days out of Greenriver, two days behind schedule. There had been a hotel here in the old days before the railroad extended to the rim of the canyon at the head of Bright Angel Trail and, knowing that it would be possible to come in on horseback, I had wondered for several days if I should cache my exposed still and motion picture films here and come back for them overland after completing the journey, rather than risk losing them in the canyons below. I thought the matter over again while looking about the abandoned camp—and drinking my fill of clear water from Diamond Creek—and decided at last to risk taking the films through in the boat. I should have enjoyed camping at Diamond Creek but, remembering the depleted stock of provisions that stood between us and the ragged edge of hunger in the canyons, I knew that we must hurry on.

We ran through the rapids below Diamond Creek, and the mile or more of riffles beyond. During the afternoon we ran one bad rapids after another. The granite walls hemmed the river in and the muddy, hurrying water fought savagely against restraint. The current swept from one side to the other of the narrow gorge and the stream roared over the rocks that obstructed its flow. There were "holes" and rocks. There were rapids where the river fell fifteen to twenty feet in a few hundred furious yards—with whirlpools lurking behind jutting spurs of rock below to swallow us if the rapids tipped us out. Dangerous traveling or running whirlpools darted out from shore, swept across the river in their mad gyrations, and threw us off our course, rendering our boats unmanageable, threatening to pile us up against rocks in the channel, or against ledges along the shore itself.

Running rapids no longer gave me a pleasurable thrill. I hated to run them with victory so near. I felt as I did the last night of the war when I lay in an open field a few miles from Verdun, listening to the explosions of heavy aerial bombs aimed at us in the darkness from enemy planes flying overhead—resentful toward the dangers that threatened to destroy me thus at the last minutes, within sight of the journey's end.

At five-twenty we ran ashore on the upper end of a pile of bowlders that had been dumped into the river from a side canyon on the left and made camp for the night.

"A hot day," I wrote in my diary, "and now the wind is blowing sand all over the place. I have on only my shoes and a pair of trousers. Camped at five-twenty about nine miles below Diamond Creek, and four miles above Separation Rapids. Hope to do both Separation and Lava Cliff to-morrow, and have all the bad rapids behind us. Camped to-night at the mouth of a beautiful side canyon coming in from the left. Weatherhead reports the discovery of a tree. I shall sleep here by the river but am going to have a look at that tree before dark. And now Carey reports a spring—a tree and a spring, that is luxury indeed—shall go up and see both of them. Much driftwood in the river, wonder if the water is rising—have set out a marker and shall know in the morning."

I went later to see the tree, a scraggly looking cottonwood, and enjoyed a cool drink from the spring. The side canyon was not more than fifty feet wide at its mouth and we could not climb out over its high walls but it was a relief to walk a hundred yards up its steeply sloping bottom—out of sight and sound of the river. I slept as usual close to shore and when I looked for my marker in the morning it was gone, the water had come up enough to cover it.

We got away, on a rising river, at six-thirty on the morning of August fourth and ran the rapids below camp without great difficulty. It was a dark, dismal day. Rain threatened and photographs were out of the question but we could not wait on that account because, before loading the boats in the morning I had checked over our diminishing stock of provisions with Adger and Seager and knew that we could not loiter on the way. Only two treasured packages of cigarettes were left. The loss of the *Powell* had deprived us of luxuries and necessities alike.

Fifteen minutes after starting we came to a rapids that presented as difficult a problem as any that we had been called upon to solve. There were rocks at the right near the top and at the left near the center of the rapids. The channel was blocked on both sides and, at the foot of the rapids was a projecting wall of rock against which the crazy stream almost certainly would force the boats if we managed to avoid the rocks in the tortuous channel. We entered along the left edge of the tongue of the rapids, passed the foam-covered rock a few feet below, pulled hard to the right to avoid the rock half way down and, after passing that so closely that Seager had to throw his oar out of the row-lock to prevent its being smashed, we swept down upon the ledge, missing it by inches. "Made it barely," I wrote in my diary at noon, "and it left me feeling a bit 'whimbly.'"

We ran another fairly bad one at seven, and another at seven-five. In this second one the cross waves turned the *Dellenbaugh* completely around while going through the rapids. The boat, of course, was out of control and it was only our good fortune that saw us through. Next, a "hole" came near to trapping us and, after that, we had a half mile of peaceful river.

The *Coronado* drew alongside and Adger called out to me, good naturedly:

"When we get to Needles I want to buy this boat and burn it."

"Why?" I asked him.

"Because," he replied, "she handles like a barge, and thinks she's a submarine. There isn't a dry place on her big enough to scratch a match."

There wasn't. We had been under way only thirty-five minutes but in that time we had run three bad rapids, had been called upon to bail the boats three times and all of us were wet from head to foot. Adger smiled when he spoke to me but I knew that there was something behind the smile—something akin to the resentment I felt toward the river for its fierce attack upon us in the last hundred miles of the journey. He had told me the night before that the trip had become a grind. He complained about the weight and clumsiness of the boat and said that all the members of his crew in the *Coronado* were weary of canyon voyaging.

"A week or two is fine," is how one of them expressed it, "but this is a long while to be out this way." At that time we had been on the river thirty-four days and had traveled 558 hazardous miles. Bartl told me that when he got home he was going to take a boat out on a quiet, peaceful lake and just sit in it for days on end.

At seven-forty we reached Separation Rapids, so named because three members of Major Powell's expedition, reaching that point in 1869, declared the rapids could not be run and, expressing the belief that Powell and all his men would be drowned there or in the granite gorges farther down, left the party and found their way finally up the canyon on the right to the rim of the plateau thousands of feet above. They discovered, by chance, one of the few places in the three hundred miles of Grand Canyon where it is possible to climb from the river to the rim, but then their good fortune deserted them. They were killed a few days afterward by Indians. Powell meantime pushed on down the river and, a few days later, completed his voyage through the canyons.

Since the morning of August 4, 1927, when I stood with Galloway and Adger on the cliff above Separation Rapids, studying its waves and currents, the place has figured in another tragedy. It was here that Kolb found the boat in which Glenn Hyde and his wife tried unsuccessfully to navigate the treacherous river in the winter of 1928. Apparently the couple had been thrown into the water and drowned or, escaping death in that form, met it in another seeking vainly for a way out of the canyon. Their fate probably never will be known.

There were rocks close to shore on either side but the center of the river was clear and we decided to enter the rapids a few feet to the left of the tip of its tongue and follow through on the apex of the current. That would take us through the waves, but would avoid the danger of being smashed upon the rocks.

We ran in properly enough but almost instantly lost control of the boat. The current caught it and threw it around broadside in the waves, bow first, stern first, every which way. There is a twenty foot drop in Separation Rapids and in running it we encountered the highest waves anywhere on the river. If they were twenty feet high from trough to crest in the Sockdolager, they were twenty-five or thirty at Separation. The *Dellenbaugh* lurched crazily, and I liked it! Here was something that I could fight against and, throwing my body first to one side and then the other to trim the boat, I snapped my teeth together and cursed the river as it tossed us about. I swore at every ugly wave that rose before us to bar our way or tip us out, its muddy water tumbling over backward into the boat. I enjoyed the battle while it lasted. "No fear or trembling afterward," I wrote at noon in my diary, "just the pure joy of conflict"—and an hour before I had found myself trembling and "whimbly" at the foot of a lesser fall. Why there should have been that difference in my behavior I shall not attempt to say. Nor was the joy of conflict to carry me, exulting, through the day.

At eight-fifteen we came to another bad rapids. At its head was a "hole" and, at its foot, the water dashed furiously against a great pinnacle of rock that extended thirty feet above the crest of the muddy waves. We started through and the *Coronado*, caught in a swifter current, swept by us at frightful speed, being saved from destruction only by a kindly cushion of water that prevented the boat from striking the bowlder below. At eight-thirty we plunged through another bad one and, at nine-fifteen, ran the boats ashore on the left above Lava Cliff—the last bad rapids and, next to Lava Falls, the worst one on the river.

Just above the rapids on the right bank of the stream there is a granite cliff which rises sheer a hundred feet above the water's edge. On top of the granite, and continuing the cliff with little break another fifty feet, is a broken, jagged mass of lava. It is from the cliff on the right—a hundred feet of granite, topped with fifty feet of lava—that the rapids derives its name. The cliff is about 150 feet long and most of it is well above the rapids, the break in the water beginning near its lower end. Then the wall falls away abruptly and there are ledges of rock, or piles of bowlders, along the edge of the rapids the rest of the way down on the right. Had it not been for the cliff at the head of the rapids it would have been a fairly simple matter to line the boats from the right bank of the river around the rapids—but the cliff was there.

So much for the right bank of the river—a sheer granite cliff, topped with lava and, below that, an easy shore from which to line the boats if one could only get to it.

Spencer Canyon enters from the left almost directly opposite Lava Cliff and it is the débris from this canyon that obstructs the channel and causes the rapids. Huge bowlders line the shore and lie submerged in the river. Below this pile of bowlders on the left bank there is another granite cliff, rising hundreds of feet above the river's edge. This cliff on the left extends the full length of the rapids and makes it impossible to line the boats from that side.

The last bad rapids and, next to Lava Falls, the worst one on the river. At Lava Falls we had found a way to take the boats out of the water and skid them along over the rocks. At Lava Cliff there was no way to do that. The wall of rock at the head of the rapids made such a procedure impossible on the right bank of the river and the cliff extending the full length of the rapids made it impossible on the left. The boats would have to stay in the water and it did not take many minutes for me to see that no boat could run safely through the rapids if it entered near the tongue and endeavored to follow the apex of the current.

When Major Powell reached this cataract in 1869 he landed as we had, on the left, and walked down to examine the rapids. He decided that the fall could not be run but thought it could be lined from the top of the hundred foot granite cliff on the right. They accordingly hauled their boats back up stream and crossed over to

The last hurdle—at Spencer Canyon. The last bad rapids and one of the worst on the river. Here it seemed safer to run through than attempt to line the boats from the cliff.

Frequent sand storms added to the many discomforts of the voyage.

the other side. They walked along the top of the cliff and Powell directed the men to line the boats from there. He then clambered over the rocks to the lower end of the cliff and discovered that the break of the fall, the tongue of the rapids, was above the lower end of the cliff and that the men could not get the boats ashore even if they should line them that far successfully.

He hastened back to warn the men but he was too late. They already had started one of the boats through, it was in swift water and the men could not pull it back. In the boat was a member of its crew, armed with an oar to keep the boat from striking against the

Soap Creek Rapids, first run successfully by the Eddy Expedition.

cliff. The men discovered that their line was not long enough for them to carry it over the top of the cliff and were compelled to tie it to a rock while one of them hurried to the other boat for more rope. Meanwhile, the current was alternately dashing the craft against the cliff and swinging it far out into the stream. It was clear that the boat could not long withstand the blows and no one realized that better than the man who was in it. He took out his sheath knife to cut the line, having decided that it was better to risk the run through the rapids than to wait for the boat to be smashed to pieces against the cliff. Then the stern-post broke away and the boat was swept into the rapids. The boat weathered the storm. Powell says it was lost from sight most of the way through the "mad, white foam below" but that it did run through successfully. Even then, however, the man in it was not out of danger. His boat was caught in a great whirlpool and Powell, not knowing how long it could remain afloat in its damaged condition, sent two men down along the shore with the rope that remained behind when the boat broke loose, while he and two others of his crew rushed back to their boat and cast off. They, too, made the run successfully though Powell said that the boat was completely out of control and that he did not know how they did it.

The government expedition negotiated the rapids in still another way. Men were let down over the granite cliff and secured themselves with ropes to the rocky wall close to the water's edge. Then the boats were let down from one man to another. The process was a dangerous one. Great difficulty was experienced keeping the boats close to shore aid time after time men barely escaped being pulled into the river. I doubted if any one of my men could hold the *Coronado* against the pull of the river—and knew that there would be no getting out of the canyon if we should lose the boats and find ourselves stranded on the shore. Here was another case where lining around a rapids seemed even more dangerous than running it.

Leaving the other men with the boats, Galloway, Adger and I went down to look the situation over. I knew what had happened to Powell, and what Colonel Birdseye's men had done. I examined Lava Cliff and wondered if any man, or any two men, in my party could possibly hold the big boat against the pull of the swollen river. I calculated the dangers of lining the boats from the cliff and hoped that some other way could be found to get them around. Then I studied the rapids and discussed with Galloway and Adger the possibilities of getting through. They agreed with me that there was no clear passage through and that if we attempted to follow through the apex of the current we inevitably would be wrecked.

After that we clambered over the pile of bowlders at the mouth of Spencer Canyon and worked our way down to the upper end of the cliff on the left. The right side of the river was closed to us, unless we wished to risk lining the boats from Lava Cliff. The rapids was impassable in the middle of the river. Was there a channel along the base of the wall on the left?

We studied it long and earnestly and, in my mind's eye, I can see us yet: Galloway, Adger and I watching the waves as they piled up against the face of the cliff below, the other members of the party grouped around the boats where they were secured to rocks 300 yards up stream, awaiting our decision. We had reached the last hurdle. Could we get over it?

Already that morning I had been depressed and frightened by one rapids, and exhilarated by another. I was about to experience another effect of long continued danger upon tired and frazzled nerves. I studied the channel close to the cliff. Thirty feet out from the wall was a great rock, below which I knew the inevitable "hole" waited with foaming jaws to engulf us. At regular intervals a wave rose from this rock, rolled over backward, swept across the thirty feet of muddy water and dashed against the cliff. Then that wave would drop back into the river, sweep with greatly lessened force back again toward the rock, to be met half way across by another wave rushing from the rock to the cliff. The waves met, spouted, subsided and for a moment the channel was clear. Then the process would be repeated from the start. Could we reach the narrow strip of water between the rock and the wall when the channel was clear? If the wave caught our boats and dashed them against the cliff, would they be smashed? If we got there just when the waves were spouting, would our boats be upset? Could we steer our boats into the channel at all or would they be drawn into the "hole," and all of us destroyed?

I looked alternately at the cliff and at the doubtful channel and then I looked up stream at the men sitting around on the rocks, smoking the last of their cigarettes, awaiting our decision. Never once in nearly six weeks of dangerous going had they questioned my judgment and I knew they would line or run with equal willingness now. Upon my decision depended defeat or victory, life or death to some or all of us.

I looked at the cliff and at the channel. Galloway had expressed his willingness to try either course and I believe now that he favored running.

I turned to Adger and said,

"Bill, do you think we can make it?"

"I don't know," he answered honestly.

Neither did I, nor did any of us. Then my frayed nerves endeavored to come to my rescue. I began to feel sick at my stomach. I had never experienced anything like it before but I knew what it meant, and how to cure it.

"Well," I thought to myself, "I'll have to make up my mind in a hurry." And I did. With a final glance at the channel along the base of the cliff on the left, I said,

"We'll run her. But we'll wait until after lunch."

The distressing symptoms subsided instantly. Galloway seemed pleased with my decision and Adger acquiesced without ever letting me know what his preference was. I went back to the boats and told the men that we were going to run through and they seemed relieved at not having to line the boats around. We then unloaded the *Coronado* and lined her down along the bowlder-strewn shore to the head of the chute that we proposed to run and hauled her up on the rocks to keep her from knocking to pieces. We followed with the *Dellenbaugh* and then prepared for lunch.

All of our duffel was piled on the rocks and, before and after lunch, I sorted it over to see what could be thrown away to lighten the boats. One tent remained and I abandoned that, figuring if we got through the rapids we would be at Needles in three or four days and could do without it, while if we did not get through, we certainly would have no further use for it. Adger found fifteen one pound cans of coffee that we did not need and left them out. But beyond that there was nothing. The journey through Cataract Canyon, the loss of the *Powell*, five weeks of battle with the river had stripped us down to bare necessities in both food and equipment.

We loaded the boats and launched them again on the river, two men from each boat holding them clear of the rocks while the others climbed in. I took my shoes off, tied them securely to the foot boards and gave the bear the full length of his leash so he would have a chance with the rest of us if the boat was tipped over in the rapids. Meantime my mind was busy with strange thoughts. I was aware that we were in grave danger, greater perhaps than we had been in at any time on the river. I examined my thoughts to see if there was in them any warning of approaching disaster, any presentiment that might give me a hint of what was going to happen. Rank superstition I know, and knew at the time, but until one has lived for days and weeks in insecurity he cannot know what a strong hold our superstitions have upon us, how quick we are to turn to magic. I thought of my wife, "Well, I left her fairly well provided for," in the past tense as if disaster already had overtaken us. I frankly threw aside for a moment the intellectual cloak that ordinarily masks my fears and superstitions and rummaged about in my mind for some "sign" or presentiment, some hint of what the future held for us—and of course found nothing there but honest realization of the danger that confronted us.

Directing the *Coronado* to follow close behind, we shoved off in the *Dellenbaugh*. There were fifty feet of easy going and, standing up in the boat, I could see all the way down through the narrow channel. We came near running into a small rock and experienced difficulty pulling the boat around it. Then, stern first as we had planned, we approached the channel between the cliff and the rock.

I watched the wave rise from the rock and sweep toward us across the channel. It struck the boat a glancing blow and swept it headlong toward the cliff. We were traveling down stream at a speed of twenty-five or thirty miles an hour and the wave carried us toward the cliff with almost equal velocity. It looked as if nothing could avert a crash and I raised my arm involuntarily to ward off the blow. Seager held his oar to serve as a buffer. We were swept so close that the oars on one side of the boat were useless and we were at the mercy of the current. The wall flashed by on our left, half a dozen feet away. Our movement toward the rock slackened, the wave struck the cliff ahead of us, dropped back into the river and cushioned us away. We slipped by the ledge and in another moment we were through.

I turned to see how the other boat was faring and saw the great rock in the foreground with the water pouring over and around it. If the boat should strike it, nothing could save her or her crew. She had started through. Following us, she floated down toward the narrow channel. As I watched, she struck the rock that we had narrowly avoided and turned broadside in the river. Her bow swung around and the wave leaped out from the rock and struck her. The boat lurched and swung toward the rocks. Then we ran into the waves at the lower end of the rapids and for a few minutes I could see nothing but the muddy water trying to tip us over, to climb into our boat, to drown us at the last.

When finally I did see the *Coronado* again she was through. They came alongside presently and I called out to Adger,

"That was pretty work, Bill."

"Pretty work—hell," Bill replied good naturedly, "that was just luck."

Whether it was luck or pretty work, it was enough to see us through and Needles seemed not so far away although we were still between granite walls and had many rapids yet to do.

By two-thirty we had run through three more bad ones and eight easy ones. At four-fifteen we reached a side canyon coming in from the right and when we ran ashore to examine the rapids below that, we found the names of the members of the government expedition painted high on the rocky wall. One after another the men were named, with their initials and the capacities in which they served—"Frank Dodge, boatman," for instance, "E. C. Kolb," and the others. But near the bottom of the list a line had been drawn and below that, all in capital letters, was one name standing alone, "MISTER _____." I cannot divulge the name. I know too little of the reasons why the others in the party set this man apart and destroyed him by calling him "Mister."

We ran through the rapids and floated cheerfully along looking for a place to camp. Each time we passed a ravine some one suggested that it might be Diamond Creek and each riffle was compared to Separation Rapids, Lava Cliff, Hance Rapids or the Sockdolager. At five-fifteen we came to a fine, big canyon on the right and as it had begun to rain we ran ashore for the night.

Rain fell intermittently all evening but our morale, at last, was proof against discomfort. After supper we sat around a sputtering camp fire, discussing the bad rapids we had run through successfully, and the few that we had lined our boats around. We had a few minutes of close harmony and I realized with a start that there had been no songs since the night, five weeks before, when the men sang in the boats at the head of Cataract Canyon.

I slept high up on a sand bar fifty feet from the river. "Won't allow myself to say it is finished until we reach Needles," I wrote in my diary, "but it looks as if we could not fail to get through now."

CHAPTER XVIII

Grand Wash Cliffs—
Through the Grand Canyon—
Black Canyon—Needles.

*T*here was no need for reveille on the morning of Friday, August
fifth. Everybody was up by five o'clock, eager to get away. It
was a cloudy morning and before we had finished with breakfast
rain was falling steadily. We started away at six-thirty and although
we had to run a long, hard rapids just below camp, and in spite of
the fact that we still were between high granite walls, floating along
in a steady downpour of rain, the men in the *Coronado* burst into
song. No rain could dampen their spirits now. What a motley crew
they were. Adger wore a red bandanna tied pirate-fashion around
his head. Carey, Bartl and Weatherhead had a five-weeks' growth
of unaccustomed beard upon their youthful faces. Three of the men
were without shirts and Weatherhead was the only one among them
wearing a hat, and trousers that reached below his knees.

At seven-thirty we were swept through three-quarters of a mile
of foaming, rock-strewn rapids. At eight we ran out of the granite. Between narrow walls of sandstone, there were cataracts, rapids, riffles—nineteen miles of dangerous going. At ten-thirty, the
walls fell away and we emerged abruptly from the Grand Canyon.
A few minutes later, looking back up stream, we could see the
almost unbroken line of Grand Wash Cliffs towering above us and

marveled that even the Colorado River ever could have cut its way through them. Within a few minutes we could no longer distinguish the narrow canyon through which we had come. How good it seemed to see the sky again, so much of it! Weatherhead was the most outspoken in his appreciation of the broadened field of view but all of us turned our eyes happily toward the south where, in one direction at least, there were no walls of rock, however beautiful, to circumscribe our view.

We ran on, monotonously, during the afternoon, making forty-two miles for the day and camped that night at the head of Virgin Canyon. We had a rapids to lull us to sleep, an easy rapids that threatened nothing more serious than a fast ride in the morning after breakfast.

I was mistaken in my calculations and thought we were much nearer Needles than we actually were.

"To-morrow night may end the expedition," I wrote in my diary, "and I shall be glad. I yearn for comforts, well cooked food, clear water. Beginning already, however, to think of the many things that I must do as soon as I get home. Have been away from the thousand cares of everyday life for a long time, but feel that they are waiting for me now, just around the corner. Now, when I'd enjoy a little rest. But no more bad rapids, no more muddy waves leaping at me, no more 'holes' and rocks.

"And now, no more adventuring, the rest will have to be steady plugging, for necessities. But it has been such a grand adventure—a voyage into story-land where dreams are real and the constant presence of danger gives richness to life—where the daily threat of death makes clear how good it is to live. No man who keeps to the beaten path can ever know the joy of home-coming after a long absence. No man who has not faced death can know how good it is to be alive. And how such an adventure reveals us to ourselves. How many times I have been afraid! What strange thoughts fear has turned up in my mind. How familiar I have been, with superstitions, and with weariness of responsibility. How many times I have faced the realization that we might not get through at all, that the river might beat us with its power or its many dangers.

"The men are less companionable than they were last night—a nervous reaction probably, though it may be because we are now quite out of tobacco. But we are all cheerful enough."

On the morning of August sixth, Galloway and I walked down to examine the rapids below camp. While we were standing there a duck came floating down stream.

"Let's see if he runs it bow first," I said to Galloway.

We watched the bird and it did go through bow first, not at all in the approved fashion of running Colorado River rapids. Still, the duck should have known the qualities of its boat, and the rapids was an easy one anyhow.

The men had been two days without tobacco, and the rations were almost gone. We had nothing left but flour, coffee and bacon—and hardly enough of those to last us through the day. However, that gave me little concern because a few hours without food would do us no harm.

The swift current carried us quickly through Virgin Canyon. The walls were narrow and steep again, though not more than two or three hundred feet high, but there were no rapids and all we had to do was to pull occasionally at our oars to keep the boat away from the rocky walls. It was warm and several men from each of the boats jumped overboard and swam alongside to cool off. I did so myself and enjoyed it. I had climbed back into the boat and was watching Holt, swimming easily along within a few feet of us, when he disappeared suddenly under the surface of the muddy water, to reappear in a moment, swimming strongly toward the boat. After he had climbed aboard he told us that a small whirlpool had "wrapped itself" around him and dragged him under. The course of the river was tortuous, the current strong and swift, and many small whirlpools were formed in the water as it swirled around the bends in the stream. We did no more swimming while we were in the canyon.

There are a number of canyons similar to Virgin between Grand Wash Cliffs and Needles. Small mountain ranges extend in parallel rows approximately from east to west and the river has cut canyons directly through them, one after another. Between these ranges of hills are wide, arid valleys where the river spreads out and, losing velocity, begins to deposit its heavy load of sand and silt. Sand bars obstruct navigation and here, for the first time, we encountered "sand waves" in the river. How the waves are formed I do not know exactly but presumably the sand in the bed of the river is drifted into ridges by the water passing over it in the same way that sand in the desert is drifted into ridges by the wind. These sand ridges in the bed of the river then affect the water that pours over them, producing great rolling waves, highest in the middle of the river and dwindling or disappearing toward the shores. Sand waves occur in the valleys where the river is wide and the waves may be ten feet or more in height from trough to crest. Where sand waves occur the surface of the water is furrowed from shore to shore, and the appearance of such waves in the river was always a signal for the men in the boats to abandon their scant clothing and leap overboard. Looking back from the *Dellenbaugh*, unless I too was in the river enjoying the sport, it would look as if the boat actually was shedding its crew. Over they would go to the last man, shouting with joy as they rose and fell on the smooth billows. The current was swift even here but it carried the men as rapidly as it did their boat and they kept abreast of it with no more exertion than the little that was required to keep themselves afloat.

We saw many abandoned mining claims along the river and once I thought I saw a dog on shore. Thinking there might be a ranch nearby I stood on the deck of the boat and called out at the top of my voice. The animal which up to that moment had been trotting toward us, stopped abruptly, answered my call and then turned tail and ran away. It was a coyote. I wonder what he thought I was.

In the distance were the Opal Mountains, range on range of desert hills, their color the color of their barren rocks. Even sage brush cannot find a foothold on their arid slopes. They were dry, barren—but magnificent. Heat waves shimmered over their ragged peaks.

During the morning we passed the mouth of Virgin River and, at ten-thirty, entered Boulder Canyon. This canyon originally was selected for the construction of a dam by the United States Government and, while it later was decided to build the dam twenty-one miles down stream in Black Canyon, the project probably always will be known as the Boulder Canyon Dam. We stopped at eleven-thirty while still in Boulder Canyon for lunch and, while we were there, watched an airplane flying overhead far away to the west of us, enroute probably from Needles to Las Vegas.

We got away again at one-thirty and an hour later, after emerging from Boulder Canyon, saw a man and woman standing on the river bank. We ran ashore and found that they were residents of Las Vegas

How to run a rapids. First, enter the rapids, stern first.

Next, hold the boat just clear of the waves, far enough out to avoid striking the rocks near shore.

Three hundred rapids conspire to make the Colorado the most dangerous river in the world.

The author's boat plunging through icy waves of North Canyon Rapids.

and that they were camping nearby in a grove of cottonwoods. They had a watermelon which they shared with us—one small melon for ten starved canyon voyagers, with enough left over for the man and his wife! Still, there was a refreshing taste all around.

The river widened below that point and we ran frequently upon sand bars which necessitated our jumping overboard and pushing the boats again into the deeper channels. The current was sluggish and the crew of the *Coronado* rigged up a sail, utilizing their oars as masts and managed in that way to keep up with us without the necessity of rowing. It was hot and many times when I looked back no one was in sight in the *Coronado*, all the men were floating alongside depending upon their life preservers to keep them afloat. The bear, riding with us in the *Dellenbaugh*, hooked his front paws over the gunwale of the boat and allowed his hind quarters to drag in the water. Half a dozen times during the afternoon I jumped overboard, clothes and all, and climbing back into the boat, allowed my clothes to dry on me.

At four-thirty we reached the head of Black Canyon and landed where we saw a dock, with a power boat moored to it on the right. We found cigarettes there, and another watermelon. When we shoved off again an hour later I was riding in the power boat, a tourist for the time, on my way to Boulder Canyon Damsite. There I transferred to the *Dellenbaugh* and our journey was continued.

We ran that night until seven, and made camp in the dark. Just as we were ready to eat, a violent wind and rain storm broke and the sand blew into everything. We had little enough to eat, and that was liberally sprinkled with sand. The rain drenched us and later while I was wandering around looking for a place to spread my poncho out in lieu of a better bed, I saw Weatherhead get his duffel bag out of the boat, look at it thoughtfully for a moment and return it, unopened. Apparently having decided that a poncho was no advantage, he felt his way through the drifting sand across the beach to some bushes growing at high water level on the shore, curled up under one of them and, so far as I know, was soon asleep. Harvard had adapted itself to wilderness ways.

We were up again at five on the morning of August seventh. The bear, after a night in the wind and rain, looked so bedraggled that I held him in my arms and petted him—and he was so wet and miserable that he permitted me to do it without protest, an unusual thing.

Breakfast consisted of flapjacks and coffee. We had no baking powder and even Galloway admitted that the flapjacks left something to be desired.

We got away at six and floated all that day on a sluggish river, running on sand bars and having to push the boats up stream again in places to get them back into deeper water. For lunch we had flapjacks and coffee again, and Seager reported to me that there was not food enough, even of what we had, to do for more than one more meal. That was reason enough to hurry and, in addition to that, I had told my wife she might expect a telegram from me on the seventh and I was eager to get the wire to her from Needles on schedule time. Accordingly, we ran late that afternoon. We ran, in fact, until dark and, even then we did not stop. Ahead of us, finally, I could see the twinkling lights of Camp Mohave, an Indian school, eighteen miles above Needles, and while there was danger of running on a sand bar in the dark and being stranded on it overnight, we hurried on. How we got around the sand bars in the dark I do not know but we did and at nine o'clock the *Dellenbaugh* came to a stop below the bluff upon which Fort Mohave is situated.

Leaving the crew of the *Dellenbaugh* lighting matches to guide the *Coronado* in, I waded ashore and, although it was late, found the superintendent and the keeper of the trading post. I sent my telegram—relayed by telephone by way of Kingman—and made arrangement for the purchase of some food. Then I went back to the boats and all the men returned with me to the trading post where we dined on cold canned beans, crackers and jam.

That night the men slept ashore and, taking with me a box of crackers and a can of evaporated milk for the bear, I returned to the boats, for my last night on the river. The little bear had long since resigned himself to going to sleep without his supper and was curled up on the after deck of the *Dellenbaugh*. But he ate greedily the mixture of crackers and milk that I prepared for him and I realized that I had grown fond of him as I watched him eating contentedly, unaware that the journey was almost ended—unaware as well no doubt that his adventures had been different from the adventures that befall every bear in his early youth. I slept in the bottom of the boat, the bear was curled up on deck and the river, sweeping listlessly by us over its sandy bed, seemed strangely quiet and unfamiliar.

Next morning, August eighth, we had the last of our food and set off on the final eighteen miles of our journey, reaching Needles at eight-forty, forty-two days out of Greenriver. No one knew we were due and no one was there to greet us. Two Indians who happened to be sitting on the bank showed not the slightest interest in us when we ran our boats ashore.

The rest is quickly told. I engaged a truck and we moved ourselves and our duffel bags to the Gateway Hotel. The bear was sold to a Santa Fe Railway engineer who wanted to take it home with him to San Francisco. Seager took an afternoon train for Los Angeles. The Rotary Club asked us to be their guests at luncheon next day at noon and I accepted the invitation. But at six o'clock on the morning of the ninth, Galloway awakened me to say that he had decided to take a seven-ten train for Salt Lake City so two of us were missing at the luncheon. At six-thirty that afternoon the remaining members of the expedition came to the station to see me off and each of them added to his farewell a request that I include him in the party when next I go exploring. Bartl had expressed a desire to keep Rags and took him with him later to Wisconsin.

As the train pulled out of Needles, I took up my diary and tried to set down in it some of the thoughts that were running through my mind.

"I am on the train," I wrote, "en route to New York. The adventure is ended. In the distance a flaming sunset is fading into night behind the sharp, arid peaks of the Dead Mountains. Before me is the Colorado River, a sluggish stream meandering about among its sand bars. Galloway by now is approaching Salt Lake City. Seager is in Los Angeles. I am crossing the railroad bridge below Needles. Adger, Bartl, Carey, Weatherhead, Holt, Callaway and Jaeger are still in Needles, having just told me good-by at the station. By to-morrow morning the last member of the Eddy Colorado River Expedition will have started for home—home with our memories, our pictures and our story of the long, hard battle with the river. And I know from past experience it is almost certain that, however much we may have in common, the members of my party never will be together in a group again.

"Already, the memories of the dangers fade and when I left them the men asked me if we couldn't do the Yukon or the Mackenzie, or go adventuring together in some other part of the world. But my adventuring probably is over—the Navy when I was a boy; the Army and France during the war; and, now, the river—it is not likely that I shall ever again go voyaging into far corners where dreams come true. I shall dream of other and less romantic things, instead, and see how well I can translate the dreams into reality.

"The adventure has not corresponded in all respects to the dream—there has been much that I would gladly have avoided. But while still within sight of my river the unpleasant incidents fade from memory and there begins to stand out in clear relief a panorama of exciting scenes. The early discouragements of Cataract Canyon are all but forgotten and I remember best the thrills of the high water there; the perils of Dark Canyon; the slow but successful voyage through the dismal Granite Gorges; the joy of passing safely through the last bad rapids of all to Mohave—and Needles.

"And so good-by to all of you who started with me six weeks ago so gayly from Greenriver—Galloway and Adger, Bartl and Carey, Holt and Callaway, Seager and Weatherhead. I am glad that I could share my dream with you."

Appendix
A Second Journey Through Grand Canyon
from Lee's Ferry to Bright Angel Creek.

*M*y second voyage on the Colorado River was the result of an effort made by a motion picture producer to use the Grand Canyon as the scenic background for a feature film. To secure the needed pictures an expedition consisting of thirteen men and six boats left Greenriver, Utah, November eighth, 1927. During the afternoon of November fourteenth I received at my home in New York a telegram from Hollywood, California, requesting me to hasten out to Arizona to assist in the search for the river party, reported lost somewhere above Lee's Ferry. Four days later I stood again on the rim of the Canyon at the head of Bright Angel Trail.

I remained at Grand Canyon until the afternoon of the twenty-third and went from there by train to Flagstaff. On the morning of the twenty-fourth my rescue expedition, consisting of a truck load of provisions, a cowboy-accoutered chauffeur, one other man and myself, started for Lee's Ferry, 145 miles across the Painted Desert. How the lost expedition was found, and why I joined it for the trip through eighty-nine miles of the Grand Canyon to Bright Angel Creek is told in the following excerpts from my diary.

Painted Desert, Arizona, November 24. Left Flagstaff at nine o'clock. Stopped to pick up George McCormick, who wants to go down the river. Am taking him along in case there are any desertions at Lee's Ferry. The road winds around the base of San Francisco Peaks through a beautiful forest of pine, spruce and fir—part of the Coconino National Forest. It grew noticeably colder as we climbed up over the divide and warmer again as we dropped down into the Painted Desert. The road led us out across Dead Man's Flat, then the open country stretched before us as far as we could see. The forest gave way to clumps of cedar, twisted and gnarled, and they in turn were replaced by sage brush. A herd of eleven antelope bounded across the road ahead of us and in the distance a coyote loped easily along. There is much petrified wood along the road and we collected specimens of it. The colors in the cliffs, buttes and mesas are magnificent. Unbelievable ribbons of red, yellow, gray, and blue wind their way across the landscape.

Stopped for lunch at the Cameron Indian Trading Post, ate sandwiches we had brought along and I remembered it was Thanksgiving Day, and that this was our Thanksgiving dinner. On to the Gap in the afternoon. The Gap is another trading post, so named because it is located in a gap in the hills. Joseph H. Lee, descendant of John D. Lee, is in charge of the trading post. Met some people coming in from Lee's Ferry and learned from them that the river party has not yet been heard from.

On to Gable's Camp, radio publicity station in the desert. The river party is equipped with radio and it was the intention that daily reports of the progress of the expedition should be sent to the desert station, to be relayed to Fort Douglas in Salt Lake City. But no word has come yet from the river and because of that silence the desert station is reporting its fear that the party has been lost in Cataract Canyon. The arrival of my rescue expedition was the subject of a special bulletin to the New York *Times*. Having seen the river party's ration list, I shall begin to feel concerned about it when I know that the men have eaten the last of their three weeks' supply of provisions—sometime after the last day of the month.

Lee's Ferry, November 25. Up at seven at Gable's Camp. Went hunting before breakfast with a forty caliber shot gun, had four shells and got three rabbits in twenty minutes—rabbits are called "phantom chickens" and are considered rare eating around here.

After breakfast we shoved off in the truck and ran out around a mesa to a little Indian camp, the home of Hoske Bancroft. The

Navajos live in dirt houses, hogans, surrounded by their sheep, goats, horses and burros. They are pastoral and doubtless live much as the Hebrews did in Old Testament times—shepherds with their flocks. Their hogans are built of cedar logs chinked and covered over with dirt. There are no windows and a piece of canvas serves as a door. The hogans, and the Indians as well, remind me of the pictures I have seen of the homes and the people of Mongolia. Doubtless the Indians are an offshoot from the yellow Asiatics who anciently wandered north along the shores of Bering Sea and south again along our own Pacific Coast. Photographed a woman weaving a rug. The Indian women are shy, the men and boys are not. According to "Preacher" Smith, whom I met yesterday at Gable's Camp, the women own the flocks and are virtually heads of the household. When a woman wants to divorce a husband—possibly to get a younger and more active one to take care of the flocks—she simply places her husband's saddle outside the hogan door. The children stay with her and the husband looks for another job, hogan and wife.

Drove on toward Lee's Ferry. Met a number of Indians on horseback, driving their flocks before them. Stopped us and asked for cigarettes. Arrived at river about one-thirty and stopped to make pictures just before we reached the Dugway. Went over to edge of canyon and looked across the river at the place where McGregory left us last July. Reassured myself again that he had no trouble getting back to Lee's Ferry. Continued on over the Dugway, a narrow ribbon of roadway clinging precariously to the cliff a thousand feet above the river. The roadway winds in and out of the ravines and is not wide enough for two cars to pass. Saw below us a truck which had toppled over the edge and rolled over and over, down the slope into the river. My cowboy-chauffeur tied open the door on the side of the car toward the cliff so he could leap out of it if the car got out of control and started over the edge. When two cars meet on the Dugway, one of them has to back up and tourists have been known to express complete willingness to abandon their cars rather than attempt to move them backward over the narrow road. When that happens some one has to walk three miles back to "Buck" Lowrey's Trading Post and prevail upon him to untangle the traffic.

Arrived at Lee's Ferry about two o'clock. The water was low and I decided best not try to take the truck across. Jerry Johnson's brother was on our side of the river and we loaded our stuff on his wagon and took it across on the ferry. Jerry Johnson is in Salt Lake City. Met "Buck" Lowrey and his wife again and arranged to stay with them until the river party arrives. Asked about McGregory and learned that he did not go back to Lee's Ferry after leaving us. Not so good. Where did he go? What happened to him? Before dinner I walked down to the place where he left us and worked my way without great difficulty down to the river. No reason why he should not have got out. Probably he walked up to the road and rather than face the people at Lee's Ferry, waited for an automobile and hitch-hiked his way ninety-five miles into Kanab.

Talked to Mrs. Lowrey during the evening and she told me that when the new bridge is finished it probably will be necessary for Mr. Lowrey to build his trading post on the east side of the river so that the Navajo Indians will not have to cross the bridge. They are afraid of the river. "River is no good for Navajos," is the way they express it and probably will be unwilling to cross even on a bridge.

In the evening I overheard a conversation between Mrs. Lowrey and a tourist. Mrs. Lowrey spoke of the river as if she fears it no less than the Navajos. She doesn't even want to live within sight of it. She told me how she hated to see us go down the river last July. Our boats seemed so small and the river was so big and muddy.

Lee's Ferry, November 26. Climbed to the top of the Vermilion Cliffs, back of the Ferry. Magnificent view up and down the river. Looking toward the south I could see, stretching across the Painted Desert, the deep and narrow gash which is known as Marble Gorge. To the north was a vast level plateau cut through by the narrow canyon. In the distance was Navajo Mountain. Occasional pinnacles and buttes rose high above the flat surface of the plateau and down through the center of it was the dark, gloomy canyon of the Colorado, with walls so steep that one might walk along the level surface of the land on top and step suddenly off its rim and fall a thousand feet into the river below. A hard, uncompromising country—the last frontier. But it is magnificent, colorful and sharply drawn, its stark outlines unblurred by vegetation or by moisture-laden air.

Lee's Ferry, November 27. Two men from Flagstaff came through to-day on their way to House Rock Valley to shoot buffalo. The herd on the reservation here has grown so large that the State of Arizona decided to have some of the animals shot. Now, holders of lucky numbers are coming in groups to shoot the animals. Men who have already been in say that the hunt is about as exciting as it would be to go out in the barnyard and shoot a cow. The buffalo are quite tame.

In the afternoon I walked along an old roadway on the other side of the river and found an ox cart abandoned half a century ago by some Mormon immigrant. Mail came to-day addressed to the river party marked, "Due at Lee's Ferry about December 1." Looks as if everybody but B— knew when the expedition was due. An automobile party came through from Flagstaff. The men said they were receiving reports nightly by radio from Los Angeles, telling about the overdue boat party. Airplanes are being sent from California to take up the search. The temperature to-day was twenty-eight degrees above zero, dropped thirty degrees in an hour and a half yesterday at sundown. . . .

Lee's Ferry and Gable's Camp, November 30. Began to-day looking for arrival of river party. Having lunch of beans, bread and tea on tailgate of wagon at Jerry Johnson's when the boats came around the bend, six of them in line. There were greetings and introductions all around. None of the men has shaved since leaving Greenriver. The expedition is in charge of C. H. LaRue. Frank B. Dodge is chief boatman, the other boatmen being Owen R. Clark, Dean C. Daily, Con Rodin, Nick Samoff and Val Woodbury. John Schubert is cook. Glen R. Kerschner and Pat C. Gannon are camera men. Sergt. Vernon T. Herrick, U. S. Army, is in charge of the radio, assisted by Devergne Barber, who also is in charge of publicity.

LaRue, Herrick, Barber and I rushed over to Gable's Camp. An airplane passed over Lee's Ferry just as the boats arrived. I tried to signal it as it went over, to notify the pilot that the expedition was in. Made a fast run to Gable's Camp and just as we arrived there the airplane returned, hit a stake and destroyed a tire on its landing wheel. Met Lieut. Walter K. Burgess, the pilot. He had driven the plane all the way up to the junction of the Green and the Colorado, 226 miles and back. "Like a ride over hell," is how he described it. Head wind at Navajo Mountain made return almost impossible. This is the first time an airplane has ever flown over the region. There is no place in hundreds of miles to make a landing. Met B— at camp and he asked me if I would go through with the expedition, in charge of photography. I am glad to have the opportunity to go through even a part of the Grand Canyon a second time.

Gable's Camp, Joe Lee's Trading Post, and Lee's Ferry, December 2. Spent Thursday, December 1, at Gable's Camp and that night at Joe Lee's Trading Post. Bought a Navajo rug, made about three miles from there. Paid $18 for it. Returned to Lee's Ferry, December second. Found everything shot to pieces when I got to camp. The checks that B— had sent to the boatmen were not countersigned and were worthless. The men were in favor of stopping at Lee's Ferry until they were paid. They looked to me because I represented B— and that placed me in awkward position. I suggested finally that we go on to Phantom Ranch and sit tight there until salaries are paid. LaRue wrote a letter to B— telling him what the decision was. I sent word to B— to have the money ready when we got there.

Badger Creek Rapids, December 3. Up early and had breakfast on the beach. Loaded the boats. I sent McCormick and the truck back to Flagstaff. We shoved off at eleven o'clock, thirteen men, six boats and a dog. LaRue and I were riding with Frank Dodge in boat No. 1. Splashed through riffles below Lee's Ferry and we are off again on the river. Pleasant, warm and sunny. We arrived at Badger Creek Rapids about three o'clock. Here I learned that I was mistaken last summer on my geography and that we had run Soap Creek Rapids successfully. We landed to-day on right and looked it over. I photographed it from same spot as last summer, when I had Holt in the foreground. Now the rapids is full of bare rocks. Dodge decided we could not run in. Crossed over to other side of river and to-night we are camped half way down with three boats drawn up on the beach. Shall run it from here.

To-night again the roar of rapids is in my ears. On this trip I feel no responsibility for the safety of the boats. Dodge takes care of that entirely. Beautiful moonlight, took a walk on the beach. Driftwood is piled high along the shore. Slept cold, awake many times. The river according to the gage at Lee's Ferry is carrying about 9000 second feet of water. Last summer when we came through here she was carrying 40,000.

Soap Creek Rapids, December 4. Up at six-ten. While Dodge and his boatmen were bringing down the last three boats I looked around and found the places where I made two photographs in July, and made two to show difference in level of water. The water was fully ten feet higher then. Badger is a bad rapids though at any level of water.

Boatmen ran boats through lower part of the rapids and the "passengers" got on below. Then we dropped rapidly down to Soap Creek. Passed the big rock where we had lunch the first day out of Lee's Ferry. It is almost ashore now on account of the low water. Reached Soap Creek Rapids at noon and stopped for lunch. The rapids is too rocky at head to be run and so my expedition continues to be the only one that ever has run Soap Creek successfully.

Got only one boat down all day. It is probable that we shall not leave here before noon to-morrow. My expedition last July passed here about two-thirty on our first day out of Lee's Ferry. It may take us ten days to reach Bright Angel after all. Either the river is more friendly at low water or I have learned to like it better. It does not seem to be the implacable dragon that it was last summer. Then she roared and threatened and knocked us about. Now she seems a little tired. The water falls over the rocks, as water should fall. Last July it fairly shouted as it plunged down stream and dashed itself furiously against the bowlders that barred its way. More rocks are visible in the rapids but it looks almost as if a man might be swept into them and escape unhurt. But the water is frightfully cold. This morning Dodge slipped on the icy bowlders along shore while lining a boat, fell into the river, disappeared under the boat and came up below it. He caught a bowlder as he was swept by, hauled himself out of the water and returned to his work as if nothing had happened. If he had not caught the bowlder when he did he would have been carried through the lower end of Badger Creek Rapids.

It is quite warm and pleasant at noon but the air chills immediately when the shadow of the cliffs cuts off the rays of the sun, which happens about two-thirty in the afternoon. Must get to work now and fix up my bed for the night, it will soon be dark. May have to wear an extra pair of trousers and a sweater to-night to keep warm. Our waterproof sleeping bags are filled with frost when we spread them out at night. We perspire during the night and because the sleeping bags are waterproof our blankets become moist, this moisture freezes during the day and our blankets are filled with frost at night. Of course, we do not take off our clothes when we go to bed but, at that, it takes a long time to warm up enough to get to sleep.

The feeling of this trip is so different to that of my first expedition. Last summer there was desert heat, sunshine, youth and gay adventure. Now it is winter. The days are short, the nights are long and cold. The men are mature, and it is a salaried performance. But the men are fine and Dodge is comparable to Galloway—quiet, strong, able and courageous. We are camped to-night on the sand bar below Soap Creek Rapids. There are five boats to be lined down to-morrow. The going is slow but we may make better time from now on. Low water is safer but adds to the difficulty of getting the boats around. Pansy, the dog, is evidently planning another trip through the canyons, she has bones buried at every camp site from here to Greenriver. We got in touch by radio with Gable's Camp but our sending apparatus is weak and the contact is unsatisfactory. Sergeant Herrick told me to-night that as the party came through Cataract he could pick up messages from Fort Douglas and from Gable's Camp but could not get messages out. Our sending radius through these walls seems to be only forty or fifty miles.

Soap Creek Rapids, December 5. Slept cold last night. Much ice along the river bank this morning. I rode through lower end of Soap Creek Rapids twice to-day, to be certain of having good shots for the feature film. Finished lining the boats about two o'clock but did not break camp at Soap Creek. We are planning to get away early to-morrow morning. It is warm enough only at noon. After two-thirty it is cool and, after six, it is cold. Had to get up last night and put on my heavy sweater and a leather coat.

During the afternoon Schubert found a cache tucked away among the rocks on the talus slope above the rapids. In it were some letters. One of them, addressed by their mother to W. E. and F. R. Mendenhall at Teardale, Utah, was dated January 12, 1894. Pack rats had nibbled at its edges but after the lapse of thirty-three years it still was legible.

"My very dear boys," wrote a worried mother, "if you could only know our great anxiety to hear from you. It is really painful when so long a time elapses between letters, yet I try to realize that you are a long, long way from the postoffice. But how is it possible for you to get supplies enough to keep from famishing with hunger? Sometimes I feel dreadfully uneasy and take a big cry over it, then try for awhile to forget it."

By what dangerous way did that letter arrive with the Mendenhall brothers at Soap Creek Rapids? Were they such a long, long way from the postoffice thirty-three years ago that their mother's anxiety for the safety of her sons never was relieved? Did they, too, die of hunger as so many others have; or meet defeat and death in the angry waters of the river? Or, did they get home finally to tell her of their wanderings?

The mother's letter indicated that her two sons had gone by boat down the San Juan River; that they had floated past Lee's Ferry and on down the Colorado to Soap Creek. A little below the cache, we found the blade and part of the handle of a crudely fashioned oar which indicated that the two men, prospecting for gold, had been swept in a flimsy home-made boat down into the turbid, swirling water—the foaming, roaring rapids—of the most dangerous river in the world.

I wonder what kind of boat carried W. E. and F. R. Mendenhall down the San Juan and Colorado rivers thirty-odd years ago! I wonder if they abandoned their expedition at Soap Creek Rapids—or went on to destruction—or by some miracle made the journey safely through the mile-deep gorges of Marble and Grand canyons. There are records of few successful voyages since Powell made the first historic journey in the winter of 1868. And the Mendenhalls are not listed among the successful navigators of the river.

Marble Gorge, December 6. Reached House Rock Rapids at ten-thirty. I went through with Dodge and Herrick and we made it nicely. Then I went through with Daily, a cross current swung us around broadside and a wave poured ice water over us and into the boat. Both of us were wet from head to foot, not so nice. The boatmen actually are wet all day. They stand for long periods in the icy water while lining the boats and get drenched when running the rapids. They are a hardy lot. Dodge sometimes does not bother to dry out even when the others are shivering around the fire.

At North Canyon Rapids Herrick volunteered to go through with me again and we spread ourselves out on our stomachs on the decks of Dodge's boat. I was on the stern and, because the boat was running stern first, my feet stuck out over the end of the boat and my head hung over the open cockpit. We were carried rapidly down into the big waves and I could see where we were going only by looking backward over my shoulder. The boat got out of control and we were swept down into the big waves in the apex of the current. I saw ourselves approaching a wave that looked as high as a house and heard Dodge say, "Look out." I tightened my hold on the life line and the current thrust us into the wave. Gallons and gallons of ice water crashed down on me, nearly washing me overboard. My feet and legs were carried over but I held tight with my hands and swung my body back into position again as soon as I could. The boat was level full of water and Dodge had a hard time getting us ashore below. Woodbury tipped over in rapids at twenty-two mile point on the map. Windy and cold to-night. Ice froze on our decks and oars this morning. The temperature of the water is thirty degrees.

Redwall Cavern, December 7. Got away at eight-thirty. This probably was the coldest morning we have had. Temperature of the water is below freezing point but it does not freeze on account of its swift motion. Ice forms on the decks of the boats and where the water drips off the oars. We passengers sit on the decks of the boats, with the seats of our trousers almost frozen to them. On account of the cold it is necessary to stop between rapids many times and build driftwood fires. Some of these fires are big enough to warm up our section of the canyon, others are small where driftwood is scarce and we make an amusing picture, thirteen cold explorers in a circle, all leaning over with our backs to the fire. Usually Schubert walks down stream, builds a fire and has it ready when the boatmen come splashing through the rapids.

Reached Cave Spring Rapids at eleven. Four of the boats ran through successfully. Then Dean Daily came along while Dodge and the others watched below. Daily was out about twenty feet farther from shore than the other boats had been. A wave struck his boat, tossed it into the air and threw Daily into the river. The boat then dropped back into the water without tipping over. Instantly Dodge and the others pushed their boats away from shore ready on the instant to risk their lives to rescue Daily. But Daily was able to save himself. He clutched the gunwale of his boat, pulled himself in and picked up his oars. In another minute he had his boat under control and the men below, ready a moment before to risk their lives to get him out, hooted at him for permitting his boat to throw him into the river. We are camped to-night half a mile below Redwall Cavern, two miles below Vasey's Paradise. There is a full moon, and it is light enough to write without any other illumination.

Little Nankoweap, December 8. Got away at eight-thirty and stopped at Royal Arches for photographs. After seeing it the second time I am certain that this section of Marble Gorge is the most beautiful part of the Grand Canyon. It has unequaled variety both in color and in form. Reached Little Nankoweap at noon and stopped for the day. Dodge and Clark, armed with an automatic pistol and a carbine, went deer hunting. Found plenty of tracks but no deer. It is cold to-night. Ice is freezing on a bucket of water fifteen feet from the fire. Beautiful moonlight. Radio working fine.

Carbon Canyon, December 9. It is not so cold to-day but we had lunch, at the mouth of the Little Colorado, and suffered from the cold on account of a strong wind blowing up stream. After lunch we started away again but the wind blew so hard that we could not make progress against it and ran ashore about a mile below the junction. Made camp on a bowlder-strewn sand bar and all the afternoon, evening and night a fierce, cold wind pelted us with sand. Sand in our eyes, our food, our beds—everything.

Hance Rapids, December 10. Schubert could not make biscuits last night on account of sand storm and we had to wait this morning until he could get his baking done. Breakfast and away at nine. Breakfast consists of oatmeal and milk, bacon, fried potatoes, biscuits, prunes and coffee. To-day we passed through the beautiful section of canyon between the mouth of the Little Colorado and Hance Rapids. Can see snow a mile above us along the rim. In afternoon rain began to fall and to-night it is pouring steadily down upon us. LaRue and Barber are planning to leave expedition here, climb to rim, go down to Grand Canyon and join us later at Phantom Beach.

Hance Rapids, December 11. LaRue and Barber started about eight-thirty for the rim. During afternoon, in steady rain, Woodbury and I climbed up to Tonto shelf along the top of the granite and went down to study the Sockdolager. Finally reached a point directly above the rapids and peered over the edge of the granite cliff down into the river, roaring and foaming a thousand feet below. Five thousand feet above us, among the cliffs along the rim, the white clouds rested on a parapet of snow. A drizzle of rain fell steadily where we clambered about on a shelf of sandstone along the top of the granite cliffs a thousand feet in height. Wisps of clouds drifted about or settled in the gloomy river trench. Everywhere there was the murky grandeur of a day half seen through clouds and fog among rocks and pinnacles and walls beyond imagining. It was a magnificent panorama of rocks and snow and clouds and rain and mist—with the river, snarling and dangerous, adding sound to perhaps the grandest, most awe-inspiring sight that I shall ever see.

LaRue and Barber were in camp when we got back, they had found the trails blocked with snow and could not get out of the canyon.

Hance Rapids, December 12. Spent the entire day portaging the boats around Hance Rapids. Took them out of the water, hoisted them on our shoulders and carried them around. Samoff injured his foot when boat crushed it against a rock and fainted dead away to-night while I was dressing it. Radio to-night said that a storm has swept Gable's tents away and that the desert radio station is being dismantled. My muscles are sore from lifting boats.

Phantom Ranch, December 13. Had sunlight for a few minutes early this morning and photographed boats running tail end of Hance Rapids. Dropped down to Sockdolager. The water was so low that we were able to approach very near head of rapids. We found a ravine there, and a way to climb to a ledge almost directly overlooking the river. Dodge asked all the passengers to walk around the rapids so the boatmen could run the boats through without the extra weight. One passenger reached a point on the cliff that he dared not pass. Dodge "rescued" him—and took him back to the boats. The rest of us got by safely but could find very little driftwood below to build a fire. We waited while boats ran through—six boats, six boatmen and one unwilling passenger. There was not enough firewood to dry all the men and I told Dodge of a place a few hundred yards below where driftwood might be found. Meanwhile the passenger had rushed up to the tiny fire and stood over it shivering.

"Come on," yelled Dodge. "Let's go."

"But _____ can't go on," answered Barber. "He has to change clothes, he's shivering with cold."

"Cold, hell," retorted Dodge. "He's just afraid."

The expedition moved on down the river.

We made our noon camp half a mile below and everybody got warm and dry around the fire.

What a grand and dangerous time we had this afternoon!

Below Grapevine Rapids two small fires were built but wood was scarce because the granite walls rose sheer from the water's edge and there was no place for it to lodge along the shore. Dodge wanted if possible to make it through to Phantom Ranch before dark and I saw no reason why we could not do so. At high water in July the going had been relatively easy. We were to find that it was not so easy with the water at low level.

We shoved off and ran one small rapids after another. All of us were wet. There was no sunshine and we were cold. It began getting dark and still we hurried on. Late in the afternoon we came to a place where the current set in against the wall of rock on the left. Dodge made it beautifully. Samoff got by. Clark narrowly escaped hitting it. By that time our boat was far below and I could hardly make out the following boats in the gathering darkness. The fifth boat, piloted by Daily, swept against the rock, tilted and I saw Barber, his passenger, roll off into the river.

"Daily has lost his passenger," I said to Dodge and we tried to run ashore.

Then we saw Daily drag Barber back into the boat.

"Now we'll have to stop," I suggested but Dodge was in favor of going on.

"How about you?" he yelled to Barber and Barber answered between chattering teeth,

"All right, go on"—and we did.

At Eighty-three Mile Rapids we landed on the right and while I held the boat against the shore, Dodge looked the rapids over. It was so dark that he must have depended somewhat on the sound to judge the fury of the rapids. Then we ran through, mostly on hope. It was a short, sharp, and vicious drop—but our luck went with us.

We came to another bad one. It was almost dark by that time. There was no driftwood to be found, we were wet and cold, we had to make Phantom Ranch. The passengers walked around and the boats went through. Dodge ran first, narrowly escaped hitting two rocks he had not been able to see from shore and all the boats followed him.

Then on down the river we drifted. It grew so dark that we had to call out to be sure that all the boats were there. We lighted matches to give encouragement to the boats following us. If there had been one more rapids we would have had to tie up and establish a fireless camp. But we had run them all and swept presently under the suspension bridge and ran ashore below Phantom Ranch.

There was a telephone at Phantom and I got in touch with B— on the rim. He told me he would send a man with the money for the crew the following day, and every one was happy.

Grand Canyon, December 14. "Shorty," a Grand Canyon guide, arrived about noon with checks but again the checks were not countersigned and the men would not accept them. I supported the men in holding out for their money and so notified B—. They had earned it. I then suggested that I go back to the rim with "Shorty" and get, in cash, the $3000 due the men and bring it back to them. I telephoned to B— to have the money ready and rode back up the trail with "Shorty." There was deep snow the last thousand feet on top and it made for dangerous going. Also, it was colder than it had been 6000 feet below on the river. B— realized finally that he would have to pay the boatmen and arranged to have the money ready for me in the morning.

Grand Canyon, December 15. Got away with "Shorty" for the long, cold ride down to the river. The snow caked under the mules' feet, they stumbled repeatedly, threatening to toss us over thousand foot precipices—and both of us walked part way. Reached Phantom Ranch at noon and I had the pleasure of handing to them, in actual cash, the amounts of money due each of the fine, brave men who had risked their lives a thousand times piloting the boats through 450 cold and dangerous miles. Then they shoved off for Hermit Falls and the end of their journey seven miles below while, my job completed, I took the up-trail toward the rim.

[The End]

ORDER FORM

Clyde Eddy
T H E   M O V I E

Down the Colorado River in a Rowboat

When Clyde Eddy undertook the expedition that is the subject of *A Mad, Crazy River*, part of the plan was to film his travels through the Grand Canyon. When Avanyu Publishing located the original edition of this book, they also discovered an original copy of Eddy's Kodak Cinegraph film that was made along the voyage. The film is titled *Down the Colorado River in a Rowboat*. This film is dated 1927, is in black and white with no sound, and is approximately 8 minutes long. Avanyu Publishing has had the original film digitally remastered and the imagery is unique.

Please use the order form below to purchase DVD copies of this film. Send your order and payment by check or money order, or purchase by credit card via our website, **www.AvanyuPublishing.com**. Please allow 6 to 8 weeks for delivery.

THE CLYDE EDDY EXPEDITION 1927: Down the Colorado River in a Rowboat

Medium	Price	Number of copies	Shipping & Handling	Total Due
DVD	$15.00 ea.	_____	$5.00	$ _____

Ship to: _____

Name: _____

Address: _____

Telephone: _____

E-mail: _____

SEND ORDER TO:

AVANYU PUBLISHING INC.
Movie Orders
P. O. Box 27134
Albuquerque, NM 87125
Fax: 505•341•1281

Avanyu Publishing Inc.